"Without a doubt, the most profound result of the Second Vatican Council has been the liturgical renewal based on *Sacrosanctum concilium*. This has been especially evident in the use of the vernacular and the simplification of the rites for Mass. But those very issues have also been at the heart of numerous disputes within the Church. Many of those arguments, however, do not reflect a great intelligence in grasping the fundamental insights of the liturgical renewal that was built upon the foundations of the pre-Conciliar liturgical movement. In his book *A Challenging Reform: Realizing the Vision of the Liturgical Renewal* Archbishop Piero Marini offers wisdom and an informed perspective as we try to better understand the Council's liturgical renewal and the ongoing task of its implementation.

"Therefore I am grateful to Archbishop Marini for what he offers us in these pages. I hope that many, through the reading of this book, will discover the inspiration that drove the liturgists in their work before Vatican II and that continues to drive the liturgists of our own day in their dedication and devotion to the service of the Church and its liturgy. Their efforts have always been characterized by a great respect for the tradition and for the celebration of the mystery of God's love for us. Without this the realization of the liturgical renewal would be impossible."

+ Godfried Cardinal Danneels
Archbishop of Malines-Bruxelles

"Archbishop Piero Marini has produced a work of considerable merit and importance. With remarkable objectivity he chronicles in meticulous detail the stages of development of the liturgical reform set in motion by Vatican II.

"This painstaking work of renewal of the liturgy deserves great respect because of the renowned expertise of those who led, took part and accomplished the work such as Cardinal Lercaro, Father Bugnini and other participants such as Josef Jungmann and Godfrey Diekmann. It was admirable, as well, because of the conscious effort to make the working group international and thus reflect the whole Church.

"It is very impressive to see in this account the great care with which the whole enterprise was conducted. Clearly it was carried out with the kind of organizational skill and discipline which marks the highest kind of scholarship.

"Archbishop Marini is commendable for providing an honest and thorough account of the history of the liturgical re█████████████████████████████ to read of the strong opposition and the persis█████████████████████████ res and groups in the Curia such as Cardinal O█████████████████████████ na and others to thwart the work of the liturgic█████████████████████ how the Curia was eventually successful in disn█████████████████████ rship as it had been initially set up by Pope Pau█

"This book, apart from its valuable history of the liturgical reform, points up two other important issues. One is the importance of the Roman Curia to the whole Church and the consequent need for its reform to enable it to respond more effectively to the needs of the world Church which emerged at Vatican Council II. The second lesson which this history yields is the importance of true ecclesial faith that is not weakened by adversity or daunted by challenges or disappointments but is enduringly confident that Christ, crucified in weakness, is risen in power and at work in every situation.

"Archbishop Marini has written a valuable work. More important, he has lived the ideals of the Church. As Master of Pontifical Liturgical Celebrations he shaped and guided the great papal celebrations seen by the whole world at St. Peter's and which so beautifully embody the ideal of the Council: noble simplicity."

Archbishop John R. Quinn

"Archbishop Piero Marini's book *A Challenging Reform* lifts the veil on the interplay of forces behind the Liturgical Reforms of Vatican II. It allows those of us not privy to the interior workings of the Roman Catholic Church to see the tussles between the liturgists, most of whom have learned their trade ecumenically where there has been an astonishing scholarly consensus, the Roman Curia and the local Bishops' Conferences. Archbishop Marini writes with unrivalled knowledge and tremendous verve of the tensions that accompanied the reform, and still do. His work, while scholarly and well-documented, reads more like a detective thriller, and keeps us on the edge of our seats. A companion to—and in part replacement of—Bugnini's classic account, Marini's work continues to raise the kind of question that liturgists all over the world are asking now: is the Roman church, in abandoning agreed ecumenical translations used for the last forty years, retreating into a pre-Vatican II Curial mindset?"

✠ David Stancliffe
Bishop of Salisbury and former Chairman of
the Liturgical Commission of the Church of England

"A penetrating analysis of the tensions which surrounded the liturgical renewal in the Catholic Church during the Vatican Council and afterwards. This book also offers fascinating insights into how the Vatican works."

Timothy Radcliffe
Blackfriars, Oxford

"The reform of worship in the Catholic Church since the Second Vatican Council has from the start engaged a whole series of dynamics: between papal primacy, curial supervision, and episcopal collegiality; between the maintenance of orthodoxy and the promotion of renewal; between historical scholarship and pastoral practice; between universal communicability and cultural variety. The stakes are high because, in the words of *Sacrosanctum Concilium*, the liturgy constitutes the source and summit of the Church's life, while the post-conciliar reform, in the words of this book, is to be reckoned 'one of the greatest liturgical reforms in the history of the Western Church.' Here we are given an inside look—with personal and documentary detail—at the early stages of this process: author Archbishop Piero Marini, since 1987 Master of Pontifical Liturgical Celebrations, served as a young priest in the secretariat of the Consilium for Implementing the Constitution on the Liturgy and then in the Congregation for Divine Worship. Among the services rendered by this important book is the abundant tribute paid to the energy and skills of Annibale Bugnini, a key figure on the official Roman scene until 1975."

Geoffrey Wainwright
Duke University

A Challenging Reform

Realizing the Vision
of the Liturgical Renewal
1963–1975

Archbishop Piero Marini
Master of Pontifical Liturgical Celebrations, 1987–2007

Edited by
Mark R. Francis, C.S.V.
John R. Page
Keith F. Pecklers, S.J.

LITURGICAL PRESS
Collegeville, Minnesota

www.litpress.org

Conversations and statements, unless otherwise attributed, are from the personal notes and memory of the author.

Cover design by Ann Blattner. Photo: View of Vatican City by Anthony Long, iStockphotos.com.

Excerpts from the English translation of *Documents on the Liturgy, 1963–1979: Conciliar, Papal, and Curial Texts* ©1982, International Committee on English in the Liturgy, Inc. (ICEL). All rights reserved.

1	2	3	4	5	6	7	8

Library of Congress Cataloging-in-Publication Data

Marini, Piero, 1942–
    A challenging reform : realizing the vision of the liturgical renewal,
1963–1975 / Piero Marini ; edited by Mark R. Francis, John R. Page,
Keith F. Pecklers.
        p.   cm.
    ISBN-13: 978-0-8146-3035-8
    1. Catholic Church—Liturgy—History—20th century. I. Francis,
Mark R., 1953– II. Page, John R., 1940– III. Pecklers, Keith F., 1958–
IV. Title.

BX1970.M327 2007
264'.02009046—dc22

                                                    2007011695

✠ Contents

Appendix

✠ Foreword

The present work is intended as a complement and supplement to the account of the liturgical reform published in 1985 by Annibale Bugnini, *La riforma liturgica (1948–1975)*.[1] Bugnini had been involved in the initial efforts, begun in 1947 under Pope Pius XII, to bring about reforms in the liturgy of the Roman church. After Pope John XXIII announced the convening of an ecumenical council in January 1959, Bugnini was named secretary of the Pontifical Preparatory Commission on the Liturgy. Soon after the council's decisive vote on December 4, 1963, in favor of the Constitution on the Sacred Liturgy (2147 to 4), Bugnini was named secretary of the body of bishops and experts charged with the task of implementing the liturgical reform. This body was known as the Consilium *(Consilium ad exsequendam Constitutionem de sacra liturgia)*. Bugnini continued in that pivotal position for the five years of the Consilium's existence. In 1972 he was named secretary of the reconfigured Congregation for Divine Worship.

Piero Marini, ordained a priest of the diocese of Bobbio in 1965, was closely involved in the work of the Consilium. Over the past four decades he has had a privileged position from which to observe, assess, and influence the conciliar liturgical reform. After his years on the Consilium staff, he went on to serve as a principal member of the staff of the Congregation for Divine Worship. After serving under five cardinal prefects of the Congregation, Marini was named Master of Pontifical Liturgical Celebrations in 1987. In preparing numerous papal liturgies in Rome under John Paul II and Benedict

---

[1] English translation: *The Reform of the Liturgy: 1948–1975*, trans. Matthew J. O'Connell (Collegeville: The Liturgical Press, 1990).

XVI, and in his travels around the world with these two pontiffs, Archbishop Marini has had a unique experience of seeing the liturgical reforms carried out in Rome and in the local churches worldwide.

Archbishop Marini ended his tenure as Master of Pontifical Liturgical Celebrations in the fall of 2007. Throughout those twenty years, he remained faithful to the renewal called for by the Second Vatican Council by keeping alive the vision that inspired the work of the Consilium. In 2005 Marini directed the dramatic and deeply inspiring liturgies that marked the death of Pope John Paul II and the election and installation of Pope Benedict XVI. The liturgical books used for these occasions are the fruit of long study and research. They were prepared under Marini's direction and take their place as milestones in the centuries-long tradition of papal liturgical celebrations.

In the forty years since the council's conclusion, its vision of the essential link between tradition and progress, between the ever ancient and the ever new, has not been without challenges. As Archbishop Marini demonstrates in this vivid account, based on extensive written sources, the reform met with resistance from the start within the Roman Curia especially, but also at times within the wider church. Elements of the Curia, protective of the prerogatives that had been theirs since the Council of Trent, were reluctant to accept the more collegial ecclesiology embraced by Vatican II.

As early as February 1964, just weeks after the solemn promulgation of the Constitution on the Sacred Liturgy, the episcopal members of the French liturgical commission stated in a letter to several dicasteries of the Roman Curia that they found themselves frustrated by those who would restrict the authority of bishops' conferences given to them by an ecumenical council. Four decades later the contention over the authority of bishops' conferences for liturgical texts in the living languages, as enunciated in the conciliar Constitution, has returned with renewed force.

After dedicated and loyal service under four popes, Piero Marini brings before us in revealing detail the struggles that accompanied the Consilium's efforts, especially in the first year of its existence, to launch the reforms in accordance with the decisions of the Council Fathers.

Mark R. Francis, c.s.v.
John R. Page
Keith F. Pecklers, s.j.

Rome
November 1, 2007
Solemnity of All Saints

✠ Acknowledgments

The editors wish to acknowledge with gratitude the work of Monsignor Leo Cushley of the Holy See's permanent mission to the United Nations, who provided Archbishop Marini with an initial draft translation in English of the text and the appendices. Subsequently, the editors reworked the manuscript in size and style in collaboration with Archbishop Marini. We also wish to express our thanks to the Jesuit Community and Theology Department of Boston College, Chestnut Hill, Massachusetts, for their hospitality during the final editing of this work.

 # Abbreviations

Archives	Archives of the Consilium, which later became the Archives of the Congregation for Divine Worship, then the Archives of the Divine Worship Section of the Congregation for the Sacraments and Divine Worship, now The Congregation for Divine Worship and the Discipline of the Sacraments.
AAS	*Acta Apostolicae Sedis*
ASS	*Acta Sanctae Sedis*
Consilium	*Consilium ad exsequendam Constitutionem de sacra Liturgia:* "a special commission with the principal task of seeing that the prescriptions of the Constitution are put into effect" MP *Sacram Liturgiam* (DOL 20).
Consulta	Meeting of the consultors of a curial Office.
DOL	*Documents on the Liturgy* (1963–1979) International Commission on English in the Liturgy. The Liturgical Press: Collegeville, 1982.
EDIL	*Enchiridion documentorum instaurationis liturgicae,* 1 (1963–1973). Ed. Reiner Kaczynski. Marietti: Turin, 1976.
Not	*Notitiae,* Typis Polyglottis Vaticani, from 1965.
OR	*L'Osservatore Romano.* Vatican Daily newspaper, since 1861. 1st English edition: April 4, 1968.
SC	*Sacrosanctum Concilium.* Constitution on the Sacred Liturgy of the Second Vatican Council.
SCR	Sacred Congregation for Rites

 Introduction

The Liturgical Movement Before Vatican II

The announcement of the Second Vatican Council by Pope John XXIII on January 25, 1959, was welcomed with great satisfaction by all who were involved in the renewal of liturgical life in the church. Work in this direction had been going on for more than fifty years.

The "liturgical movement" can be traced back to the work of the French Benedictine Prosper Guéranger (1805–1875).[1] It was thanks to him that in Benedictine abbeys, above all at Solesmes, where he became abbot, the liturgy began to be celebrated again with greater care. His volume on the liturgical year, *L'Année liturgique,* was instrumental in promoting the treasures of the liturgy. Guéranger's inspiration became a reality in Germany when Beuron Abbey was reopened in 1863. It also took root in Belgium, where monks from Beuron founded the Abbey of Maredsous in 1872, and it was brought to Farnborough, England, in 1895 with the opening of a foundation sponsored by Solesmes.

Gradually, Guéranger's ideas spread throughout Europe, particularly in those places where Benedictine life was restored. These monastic centers were responsible for publications, especially in England, thanks to the work of Fernand Cabrol (1855–1937) and Henri Leclercq (1869–1929), both Benedictines of Farnborough: *Le Livre de la prière antique"* (1900), *Monumenta Ecclesiae liturgica* (1901), *Dictionnaire d'archéologie chrétienne et de liturgie* (1903).

---

[1] See O. Rousseau, *Histoire du mouvement liturgique: Esquisse historique depuis le début du XIXe siècle jusqu' au pontificat de Pie X* (Paris: Les Éditions Cerf, 1945); see also Keith F. Pecklers, *The Unread Vision: The Liturgical Movement in the United States of America: 1926–1955* (Collegeville: Liturgical Press, 1998) 1–23.

Pope Pius X Makes Liturgical History

Another important step for the liturgical movement occurred when Pope Pius X published his motu proprio on sacred music, *Tra le sollecitudini* (November 22, 1903). With the papacy acknowledging the liturgical movement, it became a matter of importance for the whole church. In his motu proprio Pope Pius X spoke of sacred music and the liturgy, not as something reserved for a restricted circle of experts, but as something belonging to all the people of God. As a result, the Abbey of Solesmes was encouraged to continue its studies on Gregorian chant. A most important affirmation made in the document concerning "active participation in the sacred mysteries and in the public and solemn prayer of the church"[2] had very little echo. The liturgy continued to be regarded as a study of rubrics.[3]

The Liturgical Movement Between the Two World Wars

The liturgical movement that began during the pontificate of Pius X was understood and promoted by Dom Lambert Beauduin (1873–1960). Thanks to him, Mont-César Abbey in Louvain became the center of the movement in 1909, inspired by the pastoral ideas expressed in *Tra le sollecitudini*. Liturgists became active particularly in the period between the two world wars through liturgical publications, "liturgical weeks," congresses, and serious research on the theoretical, practical, and pastoral character of the liturgy. Gradually they developed a sound understanding of the liturgy. Increasingly, bishops and priests inspired lay people to take an active part in the celebration of the liturgy.

During this period the German abbey of Maria Laach became noted for its liturgical initiatives. In addition to the eminent theologian Odo Casel (1886–1948), there were others, such as the abbot of Maria Laach, Ildefons Herwegen (1874–1946); the Italo-German diocesan priest Romano Guardini (1885–1968); the Austrian Augustinian canon Pius Parsch (1884–1954); and Dom Bernard Capelle (1884–1971), abbot of Mont-Cesar in Louvain, who made their own unique contributions. The Volkliturgisches Apostolat of Klosterneuburg, for example, developed by Pius Parsch (1884–1954), had influence far beyond Austria. The liturgical movement received further

---

[2] *ASS* 36:28 (1904) 331, as given in J. Neuner and J. Dupuis, eds., *The Christian Faith in the Doctrinal Documents of the Catholic Church* (New York: Alba House, 1982) 340.

[3] A. Bugnini, "'Movimento liturgico' o 'Pastorale liturgica'?" *Not* 10 (1974) 137.

encouragement in 1928 from Pope Pius XI's apostolic constitution *Divini cultus*. The theological aspect of the liturgy was given great attention by the Innsbruck school of theology, under the guidance of the Jesuits Josef Andreas Jungmann and the Rahner brothers, Hugo and Karl.

The Liturgical Reforms of Pope Pius XII

During and immediately after the Second World War there were several initiatives of considerable importance. Two liturgical centers were opened— in France, the Centre de Pastorale Liturgique in 1943, and in Italy, the Centro di Azione Liturgica in 1948. The most important development was the publication in 1947 of Pope Pius XII's encyclical *Mediator Dei* on the sacred liturgy. A few years earlier, in 1943, there had been another great encyclical, *Mystici Corporis,* on the mystery of the church. Through these encyclicals the inseparable link between the church and the liturgy was established. This in itself was a major achievement.

But Pius XII also initiated practical reforms of the liturgy. On February 9, 1951, the Sacred Congregation for Rites promulgated a decree on the reform of the Easter Vigil. The Congregation then announced the reform of Holy Week with its decree of November 16, 1955.These two reforms introduced by Pius XII were of major importance because they underlined the paschal mystery as the center of all Christian life. The Holy Week reforms were the work of a special commission that included Annibale Bugnini and Ferdinando Antonelli, protagonists in the future liturgical reform of the council and its implementation.

In addition, Pius XII encouraged the publication of rituals with considerable allowance for vernacular languages. In 1947 a Latin-French Ritual was published, followed in 1950 by a Latin-German Ritual. In 1954 Latin-English Rituals were published in the United States and Great Britain. It was also during the pontificate of Pius XII that the eucharistic fast was shortened and the evening Mass was instituted. A new translation of the psalms was also prepared, and theological clarifications were made in the rite for the ordination of a bishop, presbyters, and deacons. The last liturgical activity during Pius XII's pontificate occurred in 1958 with an instruction issued by the Congregation for Rites on sacred music and liturgy (*De musica sacra et sacra liturgia,* September 3, 1958).[4]

---

[4] A. Bugnini, "Pio XII e la liturgia," *Ephemerides Liturgicae* 72 (1958) 375–83.

However, it was above all the publication of the encyclical *Mediator Dei* that revived interest in the liturgy throughout the church. Gradually liturgical commissions were set up, and bishops in many parts of the world became involved in liturgical initiatives. It was a time of memorable international congresses: Maria Laach, Germany (1951); Odilienburg in Alsace, France (1952); Lugano, Switzerland (1953); Mont-César in Louvain, Belgium (1954); Assisi, Italy (1956); Montserrat, Spain (1958); and Munich, Germany (1960). The liturgical movement had at last been embraced by the whole church. Thus in 1959, when the announcement of the "council" came, the movement was poised to contribute to *aggiornamento* or renewal of the church.

The Constitution on the Sacred Liturgy of the Second Vatican Council

During the preparatory period for the council, a number of initiatives on the part of the Congregation for Rites caused concern among those in the liturgical movement who had worked long and hard for renewal during the previous forty years. On July 25, 1960, a few months after the appointment of Cardinal Arcadio Maria Larraona as prefect of the Congregation for Rites, that Congregation published *Rubricarum instructum,* a new code of rubrics for the Breviary and the Missal. Soon after, new standard editions of the Breviary (April 5, 1961) and of the Missal (June 23, 1962) were published. The purpose of these measures was indicated in Pope John XXIII's motu proprio:

> After mature reflection, we came to the conclusion that the more impor-
> tant principles governing a general liturgical reform should be laid before
> the members of the hierarchy at the forthcoming ecumenical council, but
> that the above-mentioned improvement of the rubrics of the Breviary and
> Missal should no longer be put off.[5]

While these rubrics and the other books had been in preparation for some time, publishing them during the drafting of the text of the liturgical schema to be discussed by the council gave rise to a not unfounded fear that the discussion by the council would be restricted to the schema presented in *Rubricarum instructum.* Happily, this fear proved to be unfounded.[6] How-

---

[5] *Rubrics of the Roman Breviary and Roman Missal,* trans. Leonard J. Doyle (Collegeville: The Liturgical Press, 1960) 11. Trans. from *AAS* 52 (1960) no. 10 (Aug. 15) 593–740.

[6] H. Schmidt, ed., *La costituzione sulla sacra liturgia: Testo—Genesi—Commento—Documentazione* (Rome: Herder, 1966) 104.

ever, this strategy to preempt reform would be repeated again by the Congregation for Rites during the implementation stage of the conciliar reform of the liturgy.

The Preparation of the Schema on the Liturgy

On May 17, 1959, it was announced that Pope John XXIII had instituted an ante-preparatory commission for the council, which was to "trace the general lines of the matters to be discussed by the Council,"[7] after having listened to suggestions from the episcopate, from the Roman Curia, and from the theological and canonical faculties of Pontifical universities. The members of the ante-preparatory commission were curial officials: Cardinal Domenico Tardini was the president and Bishop Pericle Felice the secretary.

The responses were tabulated and published in 1960–1961 in sixteen volumes entitled *Acta et Documenta Concilio oecumenico Vaticano II apparando, Series Praeparatoria*. Replies on the subject of the liturgy were very numerous. They were a sign of the desire "to restore to the liturgy its true catechetical and formative value. These replies included the simplification of the rites, the introduction of the vernacular, adaptations to the cultural genius of the various peoples, active participation of the faithful as suitable elements for fostering an intimate understanding of the Christian mystery, celebrated by the faithful in the liturgy."[8]

On June 5, 1960, Pope John XXIII instituted commissions that were to prepare the schemas of the documents to be presented for discussion at the council. Among them was the Preparatory Commission on the Liturgy. Cardinal Gaetano Cicognani, prefect of the Congregation for Rites, was appointed its president, and Father Bugnini, who had acted as secretary of the commission for Pope Pius XII's liturgical reform, became its secretary.

This liturgical commission, which also included members and consultors,[9] began its meetings in Rome on November 12, 1960. That day thirteen subcommissions were set up according to the various topics. The

---

[7] AA.VV., *La Costituzione sulla sacra liturgia*. Genesi storico-doctrinale. Testo latino e traduzione italiana. Esposizione e Commento. Norme de applicazione. Riforma liturgica nel mondo (Turin: Elle Di Ci, 1967) 53.

[8] Ibid., 67.

[9] H. Schmidt, *Costituzione,* Appendix A. Commissione Preparatoria della Sacra Liturgia, 359–63.

only serious difficulty encountered in the work of preparing the schema on the liturgy was the subject of the vernacular, since there was a campaign in support of maintaining Latin as the liturgical language of the church. Apart from this, the work was done without particular difficulty. The commission's last plenary session was held January 11–13, 1962. The final text of the schema, ready on January 22, was given by Cardinal Cicognani to the General Secretariat of the council on February 1. Four days later the Cardinal died.

On February 22, 1962, Pope John appointed Cardinal Arcadio Larraona, the new prefect of the Congregation for Rites, as president of the Preparatory Commission. He had never dealt with liturgical matters and knew nothing of the work carried out by the commission. The schema was then submitted to the Central Commission (Pontificia Commissio Centralis Praeparatoria), instituted by the Pope on June 5, 1960, to revise the work done by each commission, and then to submit it to the Pope and to the council. This Central Commission made no decisions but submitted the schema with the minutes of the meetings to another subcommission, which would then amend the schema. It was here that the Preparatory Commission's text was altered. The *declarationes,* or explanatory notes, were removed; these were intended to help the Council Fathers understand the schema. Moreover, several articles had been changed so much that their original content was unrecognizable.

A meaningful statement had been placed on the title page: "The sole purpose of this Constitution is to provide general norms and 'the fundamental principles governing general liturgical reform' (see John XXIII, motu proprio *Rubricarum instructum* of July 25, 1960). The practical implementation of the individual cases is to be left to the Holy See." This was a return to the theory of centralization already expressed by the Congregation for Rites in the motu proprio issued with the new code of rubrics published two years earlier.

Once the opening date of the council had been set for October 11, 1962, and the preparatory period was over, it was time to replace the preparatory commissions with the conciliar commissions. On September 4 Pope John XXIII appointed Cardinal Larraona president of the Conciliar Commission on the Sacred Liturgy. On October 20 the Council Fathers elected sixteen members of the Conciliar Commission. On October 21 the president appointed two vice-presidents, Cardinals Paolo Giobbe and André Jullien, and a new secretary, Father Ferdinando Antonelli, O.F.M., Promoter of the Faith at the Congregation for Rites.

Immediately, two matters aroused attention: Cardinal Giacomo Lercaro, archbishop of Bologna and one of the world's most esteemed liturgists, who had been elected by an overwhelming majority as a member of the Preparatory Commission,[10] had not been appointed vice-president; and the demotion of Father Annibale Bugnini to *peritus,* or expert, of the commission rather than as secretary of the Conciliar Commission. Father Bugnini was also removed from the chair of liturgy at the Pontifical Lateran University because his liturgical ideas were seen as too progressive. In the words of the historian of the liturgy Enrico Cattaneo,

> It was clear to everyone that the Roman curial circles had scored a victory by practically eliminating two outstanding and reputable people equipped to help bring about a truly pastoral liturgical reform. . . . This fact appeared all the more grave and ominous considering that a further thirty-two experts who had been involved in the preparatory Commission had not been confirmed among the *periti* for the Council.[11]

Both Lercaro and Bugnini would not be reinstated until the election of Pope Paul VI, who before the end of 1963 had tried to position them as leaders of the implementation of the reform.

The schema of the Constitution on the Sacred Liturgy *(Sacrosanctum Concilium)* was the first to be discussed at the council. During the first general congregations several Council Fathers asked for the original text drawn up by the Preparatory Commission and the *declarationes* that had been removed by the Central Commission.

Discussion on the schema began on October 22, 1962, after which fifteen plenary sessions took place before November 13.[12] A total of 685 interventions were made. The majority declared themselves in favor of the proposals made because they were based on pastoral criteria. The only unfavorable opinions came either from members of the Roman Curia, motivated by a

---

[10] See Giacomo Lercaro, *Lettere dal Concilio 1962–1965,* ed. Giuseppe Battelli (Bologna: Dehoniane, 1980) 35.

[11] E. Cattaneo, *Il culto cristiano in occidente. Note storiche* (Rome: Edizioni Liturgiche, 1978) 629–30.

[12] On November 11, 1962, Cardinal Lercaro expressed his frustration to the Secretary of State for the lack of progress of the work of the Conciliar Commission. He also raised the specter of an even greater division being created between the Roman Curia and residential bishops, who would blame the curialists for their foot dragging. Lercaro, *Lettere dal Concilio,* 104.

concern to protect the Apostolic See's juridical prerogatives against bishops' conferences, or from diocesan bishops anxious to safeguard traditional liturgical practices.[13] When the interventions were over on November 14, 1962, a vote was taken on the General Declaration, which entailed accepting or rejecting the liturgical schema. Of the 2,215 Fathers present, 2,162 voted in favor, 46 opposed, and there were 7 blank votes.

The separate parts of the Constitution were then examined. In order to carry on this study, the delegates received two versions of the text—one prepared by the Central Commission and the other by the Preparatory Commission. On November 17, Cardinal Lercaro announced that the Conciliar Commission had obtained the presidency's permission to include with the text the *declarationes* or explanatory notes that had been provided in the Preparatory Commission's redaction and later removed by the Central Commission. The Conciliar Commission judged the statement that the Central Commission had placed on the schema's title page as not pertinent. This was indeed a triumph for those bishops at the council who were anxious to overcome the exaggerated liturgical centralization inherited from the Council of Trent and to move to a liturgy that would be both more pastoral and open to the needs of the contemporary world.

On December 8, 1962, Pope John XXIII closed the first session of the council. On June 3, 1963, while the council was in recess, Pope John died. He was succeeded by Cardinal Giovanni Battista Montini, who was elected pope on June 21 and took the name Paul VI. He opened the second session of the council on September 29. Interventions and votes on the separate parts of the liturgy schema continued until the end of October. All the proposed modifications were considered by the Conciliar Commission. On November 22 the schema was submitted to the Council Fathers for a final vote. The results of this vote were overwhelmingly positive: of the 2,178 voting, 2,158 were in favor, 19 opposed, and 1 blank vote.

Nevertheless, Pope Paul VI asked the Fathers to give the text additional consideration until December 4. At that time a definitive vote was taken before the solemn promulgation of the Constitution on the Sacred Liturgy. Again the results were overwhelmingly positive: 2,147 in favor and only 4 opposed. At long last the hopes and dreams of the liturgical movement had borne fruit. Now came the task of the pastoral implementation of the conciliar decisions, which would bring its own challenges and opportunities.

[13] Cattaneo, *Il culto,* 631.

As we shall see, the more traditionalist members of the Curia would try to circumvent the process of implementation by opposing real liturgical change and maintaining the status quo, a stance rejected by the council.

There were, however, positive factors for those convinced of the need for liturgical reform. For one, at the council the new Pope had been among the most ardent supporters of a liturgy open to the needs of the modern world and in favor of vernacular in the liturgy.[14] Secondly, because the council was still in session, it would be able to exercise some "control" over the Curia's attempts to interfere in the implementation of the reform.

---

[14] Cattaneo, *Il culto,* 616–17.

Chapter One

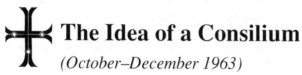

The Idea of a Consilium
(October–December 1963)

The *Primitiae* Document

The Consilium *(Consilium ad exsequendam Constitutionem de sacra Liturgia)* is known above all as the group that directed the implementation of the liturgy of Vatican II for a number of years, beginning in 1964. In the past, most historians have devoted their attention to what the Consilium accomplished rather than to the group itself. That is why so little is known of this group and of the inside story of the reform. From October to December 1963, several significant events occurred that paved the way for establishing the Consilium.

The beginning of what was eventually to become the Consilium can be traced to a few words in Father Bugnini's handwriting on a single sheet of paper stored in one of the many files in the archives of the Consilium. They were merely calendar notes on events between October 10 and October 20, 1963. Bugnini noted the following:

> The Holy Father expressed to the four moderators the desire that the 2nd Session of the Council close with a "partial law" on the liturgy, and entrusted the task to Cardinal Lercaro[1] (Thursday, October 10). Cardinal Lercaro calls for Bugnini and tells him of the Holy Father's desire and asks him to

---

[1] This is mentioned by Cardinal Lercaro in a letter dated October 10, 1964. He notes that the Pope thought that some of the more simple liturgical reforms should take place immediately, without waiting for the conclusion of the work of the Consilium. (*Lettere dal Concilio 1962–1965,* ed. Giuseppe Battelli [Bologna: Dehoniane, 1980] 177).

suggest a group of *periti* to help him in this task (October 11, 8:00 p.m.). Bugnini presents Cardinal Lercaro with the list of liturgists (October 12, 8:30 a.m.). The *periti* (including Josef Jungmann) are called to Cardinal Lercaro's residence during the Council, located at the Benedictine convent of Santa Priscilla on the Via Salaria, and the work was assigned (5:00 p.m.). Letter from Father Bugnini to the *periti*.—Visit to His Eminence asking him to request from the Pope permission for concelebration (October 15). At S. Gregorio al Celio, a meeting was held to examine proposals for chapters 1 and 11 (October 19, 4:00–8:00 p.m.) At S. Gregorio al Celio, the rest of the work was examined (October 20, 4:00–8:00 p.m.).

The first list of *periti,* with the distribution of the work, was as follows: Father Cipriano Vagaggini, O.S.B., and Father Frederick McManus (sacraments); Monsignor Johannes Wagner (art and music); Canon Aimé-Georges Martimort (general principles); Father Josef Andreas Jungmann, S.J. (Mass); Father Herman Schmidt, S.J. (Divine Office); Father Ansgar Dirks, O.P. (liturgical year and sacred furnishings); Monsignor Emmanuel Bonet (liturgical law); Father Annibale Bugnini, C.M. (secretary).

The objective of their work had been indicated by Pope Paul himself: to complete an overview of the salient elements having to do with the implementation of the liturgical reform already contained in the not-as-yet-approved Constitution on the Sacred Liturgy. These were to be brief, simple proposals. Several drafts of the document were prepared during the month of October. Two further versions were drafted during the month of November—one dated November 1 and the other November 24. The final version was then presented to the Pope.

The draft foresaw the joint publication of two documents: the Pope's motu proprio authorizing the establishment of the Consilium and the instruction, given the working title *Primitiae,* with the details of the implementation. The instruction dealt with the following sections of the Liturgy Constitution: On the Most Holy Mystery of the Eucharist, the Sacraments, and the Divine Office. The publication of the motu proprio and instruction was planned for early December, but this was not to be. What exactly happened next is not known. It is certain that there were numerous observations made by various advisors and that the group of *periti* met to prepare answers to each of the observations. The Pope was kept constantly informed.

The Consequences of the First Draft

At first glance it could seem that the initial draft of the *Primitiae* instruction constituted a failure in implementing the Constitution on the Sacred Liturgy.

In fact, the text was never published. But this attempt involved both the key elements of the reform and the people who would later be its greatest supporters. This first draft reflected the reform's complexity and the need to expand the commission. The expertise and organizational skills of Cardinal Lercaro and Father Bugnini would later prove to be invaluable to the process of renewal because of their transparency and open-mindedness.

The following changes were indicated in this version of the instruction. In regard to the Mass: the chants of the Proper and the Ordinary of the Mass, if sung, were not to be read privately by the celebrant; at the beginning of Mass, in the prayers at the foot of the altar, Psalm 42 was to be omitted; the prayer over the gifts was to be sung or said aloud; the text of the Canon of the Mass, from *Qui pridie* up to *calicem salutis perpetuae,* could be said aloud, and there were alterations in the rubrics regarding the doxology of the Canon; in distributing Communion, the simple formula *Corpus Christi* was to be used; at the end of the Mass the *Ite, missa est* was to be said after the priest's blessing and the last gospel and the Leonine prayers (i.e., Hail Mary, Hail Holy Queen, Prayer to St. Michael . . . were to be omitted [art. 50]). In addition, before the offertory, the prayer of the faithful could be offered (art. 53). The vernacular language was to be used for the readings of the Mass, which were to be proclaimed facing the people and, if possible, from a lectern. Provisionally, the vernacular text was to be approved by the local bishop. The vernacular language was also to be used for the prayers of the faithful. The Our Father was to be said in the vernacular only when the Mass was not sung (art. 54). Concelebration was to be permitted in the cases provided for by the liturgy Constitution only after publication of the revised Order of Mass (art. 57).

With regard to the sacraments, directions were given for the use of bilingual Rituals already approved (art. 63b); instructions were given for the omission of certain exorcisms in the rite of baptism (arts. 66, 69); the celebration of confirmation during Mass after the homily was permitted (art. 71); when celebrated together, the anointing of the sick was to precede Viaticum (art. 74); during the consecration of a bishop, all the bishops present could impose hands (art. 76); normally matrimony was to be celebrated within Mass after the homily; and the prayer over the couple after the Lord's Prayer could be given in the vernacular (art. 78); with a few exceptions, most of the blessings in the Roman Ritual could now be imparted by any priest (art. 79).

While waiting for the reform of the entire Breviary, the following changes were indicated: the Hour of Prime could be omitted, although its celebration was still encouraged so as not to completely omit certain psalms and prayers; those who were not bound to the choral recitation of the Office were encouraged to pray only one of the three Little Hours—Terce, Sext, or None—but at the appropriate time.

Mention was made also of a few proposals not included in the first draft of the instruction that would be dealt with later on. For example, in the Mass, it was recommended that the number of offertory prayers be reduced and there be new prefaces. The holding of the paten by the subdeacon was also to be abolished, as were some bows and signs of the cross. In the context of dealing with the sacraments, missionary clergy were invited to study possible adaptations in light of local cultural elements as well as the appropriate use of the vernacular in the celebration of the sacraments. In its treatment of the Divine Office, indications were made as to the time to celebrate the Hours and the relationship of the Divine Office to other liturgical actions, for example, during Holy Week.

Moreover, a draft ritual for concelebration had been prepared. This draft was not accepted because concelebration was considered such a delicate issue that its application would require more careful consideration. Those responsible for the draft proposed a period of experimentation of the new rite in three or four abbeys (Montserrat, Solesmes, En Calcat, Maria Laach were suggested). Only after several months of experimentation would it be possible to fine tune and then promulgate the rite for the whole church.

Had the motu proprio and the instruction been implemented in December 1963, especially given the drafters' understanding of the term "territorial episcopal assemblies," more problems than solutions would have ensued. The practical implementation would have required much more explanation and would have needed to be set in a much wider context of reform. Otherwise these changes would have given the impression of a hasty, superficial attempt at renewal that would certainly have disappointed those who wanted a more profound and thoughtful reform as envisaged by the council.

To appreciate just how limited this first attempt at reform proposed in late 1963 was, it is enough to remember that the Consilium had to work for most of 1964 in order to draw up the instruction *Inter oecumenici,* which contained the basic guidelines for applying the principles of the Constitution on the Sacred Liturgy. Therefore, not to publish this initial draft instruction was a wise decision.

Constituting the Commission

The idea of establishing a larger commission of *periti* or experts that would be independent and international was already present in the minds of those who worked on the first draft of the instruction, such as Cardinal Lercaro.[2] Even while working on the first schema of the document, it became clear that there was a need to constitute a postconciliar commission for the liturgical reform. It was logical to foresee that as soon as the motu proprio and the instruction were published, questions would be raised regarding carrying out the reform. For example, which office was to deal with the queries and give appropriate indications? The Sacred Congregation for Rites hardly seemed to be suitable. Its polemical attitude toward the Constitution on the Sacred Liturgy was quite evident.[3]

Many thought that it was important to avoid a similar attempt at liturgical reform that had taken place between 1948 and 1959 during the pontificates of Pius XII and John XXIII. In this case, the Congregation for Rites was intimately involved in the implementation of changes in worship approved by the Pope, which proved to be problematic for the following reasons. First, the work of reform was entrusted to persons who had other time-consuming jobs in the Congregation for Rites. Their work on the reform always took second place. Second, the president and the secretary of the commission were, respectively, the prefect and secretary of the Congregation for Rites. Their many commitments made the organization of meetings very difficult and impeded progress. Third, the situation was further complicated because certain problems of the Congregation for Rites were passed on to the commission for study and deliberation. This, too, slowed down the process of implementation. Fourth, the project lacked clarity, and there was not sufficient outside help.

This situation, with the difficulties listed above, was well known to Father Bugnini, who was the secretary of the Commission for the Liturgical Reform established by Pius XII. Consequently, while the first version of the *Primitiae* instruction was being drafted, the idea of setting up a postconciliar commission for the implementation of the liturgical reform that would be independent of the Sacred Congregation for Rites found favor. There was reason to believe that Pope Paul VI himself approved of the idea of this new commission.

In the establishment of a postconciliar commission for the liturgical reform, several concrete details needed to be considered. Three possible models were proposed. The first possibility was the institution of a completely new

[2] Lercaro, *Lettere dal Concilio,* 177.
[3] Ibid., 47–48.

commission that would have the advantage of allowing freedom in appointing competent experts who would ensure that the work of the commission was efficient and reliable. The commission could set up its offices in the Palazzo Santa Marta in the Vatican, where the conciliar commissions already had their offices. Because this location was distinct from the location of the Congregation for Rites, it would both facilitate the working process and guarantee its independence. This model, however, had the disadvantage of creating an inevitable tension with the Congregation for Rites, which would undoubtedly lead to misunderstandings, suspicion, and unpleasant situations.

The second model was to reconfirm the Pontifical Commission for the Liturgical Reform instituted by Pope Pius XII. Its activity had been suspended two years earlier with the opening of the council. This possibility had the advantage of avoiding turmoil in the circles involved and of making an already existing office more efficient. But the disadvantages were obvious. The commission was connected to the Congregation for Rites, and most of its members were inactive. As mentioned above, they were already overburdened with other responsibilities, so work on the liturgical reform would lie stagnant. Consequently, this model would only be acceptable under the following conditions. The commission would have to be formally established (which had never been the case—things had always been done informally). It would have to be made autonomous in order to ensure that it would function properly and accomplish its task in a reasonable amount of time. The commission would need to be directed by people who were dedicated to the work full time and not employed in other curial offices.

The third model was to divide the Congregation for Rites into two distinct sections: one working with the causes of beatifying and canonizing saints, and a second section dedicated solely to the sacred liturgy. This was the most radical and permanent solution. To many it was also the most logical and satisfactory solution. The time seemed ripe for this solution. The need for such a division of the Congregation for Rites had already been discussed in 1953, and the idea surfaced again a few years later. Finally, when Pope John XXIII was elected, on October 28, 1958, the division of the Congregation for Rites seemed a certainty, but the plan was never implemented. The already-announced reorganization of the Roman Curia could have also provided the framework for such a division of the Congregation for Rites.

It is not difficult to see that the models considered in 1963 contained the blueprints for the establishment of the Consilium and for the later reorganization of the Congregation for Divine Worship. The Consilium emerged from the first model and brought with it the advantages and the disadvantages foreseen in 1963: efficient and reliable work, obstructed, however, by misunderstandings and suspicion. The Congregation for Divine Worship instituted in 1969 was the realization of the third model.

The proposed Pontifical Commission for the Liturgical Reform was to have the following characteristics. First, it was to be autonomous and deal solely with the reform. For this reason it would be necessary to exclude from the commission all those already permanently engaged in offices and positions of responsibility, such as those of the Roman Curia.

Second, it was to work efficiently in order to accomplish the reform within a reasonable period of time. It was recalled that the liturgical reform of the Council of Trent took around fifty years, although the reform of the primary liturgical books required eight years of work. For the liturgical reform of Vatican II, it should also be possible for the commission to complete its work within eight years, but much would depend on its efficiency and organization.

Third, the commission was to have an international character—an indispensable condition for expressing and interpreting the needs of the whole church and for bringing about a reform acceptable to all.

Fourth, it would be composed of a secretariat, a large group of experts divided into a number of subcommissions, and a group of around thirty bishops and cardinals to oversee and pass judgment on the proposals of the experts. It was envisaged that after the drafts of the proposed revisions had been examined in light of various disciplines (pastoral, theological, anthropological, etc.) by the commission, they would then be sent to the presidents of the bishops' conferences and then to the Holy Father.

A Group of Experts

The draft instruction provided certain experts the opportunity to meet and to work together on the implementation of the reform. Conversations and meetings began to take place between Cardinal Lercaro and Father Bugnini. The meetings were private and were held mostly at the Convent of Santa Priscilla, where Cardinal Lercaro stayed when he was in Rome. It was because of these meetings that the two men developed a sense of mutual understanding and trust that was to continue for years to come. Lercaro was also able to have frequent conversations with Pope Paul VI on matters of reform, since he was one of the four Moderators of the council. Developing the draft instruction was the catalyst for establishing a relationship of trust between the Pope, Cardinal Lercaro, and Father Bugnini that would see them through many difficulties and would carry forward the reform. But it was Bugnini who most came to the fore, thanks to the draft instruction.

In addition to Bugnini and Lercaro, key collaborators included Cipriano Vagaggini, Aimé-Georges Martimort, and Johannes Wagner. Vagaggini was the secretary for the group that wrote fundamental documents such as the Rite of Communion Under Both Species, the instruction *Eucharisticum mysterium,* and drafts of some of the new Eucharistic Prayers of the Roman Missal.[4] Martimort was in charge of the revision of the Breviary, and Wagner of the Roman Missal. This first group of experts would constitute the nucleus of what would later become the Consilium. Therefore, although the draft instruction of October 1963 was never adopted, it nonetheless provided the context for appreciating the complexity of the work ahead.

Plans for the Organization of the Reform

By mid-December 1963, it was clear to those involved in the liturgical reform that it was necessary to draw up a systematic plan of work and to organize a means of carrying it out. Two projects of reform were commissioned by Pope Paul VI: one to be developed by the Congregation for Rites (which we will call Project A) and the other by Father Bugnini (which we will call Project B).

Project A was a well-structured program. The introduction, which stressed the need to divide the preparatory work among various groups of experts, each of whom would be charged with a specific sector of the work, was followed by a list of the fourteen study groups that were to treat various elements of the reform mandated by the Constitution on the Sacred Liturgy. The first was to deal with a definitive revision of the Psalter, and a second group was to treat the revision of the liturgical calendar. Five groups dealt with the reform of the Breviary: the distribution of the Psalter over a longer period of time than one week; the revision of the biblical readings; the revision of the patristic readings; the revision of the accounts of the lives of the saints; and the revision of the hymns. Additional groups dealt with the revision of the Order of the Mass, with new prefaces and prayers of the faithful; distribution of the Lectionary readings used at Mass in a three-year cycle; rubrics for concelebration and

---

[4] For Vagaggini's activity in the Consilium, see A. Bugnini, "Lettera all'Editore," *Lex Orandi Lex Credendi: Miscellanea in onore di P. Cipriano Vagaggini,* ed. Gerardo Bekés and Giustino Farnedi (Rome: Editrice Anselmiana, 1980) 11–15.

Communion under both species; the revision of the Roman Pontifical; the revision of the Roman Ritual; completion of the *editio typica* of the books of Gregorian chant; and the revision of the Roman Martyrology.

Now came the task of organizing the work. It was agreed that while the council was in session, it was not advisable to ask the Congregation for Rites to direct the work, although some staff members of that congregation could be consulted because of their knowledge and experience of the subject. Neither did it seem advisable to give the direction of the work to the Conciliar Commission on the Sacred Liturgy, because many of its members lacked the proper preparation for such work. It would also have been difficult to convoke meetings because the members were numerous and lived in so many different parts of the world. It simply was not practical. Nevertheless, the members and the experts of the commission were aware of the challenges, limitations, and objectives of the liturgical reform.

In the end it was proposed that the work on the reform be entrusted to a reduced commission whose members, because they were on the Conciliar Commission, were also familiar with the problems that had arisen in the conciliar discussions. The first name indicated was that of Cardinal Arcadio María Larraona, prefect of the Sacred Congregation for Rites and president of the Conciliar Commission. Then came Cardinal Giacomo Lercaro and three other bishops: Francis Grimshaw, archbishop of Birmingham, England; Joseph Martin, bishop of Nicolet, Canada; and Franz Zauner, bishop of Linz, Austria. The cardinals and bishops were to be assisted by a few technical experts: Martimort, Wagner, Borella, Frutaz, Bugnini, Vagaggini, Dirks, and Antonelli. The duties of the commission were to set general criteria for the work and distribute it to the various study groups. It could have been convoked from time to time if important questions arose and to clarify doubts regarding interpretation of the Constitution.

This section of Project A concluded by noting that the secretariat of the Conciliar Commission on the Sacred Liturgy could also easily function as secretariat to this commission, since it already had all the necessary materials. The third section of the document gave the composition of the various study groups listed in section one.

It was rather easy to evaluate Project A. The most important feature of this project was not so much in distributing the work as in establishing the office to oversee it. At the same time this was the weakness of Project A. The intention was to give the impression that a new Office was being established, an Office that was neither the Congregation for Rites nor the Conciliar Commission on the

Sacred Liturgy. But on careful consideration of the project, it seems legitimate to wonder if the new Office was really new at all. First of all, it was to include a number of officials of the Sacred Congregation for Rites and would be directed by Cardinal Larraona, prefect of the Sacred Congregation for Rites and also president of the Conciliar Commission on the Sacred Liturgy. Finally, the least innovative aspect of the project stipulated that its secretariat was to be the same as that of the Conciliar Commission on the Sacred Liturgy. This secretariat was still tied to the Congregation for Rites and was located in Vatican offices apart from the other secretariats of Conciliar Commissions. Thus the Office would have been largely under the direction of the Congregation for Rites.

Project B, proposed by Bugnini, looked more like a collection of notes for personal use than a well-organized proposal for official presentation. It is, however, interesting to see how the future secretary of the Consilium envisaged how the work was to be carried out as well as the structure of the new Office. Bugnini's project was limited to presenting how the work was to be carried out. The question of appointments to the commission, whether of bishops or experts, was not broached. Almost certainly Bugnini already had in mind the names of the bishops and experts capable of carrying out the work of the reform, although at that stage he could not be certain who would be chosen to direct the commission.

The project presented a page-size diagram with the Holy Father at the top, followed by the bishops' conferences, then the commission, the secretariat, and the first group of liturgical books to be reformed: Breviary, Missal, Pontifical, Ritual (phase one). Next came the second group of books to be revised: the Ceremonial of Bishops, the Code of Liturgical Law, and the Martyrology (phase two). Placed between the two groups were the theological, pastoral, musical, and historical sections.

Phase one would be carried out in four stages. First, there would be the technical structuring by various subcommissions and sections. Next, the subcommissions would need to revise the theological, pastoral, musical, and historical dimensions of the work. Third, the commission would need to do a final review of the work. Lastly, with the approval of the Pope the draft of each ritual would then be sent to the bishops' conferences.[5]

---

[5] This two-phased process was also the case for previous liturgical reforms of the Roman Rite: after the Council of Trent and again in preparing the revision of the rites of Holy Week that began in 1948. The basis for these reforms was the liturgical calendar itself, since it affects both the Breviary and the Missal.

Phase two would begin once the revision of the primary liturgical books had taken place. The revision of the secondary texts important for the reform—the Ceremonial of Bishops, the Code of Liturgical Law, and the Martyrology—would constitute the work of this phase. There was a question of whether it was worthwhile to plan a reform of the Martyrology. If it was to be reformed, the work would have to precede the other revisions because it would affect the calendar of the Breviary and of the Missal. But the reform of the Martyrology hardly seemed that urgent.

Conclusion

The year 1963 closed with an event of fundamental importance in the history of the liturgy of the church: the approval of the Constitution on the Sacred Liturgy by the council on December 4, during its third public session. In that same month the implementation of the liturgical reform began in earnest with the draft proposals for the organization of the Consilium, the organization that would direct the revision of the liturgical books and the implementation of the reform. Despite some initial obstacles, the reform was launched and began at a slow but steady pace. A network of relationships had been established that inspired confidence and optimism in the future of the liturgical renewal.

The last three months of 1963, however, remain the least-known period of the history of the implementation of the Vatican II liturgy. The names of the people who worked together in preparing the drafts remain anonymous. Of the work achieved at that time, no trace is found in any official document.

Nevertheless, although it produced no results of an official character, that period is fundamental to an adequate understanding of the subsequent story of the Consilium and of the liturgical reform. It was precisely in the final months of 1963 that certain people began to meet and challenges were brought to light. The challenges that emerged were essentially the following: the complexity of the liturgical reform to be carried out; proposing a general plan of reform; establishing an international commission to which the reform would be entrusted. These people and challenges were to constitute the basis of the future Office and of the eventual reform of the liturgy.

As we have seen throughout the previous pages, the most important factor in these early years of renewal was the bringing together of those charged with studying the implementation of the liturgical reform. It was they who constituted the nucleus and the spirit of the future Consilium and of the reform itself. These internationally respected figures, wisely appointed by Pope Paul VI and known for their leadership and open-mindedness, were just the kind of individuals needed to advance a liturgical reform that would respond to the needs of the contemporary world.

The discreet appointment of Lercaro and Bugnini, officially confirmed at the beginning of 1964, was essential for the success of the reform. These appointments by Paul VI demonstrated not only open-mindedness on the Pope's part but also a fair degree of courage. Lercaro enjoyed greater prestige internationally than in Italy. Within the Roman Curia and beyond, he was often seen as being too progressive, both in terms of his politics and his liturgical views. As for Bugnini, his appointment was truly a vindication, since it was only one year before that he had been sidelined by the Curia. From that moment on, he would remain at the helm of the liturgical reform of Vatican II until 1975, when the Congregation for Divine Worship was restructured.

Working with Lercaro and Bugnini in those months were also others, as we have seen, who were to play an important role in the work of the reform: Cipriano Vagaggini, who directed the work on the rite of concelebration and Communion under both species, on the instruction *Eucharisticum mysterium,* and on the new anaphoras of the Missal; Aimé-Georges Martimort, who directed the work on the new Breviary; and Johannes Wagner, who directed the work on the new Missal.

The Pope's idea of revising liturgical law led to the immediate preparation of a draft for a motu proprio and a related instruction. It was precisely this *Primitiae* project and its instruction concerning those elements of the reform which could have been put into practice from December 25, 1963, that necessitated a comprehensive revision of almost every aspect of the reform: the Mass, the Divine Office, and the sacraments. The preparation of the project offered the first clear picture of the breadth and complexity of the future reform.

Those who worked on the motu proprio or *Primitiae* project, Bugnini in particular, were seriously considering the establishment of a Postconciliar Commission for the Liturgical Reform. This pontifical commission was to be independent of the Congregation for Divine Worship's control, concerned only with the reform, and was to be international in character. The internal structure of the new organization was also indicated: working groups composed of bishops and a secretariat assisted by experts. The draft documents elaborated by the commission would be submitted to the national bishops' conferences and then to the Pope.

It was probable that the Pope himself agreed with the idea of instituting a new commission of this type, since he had requested the drafting of a general plan of reform. The responsibility was given to two individuals who were representative of two points of view: Bugnini for Project B and an expert from the Congregation for Rites for Project A. The two plans, very similar in regard to the revision and organization of the liturgical material to be entrusted to various study groups, differed both as to the nature of the organization to which the reform was to be entrusted and as to the individuals who would be responsible for its direction.

Project B, which supported the ideas expressed earlier, laid more emphasis on the international aspect of the Office and its independence from the Congregation for Rites. Project A, on the other hand, envisaged a restricted commission under the direction of the Congregation for Rites. Essentially the possibilities were two: to entrust the reform to the Congregation for Rites by means of an Office dependent on the Congregation or to create a new Office independent of the Congregation for Rites. As it turned out, the problem would be solved at the beginning of the new year. The choice had already been made to develop the Office envisaged by Bugnini.

Finally, not to be overlooked was the difference of opinions that already existed regarding the nature and method of the reform, which were later to become so important. On the one hand, the Congregation for Rites was anxious to discover a way of retaining the leadership of the reform. On the other hand, Lercaro and Bugnini both had a wider vision and not a great deal of faith in the Congregation. The fact that both Bugnini and an official from the Congregation for Rites were given the task of drafting a general project of reform probably indicated an intention not to exclude the Congregation for Rites completely from the work of reform and to favor a compromise between the two points of view. This compromise would prove problematic in the future.

Chapter Two

The Consilium Is Born

(January–March 1964)

The Preparatory Consilium

Early in 1964 senior Vatican officials set out to deal with the challenge of the practical implementation of the liturgy Constitution just approved. The efforts at setting up a working group for directing the implementation of the reform made the complexity of the task apparent, but it must be admitted that the group did not have a clear idea of exactly what they wanted to accomplish. Only a handful of people knew the kind of structure and characteristics the future working group would need to have. That is why the birth of the new organization had to mature through various phases, amidst difficulties and disagreements.

None of the few existing studies on the Consilium has adequately explored its origins and evolution. Indicative of this lack of information is confusion over the actual date the Consilium was established. The most frequently recurring dates are January 13, January 25, and February 29, 1964. Bugnini himself offers some clarity on the matter:

> February 29, 1964, was the date of birth of the *"Consilium ad exsequendam Constitutionem de sacra Liturgia,"* a title which smacks somewhat of Baroque, if you will, but which indicates well the features of the institution: the boldest and most fundamental liturgical reform of all times, desired by the Second Vatican Council, will remain linked with this organization, born

of the will, the intelligence and the attentive and far-sighted circumspection of the Holy Father Pope Paul VI. . . . An organization of humble, modest origins, just like all authentic works of God, St. Vincent would say. . . . On February 29 it was born on paper, not officially. The foundations had been laid six weeks earlier, on January 14,[1] with the formation of a pre-Consilium, or one could say more importantly, of a "subcommittee" of the Consilium. . . . This subcommittee had the task of preparing not the Constitution which already existed, but the larger working group that would render it operative. It was made up of three Eminent Cardinals—two from the Roman Curia and one a diocesan bishop: Larraona, prefect of the Sacred Congregation of Rites; Giobbe, datary of His Holiness, and Lercaro, archbishop of Bologna, one Spaniard and two Italians. The former secretary of the "preparatory" commission was also asked to serve as secretary for this group as well. Each of the members of the subcommittee had been appointed by the Pope.[2]

The most popular and accepted date for establishment of the Consilium is January 25, 1964,[3] the same date that the motu proprio *Sacram Liturgiam* was promulgated. It mentions the Consilium in these words:

Many of the prescriptions of the Constitution clearly cannot be put into effect in a short period of time, since some of the rites must be first revised and new liturgical books prepared. In order that this work may be carried out with the wisdom and prudence required, we are setting up a special commission with the principal task of seeing that the prescriptions of the Constitution are put into effect.[4]

The reference to *Sacram Liturgiam* as the document that instituted the Consilium was later officially confirmed by the instruction *Inter oecumenici*.[5] It should be kept in mind that the Consilium was not born in a day but evolved gradually over a period of time. Bugnini described this evolution by noting the phases of its initial development: the period of its preparation

[1] Certainly a mistake. The correct date is January 13, 1964.

[2] A. Bugnini, "President of the Consilium," *Miscellanea liturgica in onore di Sua Eminenza Cardinal Giacomo Lercaro,* I (Tournai: Desclée, 1966) 11.

[3] See Carlo Braga, *Rinnovamento della Liturgia* (Rome: Edizioni Liturgiche, 1965) 13. Enrico Cattaneo, on the other hand, maintains that the Consilium was instituted on February 29. *Il culto cristiano in occidente* (Rome: Edizioni Liturgiche, 1978) 637.

[4] English text from *DOL* 278; for the Latin see *EDIL* 179.

[5] *EDIL* 200; *DOL* 294.

and its establishment, when the names for the composition of the Consilium were presented to the Holy Father and the secretariat was organized.

The Preparatory Period

On January 13, 1964, a letter written by the Cardinal Secretary of State appointed three cardinals to the Consilium—Lercaro, Giobbe, and Larraona —with Father Bugnini as secretary. In a letter dated January 10 addressed to Cardinal Lercaro, Bugnini raised a number of questions. First, deciding on the name of the Consilium. Bugnini thought it wise to avoid the adjective "postconciliar" and preferred a variation on the name used for Pius XII's liturgical commission: The Pontifical Commission for the Liturgical Reform or Consilium for the Reform of the Sacred Liturgy. Second, that cardinals and bishops should make up the Consilium, along with a few priests of particular distinction. As for the Consilium's consultors, they would be taken both from the Preparatory and Conciliar commissions. While there would be an attempt to make the group of consultors as international as possible, special attention would be given to competence. The secretariat still needed to be organized with regard to personnel and location. Finally, the presidency of the pre-Consilium still remained uncertain. While three cardinals had been named, it was not yet clear as to how the three would collaborate: as a triumvirate, with one as a *primus inter pares* (perhaps the eldest) or with one person directing the work as president. Bugnini describes the first meeting:

> The first meeting was held on January 15, 1964,[6] at Santa Marta, in the shadow of St. Peter's, where a small room had been put at our disposal by the local section of the General Secretariat of the Council. There was a discussion among the three members which was recorded verbatim by the secretary. This was the pre-Consilium's first meeting. The order of the day included several communications by Cardinal Lercaro, as well as drawing up a plan for the future functioning of the pre-Consilium along with other proposals.[7]

Lercaro's communications concerned the pre-Consilium itself. He discussed the purpose of the commission instituted by the Pope for the implementation of the council's Constitution on the Sacred Liturgy and the importance of the pre-Consilium's mandate. Regarding the program, the secretary prepared

[6] The original text reads incorrectly "February."
[7] Bugnini, "President of the Consilium," 11.

a draft of two typewritten pages that broadly reflected Project B, which we examined earlier (see p. 10). The discussion focused on the two new possible drafts for the motu proprio. Neither Lercaro's communications nor the program could be given serious consideration at that stage.

The pre-Consilium lacked a clear organizational structure. All three cardinals were equally responsible, but Cardinal Giobbe, as datary of His Holiness, had little status. He was a gentle man who shrank from the intrigues within the Curia. From that day on he took part in almost all the pre-Consilium's meetings. Although he was not an expert in liturgy, he was always a man of discretion and balance. Thanks to those very qualities, he supported the line of reform carried forward by the majority of the Consilium. Lercaro possessed two great advantages: he was recognized internationally as an expert on liturgy,[8] and he was one of the four moderators of the council. At that first meeting, however, neither of these two qualifications gave him particular authority. His principal authority was in being spokesperson for the Pope. Nevertheless, without an explicit mandate, all that he could hope for from the other members was respectful attention.

The one with the greatest authority was Cardinal Larraona. He was appointed president of the Conciliar Commission on the Sacred Liturgy on September 4, 1962, and was still prefect of the Sacred Congregation for Rites. Therefore, it was understandable that he would wield significant power within the pre-Consilium. It was also noteworthy that the meeting was held at Larraona's apartment.

The secretary is always the key person of any office, but Bugnini was relegated to an unusually inferior position as a secretary to three cardinals for an office that really did not yet exist. As he noted in his memoirs, the beginning of the Consilium was rather disconcerting and got off to a bad start.[9] Given the reality he had to confront, it is hard to disagree with this opinion.

If the first meeting was uneventful, the second meeting was even more so. All that happened was an examination of the names to be proposed to the Pope as members of the Consilium. The list was unanimously approved. Cardinal Lercaro also proposed the names of members for the study group on the Psalter. This second meeting took place simply to examine a list of names that could have been drawn up in twenty-four hours. This way of proceeding certainly did not appear to be consonant with the program of liturgical renewal mandated

---

[8] See Lercaro, *Lettere dal Concilio,* 35.

[9] Bugnini, "President of the Consilium," 12.

by the council and envisaged by the Pope. The beginning of the pre-Consilium a month earlier had been bad enough—but this was even worse!

Probably none of those involved had much faith in the pre-Consilium. Lercaro and Bugnini, well aware of the vast program of liturgical reform mandated by the council, could not possibly have considered this initial structure a suitable instrument for carrying out such an immense task. Larraona, prefect of the Sacred Congregation for Rites and president of the Conciliar Commission on the Sacred Liturgy, had nothing to gain from promoting an Office that would necessarily encroach upon the territory of the Congregation of which he was prefect. That is why the second meeting lasted barely an hour. The participants realized that the future of the reform depended, not on any decision that might be taken within the pre-Consilium, but on what was happening outside of it. Everyone was eager to return to a more open forum where the fate of the reform was really being decided.

Now we must examine the course of events during the month that elapsed between the first and the second meetings and return to the subject of the task given to the pre-Consilium to draft the motu proprio, an agenda item at the group's first meeting.

The Motu Proprio Sacram Liturgiam

In Bugnini's letter of January 10, 1964, to Lercaro, the secretary said among other things, "With regard to the motu proprio, Your Eminence, I feel it would be better to give it no further thought." He was still referring to the *Primitiae* draft. In its place at the beginning of January 1964, we find other drafts: one from the Secretariat General of the council (January 11, 1964); one from the Congregation for Rites (January 14, 1964); and one from the pre-Consilium (January 17, 1964).

After the failure of the *Primitiae* draft, Pope Paul did not abandon his intention but entrusted Archbishop Felici, secretary general of the council, with the task of preparing a motu proprio. The draft prepared by the secretariat of the council was barely finished when it came to the attention of Cardinal Larraona, who, instead of examining and correcting the text, decided to order a new version of the draft by the Congregation for Rites, with the collaboration of the *periti* belonging to the Conciliar Commission on the Sacred Liturgy. Bugnini, still a member of that commission, was among those called to attend the meeting of the Congregation for Rites on January 11, 1964, to discuss a draft of a motu proprio.

As a result, for the Consilium's first meeting, there were two different drafts: the first, by the secretariat of the council, prepared at the Pope's request and passed on officially to the cardinals and the secretary of the Consilium, which had been instituted in the meantime; the second, the work of the Congregation for Rites, in the hands of Cardinal Larraona, meant to replace the first draft.

The draft of the council's Secretariat General consisted of four typewritten pages, which were limited to general concepts and avoided going into specifics. It was made up of a lengthy introduction followed by the body of the document, which comprised five major sections: liturgical education (arts. 15–17); the setting up of diocesan commissions (arts. 45–46); the obligation of a homily for certain Masses (art. 52); the celebration of matrimony during Mass after the homily (art. 78); the "public" character of the Office on the part of those mentioned in article 98; and a conclusion. After a few slight alterations, the introduction and the conclusion of this project became part of the promulgated motu proprio.

The draft of the Congregation for Rites, on the other hand, consisted of practical dispositions corresponding roughly to articles 1–9 of the eventual motu proprio. This version, as it was presented by Cardinal Larraona during the first meeting of the Consilium, focused on a collection of texts prepared by the Conciliar Commission on the Sacred Liturgy. This commission, before the closing of the council's second session, wanted to distinguish those liturgical norms that could be applied immediately after the *vacatio legis* (the interim period between a law's promulgation and its entry into force) and those that instead would require either the intervention of the territorial ecclesiastical authorities or the revision of the liturgical books.

All that remained to the newly constituted Consilium, therefore, was to try to reconcile the two versions of the motu proprio. During the meeting of January 15, already mentioned, it was decided to draw up a text that would follow Archbishop Felici's formulation for the beginning and the conclusion, and the version drawn up by the conciliar *periti* for the central part, which contained the norms. Therefore, two days later there was a new draft of the motu proprio adopted by the Consilium that was actually a juxtaposition of the two versions described above. This text drawn up by the Consilium was published in *L'Osservatore Romano* with some corrections.

The sequence of events that led to the final version of the motu proprio published by *L'Osservatore Romano* was quite complex. Above all, it must be kept in mind that the Office that was to carry out the liturgical reform was working under confusing circumstances. In a letter dated January 10 to Cardinal Lercaro, Father Bugnini observed that there was kind of "a scramble to get on board." This was due to the fact that the secretariat of the council had received a mandate from the Pope to deal with the *vacatio legis* of a conciliar document, the Constitution on the Sacred Liturgy. The Sacred Congregation for Rites, however, was still in charge of liturgical matters, but while the council was meeting, the Congregation had been forced to suspend its activity. Some believed that this was the opportunity for the Congregation for Rites to resume dealing with matters liturgical.

The secretary of the Consilium, after the failure of the *Primitiae* initiative, kept prudently out of the way. He knew full well that because of the weakness of his position and the strength of the opposition he had little chance of success.

On January 29, 1964, *L'Osservatore Romano* published the Latin text of the motu proprio *Sacram Liturgiam;* the Italian translation followed on January 31. Compared with the Consilium's version, the promulgated motu proprio contained various corrections of style and explanations that clarified certain expressions. There were two significant additions: a supplement concerning the institution of a special commission to implement the provisions of the Constitution on the Sacred Liturgy, and the rewriting and amplification of article IX, which provoked much consternation and difference of opinion. The special commission was described as follows:

> Many of the prescriptions of the Constitution clearly cannot be put into effect in a short period of time, since some of the rites must be first revised and new liturgical books prepared. In order that this work may be carried out in the wisdom and prudence required, we are setting up a special commission with the principal task of seeing that the prescriptions of the Constitution are put into effect.[10]

The Pope's use of the word "clearly" was a sign that he was more than ever convinced of the need to establish the Consilium after the *Primitiae* attempt and the various drafts of the motu proprio *Sacram Liturgiam*. The will to institute the Consilium had thus been supported by the Pope; it only remained to organize the Office. Nevertheless, another month would pass before it became a reality. The last resistance of the Roman Curia was finally overcome only because of the pressure of the events. All the other norms in the motu

[10] *DOL* 278.

proprio were taken from the drafts mentioned above. The date established for the norms to take effect—February 16, the First Sunday of Lent—was the same indicated earlier as the date for the *vacatio legis* to cease.[11]

Bugnini was convinced that something in the drafts of the motu proprio had been amiss. In a letter to Cardinal Lercaro dated January 10, he observed that "the two drafts that I examined are equivalent: juridically they are quite good, but they are not completely in agreement with the Constitution." The subsequent publication of the text in *L'Osservatore Romano* would bring to light the contrast between some of the motu proprio's norms and the principles of the Constitution on the Sacred Liturgy.

On January 31, 1964, the day after the publication of *Sacram Liturgiam*, *L'Osservatore Romano* carried a commentary on the motu proprio by Salvatore Marsili of the Pontifical Liturgical Institute of Sant'Anselmo, one of the most qualified scholars in liturgical matters. After describing the instructions given in the motu proprio, the article attempted to head off a few possible objections that might arise. The *vacatio legis* could not have been postponed until the postconciliar commission had finished its lengthy task because the liturgical renewal demanded new texts and new rites. Furthermore, the bishops were now responsible for the reform, and the new processes for renewal needed to be implemented and tested. Regarding innovations that could have been authorized by territorial ecclesiastical authorities (such as a wider use of the vernacular language or a greater simplification of the rite of the Mass), the article emphasized that the reform was so complex and required such coordination that it would necessarily demand time and moderation. Bishops, however, could always request Vatican authorization for special cases.

The article ended by admitting that the motu proprio could cause frustration for the impatient, since it appeared to be rather hesitant in applying the new principles of the liturgical reform. Marsili, then, accepted *Sacram Liturgiam,* but as a starting point that needed to be sustained with courage

---

[11] On December 4, 1963, after the promulgation of the Constitution on the Sacred Liturgy, the secretary of the council read out the following decree: "The Holy Father has decided that the Constitution on the Sacred Liturgy, which has just been approved, will come into force on February 16, 1964, the first Sunday in Lent. In the meantime, the Holy Father himself will decide when and how the decrees of this Constitution will be implemented; no one, therefore, has the right to put the new provisions into practice of their own authority before the established date." (See A. Bugnini, *Verso la riforma liturgica* [Rome: Libreria Editrice Vaticana, 1965] 54.)

and confidence by the very commission that this motu proprio established. According to Marsili, this document was very timid when compared with the global vision of reform indicated by the Constitution on the Sacred Liturgy. The thing to do, however, was to accept it and have confidence in the Pope, who would certainly not block the reform desired by the council.

But while Marsili looked toward the future, others preferred to remain anchored in the past. On February 5, 1964, *Il Tempo,* one of Rome's daily newspapers, published an article whose polemical title in English reads: "Argument over the Liturgical Reform breaks out—the Vatican newspaper 'disagrees' with the Pope." After examining several of the norms in *Sacram Liturgiam,* particularly the provision requiring the Holy See's approval of the translations of all liturgical texts, the article criticized Marsili's questioning of this provision, calling it "a disrespectful observation." "It is unbelievable! *L'Osservatore Romano,* the official Vatican newspaper, has published an article criticizing a pontifical decision!"

The article provoked more negative reaction than could be imagined. Using the pseudonym "Helveticus," those in the Curia who disapproved of the conciliar liturgical reforms wrote withering attacks against the provisions of the motu proprio. This was the first indication to those who were about to launch the reform that the path would not be easy.

The French bishops were criticized for having issued some regulations on liturgical matters that seemed overly progressive. After the first scathing article in *Il Tempo,* the same newspaper ran a second article several days later that attacked the French bishops for having introduced the readings of the Mass in the vernacular.

The attack did not go unanswered. In the February 1964 issue of *Questi-talia,* a journal published in Venice, an article appeared under this heading, in English translation: "The Strange Story of a Motu Proprio." The article was penned by Marsili to defend the reform mandated by the Constitution on the Sacred Liturgy. He critically focused on two points—the article in *Il Tempo* mentioned above and the motu proprio itself. He spoke quite openly of "anti-reformist intriguers who at fascist instigation have cried scandal" and of an "article by a newspaper yearning for the good old days." As for the motu proprio, the conciliatory tone of the article in *L'Osservatore Romano* had disappeared.

Writing under the pseudonym "Pascasio Minuto Negri," Marsili laid bare every one of the contradictions in *Sacram Liturgiam.* Among the many inconsistencies, he pointed out that the Constitution on the Sacred Liturgy had given the national bishops' conferences the authority to approve vernacular translations of the liturgy (*SC* 22, 36), while the motu proprio required the confirmation of the Holy See (art. 9). Thus, even though the Constitution had envisaged greater juridical importance given to "competent territorial bodies of bishops," the motu proprio limited that authority. The article also criticized the fact that the motu proprio had omitted certain conciliar provisions such as the prayer of the faithful at the conclusion of the Liturgy of the Word. The author ended the article by strongly criticizing both the curial agencies and others involved with the document's preparation. He emphasized the many obscure points in "this rather absurd story," not least of which was the request for a postconciliar document that would have required only "the collaboration of one or two liturgists, a couple of canon law experts, and a Latinist." The article was essentially a warning to be on guard against the danger of the Roman Curia, which had historically tended to impede the reforming impetus of councils and bishops.

These journalistic duels over *Sacram Liturgiam* had their own particular importance because they heralded the onset of the opposition by those reactionaries who would stand in open disagreement with the liturgical reform mandated by an ecumenical council. The polemic, which reached its climax a few years later with publications by ultraconservatives, which were then echoed by some cardinals and Curia members, found its logical conclusion in the schism provoked by Archbishop Marcel Lefebvre in the mid-1970s.

The controversy was not limited to the Curia and definitely not confined to Italy. For the record, Marsili accurately read the situation. Beginning in February 1964, a long series of protests and authoritative interventions began to reach the Offices of the Roman Curia and the Vatican Secretariat of State. In a report dated February 13, 1964, Monsignor Johannes Wagner of Trier noted the disappointment that the motu proprio had caused in Germany: "The hope and expectations of many Catholics and non-Catholics have remained unfulfilled, and there is now widespread anxiety and sadness." The report criticized the style of Latin used and pointed out some of the Latinists' errors. In his opposition to article IX of the document, Wagner argued that the Council Fathers purposely intended to do away with the need for texts translated into the vernacular to be submitted to the Holy See (*SC* 36 §4). Lastly, Wagner proposed that there be a general instruction on the principles of translating from Latin into the vernacular. Cardinal Joseph Frings, archbishop of Cologne, in a statement criticizing article IX of the motu proprio, insisted that the bishops' conferences should have control over vernacular translations. The Austrian bishops of Linz and Graz-Seckau offered the same criticisms in no uncertain terms: "Less than two months after the solemn and unanimous vote of the council, it [the Constitution] is being made ineffective by a decision from Rome that touches that point so dear to the Fathers' hearts: the decentralization of the church—the vernacular language."

But what caused the greatest clamor was the position taken by the French bishops. At the end of their plenary assembly held in Rome (November 30–December 2, 1963), they had approved a number of decisions for the application of the Constitution on the Sacred Liturgy. Those decisions were much more advanced than what would later be conceded by *Sacram Liturgiam*. For example, they decided to permit use of the French language not only in the readings of the Mass but also in other invariable parts of the Mass as well, such as the *Kyrie,* the *Gloria,* the Creed, the *Sanctus,* and the *Agnus Dei*. It should be noted that these decisions were almost unanimous. Of the 106 bishops voting, 97 voted in favor, 8 were opposed. Pending the availability of the definitive French translation, the translations found in various people's hand missals used at that time were permitted for use.[12]

At the end of January, the French bishops were faced with a motu proprio that not only curtailed decisions they had already made but imposed the authority of the Holy See to revise and approve all vernacular texts. They reacted with great firmness. In a letter dated February 7, Joseph-Marie Martin, archbishop of Rouen and president of the bishops' liturgical commission, wrote to several Roman curial Offices, summarizing the reflections made by the bishops of the commission that had met in Paris the previous day.[13] Essentially it reaffirmed the bishops' right, sanctioned by the council, to approve the vernacular versions without confirmation from Rome. Public opinion in France was alarmed: "They say that just two months after its promulgation, the Constitution is beaten in the breach; that the decisions made by the episcopal assemblies may be effectively neutralized by the Roman Curia; that the role of the bishops' assemblies is being undermined

---

[12] The French bishops' decisions were to have gone into effect the moment the Apostolic See published the motu proprio. However, in order to understand what happened, it must be remembered that those decisions were reached by the French episcopate while the *Primitiae* text was being prepared. That text did not consider the question of the confirmation of the translations by the Holy See; on the contrary, it affirmed that *ad interim* ("meanwhile") the vernacular versions could be approved for liturgical use by the bishops.

[13] See Appendix I, Document II.

at the very moment of its establishment by the council; that the decisions of the council are being challenged even before the council has finished."

This state of affairs could not continue. The arguments were spreading ever wider, and the bishops themselves were being drawn into the controversy.[14] The text of the motu proprio needed to be reexamined in order to find an acceptable solution to the problematic article IX.

None of the draft versions of the motu proprio contained anything contrary to the council's giving bishops' conferences authority to approve vernacular translations found in *SC* 36 §4. The draft by the secretariat of the council made no mention of the question concerning the use of the vernacular. The draft prepared by the experts of the Congregation for Rites simply stated that the episcopal conferences could approve vernacular versions for use in the liturgy. That phrase did not appear in the final version submitted by the Consilium. It had been purposely removed in order to avoid raising the problem of translations needing further consideration.

It is clear that members of the Consilium, directly responsible to the Pope for drafting the document, were still part of the Secretariat General of the council, but there is a possibility that the final formulation of the text, and in particular the problematic article IX, may very well be attributed to the Sacred Congregation for Rites.

Given the arguments and pointed criticism of early February, there needed to be a response. The challenge for the Consilium was to save the motu proprio while taking into account the numerous amendments proposed mainly in regard to article IX. The problem was particularly felt in the Secretariat of State. So it was decided to turn to Father Bugnini, who until then had remained on the periphery of the debate.

Bugnini had the amendments for the motu proprio ready on February 12. The text published in *L'Osservatore Romano* had in fact not officially taken effect, because it had yet to be entered into the *Acta Apostolicae Sedis*. Twenty-one amendments were proposed. Of these, nineteen were accepted and inserted into the text of the *Acta Apostolicae Sedis*. Of the nineteen that were accepted, fifteen were inserted as they had been proposed, and only four were altered slightly, mainly in the style of the Latin. Bugnini had included with the text of the corrections seven pages of "annotations," in

---

[14] For example, a memorandum was also presented by the Mexican bishops and reached the Consilium through the Consistorial Congregation. The whole story of the motu proprio was also published in the magazine *Il Regno* (February 1964) 38–39.

which he explained each proposed change. The most interesting annotation was the one regarding the famous article IX, about which there was so much discussion. Relations between the council and the bishops on the one hand and the Apostolic See on the other were at stake.

In order to appreciate the negative reaction to this part of the motu proprio, it is necessary to know the discussion that took place at the council regarding what was to become that part of the Constitution on the Sacred Liturgy.[15] Paragraph 4 of article 36 §4 of the Constitution on the Sacred Liturgy, granting approval of translations of liturgical texts to the "territorial ecclesiastical authority," was approved at the council by a vote of 2041 to 30.

In the period prior to the council, when bilingual texts began to be produced for the rite and the celebration of the sacraments, liturgical translation was handled in one of two ways. Either the translation of the Latin liturgical book was commissioned by local ecclesiastical authorities (this most often happened in mission territories under the responsibility of the Sacred Congregation for the Propagation of the Faith [Sacred Congregation de Propaganda Fide]), or the translation into the vernacular was provided by translators in Rome appointed by the Sacred Congregation for Rites.

The approach used by the Congregation for the Propagation of the Faith had the disadvantage that the Holy See was not at all involved in the process of approving the translation, a prerogative that had been deemed essential by canonists and others since the Council of Trent. The approach favored by the Sacred Congregation for Rites, which required its central role in translation, was more complicated than might first appear. For example, when the Polish bilingual Ritual was being produced, the Congregation for Rites searched all over Rome for a person competent in liturgy, the Polish language, and Latin literature. A translator who appeared capable was engaged by the Congregation

---

[15] Until now the Holy See, with regard to translations, had maintained two attitudes: one for mission countries and another for those territories that depended on the Congregation for Rites. For the mission countries, the Sacred Congregation de Propaganda Fide, in 1941 and then again in 1948, issued a provision that in every nation a bilingual Ritual should be compiled. The apostolic delegate to India, H.E. Mgr. Kirkels, on July 8, 1949, communicated to the bishops that they should form a commission of "priests having a knowledge of the languages at issue," in order to prepare an Indian Ritual. The translation would then be approved for a decade "without it being sent first to Rome." The commissions were held responsible for the approval. The approval, however, was given by the bishops concerned. See *Documenta pontificia ad instaurationem liturgicam spectantia* (Rome: Edizioni Liturgiche, 1953) 173–74.

to judge the quality of a translation provided by the Polish bishops. Having examined the Polish text, he wrote several pages of observations to the Congregation that were very critical of the translation. These observations were transferred to the official stationery of the Congregation and then sent back to the Polish bishops' conference.

The reaction to this critique on the part of the Polish bishops was immediate and strong. How was it possible that the text they submitted, produced by a team of outstanding scholars from the Universities of Lublin and Warsaw, assisted by a group of priests, could be so peremptorily dismissed by a Vatican congregation that had no experience of Polish life or culture? Every one of the observations sent by the Congregation was challenged, and nearly all were rejected. In the end the Congregation was forced to concede and accept the texts proposed by the Polish bishops.

A similar exchange took place when the translation of the Hungarian Ritual was submitted to the same Congregation for approval. After some time the Holy See found a Hungarian Benedictine monk at the Athenaeum of Sant'Anselmo who agreed to revise the lengthy manuscript. Unfortunately, his patriotism and enthusiasm were greater than his competence. However, due to a lack of alternatives, the Congregation was forced to accept the monk's revision and approve the Ritual. Nevertheless, given the inferior quality of the work, one could question the value of this official approval. Many believed that it was inappropriate for the Holy See to authorize a liturgical book in this way.

It seemed to Bugnini, therefore, that the best solution to this complicated problem of translation that would do justice to both the bishops' conferences and the Holy See would be as follows. The bishops' conference—or other territorial ecclesiastic authority—would form a commission of experts to prepare the work, taking responsibility for the commission's translation: its fidelity to the content of the Latin text and its integrity. This translation would then be submitted to the Holy See for confirmation. This confirmation would entail assuring that the translation had been done following the norms of the Holy See, leaving primary responsibility for this translation in the hands of the local bishops' conference. This solution would not involve the authority of the Holy See until the final stage of approval. At that point, if doubts or difficulties concerning the translation arose, the Holy See would serve as an arbiter for a solution to the problem.

A question still remained as to what norms the Holy See should follow to grant that approval or confirmation. The norms had yet to be established, but they would be based on article 36 §3 of the Constitution on the Sacred Liturgy and would establish instructions regarding the specifics of the confirmation by the Holy See.

The corrections to the motu proprio were noted in a diplomatic article written by Bugnini himself and published in *L'Osservatore Romano* of March 2/3, 1964. The article, "For the Implementation of the Conciliar Liturgical Constitution—The Motu Proprio *Sacram Liturgiam*," was a positive, moderate commentary on the motu proprio. The publication of this article marked the end of the controversy over the motu proprio.

In the Wake of the *Motu Proprio*

The motu proprio *Sacram Liturgiam* was the first document drafted by the Roman Curia to implement the liturgical reform mandated by the Second Vatican Council. It marked a delicate step: the "new" liturgy's passage from decisions of an ecumenical council to its practical implementation under the leadership of the Curia. The controversy that surrounded the document proved the importance of this transition.

In addition to constituting an important moment of passage, the document became a catalyst for several developments that would continue to haunt the liturgical reform. It was obvious from the beginning that the traditional structure of the Curia was inadequate to plan the implementation of the reform according to the expectation of the council. Given the legitimate protests, amendments to the motu proprio had to be made.

The absence of a single Office designed to coordinate in a competent manner the implementation of the conciliar liturgy became even more apparent. The various drafts that preceded the final text of *Sacram Liturgiam*, prepared by several different Offices, were proof that there was confusion on the institutional level regarding the implementation of the reform. There was a tendency in some curial circles to attempt to thwart aspects of the liturgical renewal approved by the council and supported by the Pope.

A new awareness was emerging that the liturgy could no longer be imposed from above by a few Offices of the Roman Curia, but rather needed to be received and implemented by the faithful on the local level. It was at this time that the liturgical movement had been officially sanctioned by the promulgation of the Constitution on the Sacred Liturgy. Both episcopal conferences and national liturgical commissions had been established. Moreover, they were aware not only of their duties but also of their rights. Without their collaboration, the liturgical reform could not be carried out.

There was, consequently, an urgent need to establish an international agency made up of experts able to guide the implementation of the reform in accord with the spirit of the council. Father Bugnini's role in this process became increasingly important. After the aborted first draft of the motu proprio, he had almost disappeared from the scene; he only reemerged when the controversies broke out over the formulations of *Sacram Liturgiam* as the one person capable of reconciling both the demands of the bishops' conferences and the position of the Holy See.

It is unquestionable that Bugnini's point of view was closer to that of bishops and parish priests on the local level than to that of the cardinals and other curial officials. It was becoming clear which direction his work would take: the council's reform would be carried out with the support of the bishops, the experts, the national commissions, the liturgical institutes and centers—in other words, with the local church. In fact, this was none other than the renewed and broader vision of the church understood as the People of God, so well expressed by the documents of the Second Vatican Council.

Conflict with the Roman Curia was inevitable; nevertheless, Bugnini, as secretary of the Consilium, could count on the Pope of the council. One particular incident illustrates this. In mid-February the Congregation for Rites could wait no longer. Ignoring the existence of the Consilium, it undertook a series of initiatives to settle the uncertainties of the situation to its own advantage. These initiatives found expression in a rescript dated February 14 and sent by the Congregation to the French bishops. The document's prologue illustrates the strategy of the Congregation:

> This Sacred Congregation of Rites, through the competent section in charge of the postconciliar liturgical movement, having consulted the Council for the Implementation of the Constitution on the Sacred Liturgy [Motu Proprio *Sacram Liturgiam,* January 25, 1964], and having heard the deputation from the conciliar commission on the sacred liturgy, and being provided with the necessary faculties in accordance with Canon 244, 1 and 2, of the Code of Canon Law, and having duly weighed the documentation you sent regarding the measures taken by the French episcopate on January 14, 1964, and in view of the fact that the Motu Proprio *Sacram Liturgiam* has appeared in the interim—this Congregation has thought it necessary to declare to you . . .[16]

---

[16] Translation by Matthew J. O'Connell from A. Bugnini, *Reform of the Liturgy: 1948–1975* (Collegeville: The Liturgical Press, 1990) 70–71.

The rescript was signed by Cardinal Larraona. The Offices that were to carry out the reform were described as follows: the sole responsible and decision-making agency was the Sacred Congregation for Rites, which already had an executive division with the task of overseeing the postconciliar liturgical renewal. Two other agencies followed: the *Consilium ad exsequendam Constitutionem de sacra Liturgia* and the Conciliar Commission on the Sacred Liturgy. These last two Offices, however, were to have purely consultative functions; decisions were to be made by the Congregation for Rites in consultation with the Consilium and after informing the Conciliar Commission.

The plan was clear: to relegate the Consilium to a subordinate role even before it could begin to operate. This became clear by reviewing the events as they unfolded. On Thursday, February 13, 1964, the Congregation for Rites convoked some *periti* (experts) of the Conciliar Commission to discuss the problem of the motu proprio *Sacram Liturgiam*. The *periti* present were Monsignor Johannes Wagner, Monsignor Aimé-Georges Martimort, and Father Annibale Bugnini. They were ushered into the committee room of the Congregation for Rites, where all the members of the Congregation had assembled. Cardinal Larraona spoke first, affirming that there existed no conflict between article IX of the motu proprio and the Constitution on the Sacred Liturgy.

Wagner and Martimort were then given permission to speak. Wagner read a report in Latin in which he underlined the disappointment caused in German-speaking countries by the motu proprio *Sacram Liturgiam*.[17] Martimort expressed similar feelings and proposed that a solution acceptable to both the Holy See and the episcopate should be found. Supporting Cardinal Larraona's position, several committee members made their interventions. The discussion was closed a little before noon, only an hour after it had begun.

It was evident that the purpose of the meeting was not so much to listen to the opinion of the experts as to inform them of a decision that had already been made. This was an example of procedure that, according to the rescript addressed to the French bishops mentioned earlier, the Consilium was to be consulted and the Conciliar Commission on the Sacred Liturgy was to be informed. But in reality the reply to the French bishops was given without the knowledge of the Conciliar Commission, and certainly without consulting the Consilium. Bugnini only came to know of the rescript on February

[17] See as above, p. 24.

23, when the text was sent to him from France by Canon Martimort, who had this to say about it:

> Actually, as you can see in the first paragraph of this letter from Cardinal Larraona, the Congregation of Rites has, on its own authority, constituted a section to preside over the postconciliar liturgical renewal, and this section, as you were able to see for yourself when you were convoked, comprises exclusively officials of the Congregation, namely, all those who up to the very end were hostile to the Constitution on the Liturgy. The document then claims to have consulted the Consilium, perhaps due to the fact that you were present at the meeting in question. Lastly, it affirms having heard a "deputation of the Conciliar Commission"—that deputation must be Mgr Wagner and myself. On this last point it should be said that we can hardly be deputies, seeing that the commission, which has not met since December 1, has given us no such charge.

> Cardinal Larraona hastened to carry this document and several others of the same kind, for Belgium and Chile in particular, to the Pope in order that he might see that two things have already been definitively settled: (1) the existence of this new section of the Congregation of Rites; (2) the text of the motu proprio and the interpretation which the Cardinal has given to it and to the Constitution in view of restricting as much as possible the effectiveness of the conciliar Constitution.

The preamble was intended, on the one hand, to reduce the Consilium to a mere consultative body and, on the other, to convince the bishops of the credit and authority of the responses of the Congregation. The situation was definitely confused. Which Office was responsible for the interpretation of the Constitution, the examination and approval of the decisions of bishops conferences, and for answering the queries that were being sent in, some to the Secretariat of State, others to the Congregation for Rites, others to the Consilium?

It often happened that decisions of bishops' conferences, such as those from Brazil and Chile, were passed from one Office to another while they tried to decide who was responsible for examining the texts. Reasons for designating the Office responsible for the interpretation of the Constitution on the Sacred Liturgy were collected by Bugnini in a *promemoria* (memo) addressed to the Pope. But the *promemoria* was never sent.[18] The Congregation for

---

[18] Cf. Appendix I, Document Number III, pp. 171–72.

Rites, and particularly its prefect, had taken this step in the hope that the Holy Father would eventually confirm the state of affairs that had been created. The Congregation was convinced that just as in the post-Tridentine period, the Congregation for Rites was to maintain its role in the church as the agency charged with safeguarding the orthodoxy of the rites.

The officials at the Congregation for Rites obviously failed to realize that times and circumstances had changed. It was no longer simply a matter of defending orthodoxy but also of promoting renewal. Fortunately the Pope was well aware that times had changed and that the present challenges were different from those of Trent. A new agency for promoting liturgical renewal was needed. It is likely that as far back as October 1963 the decision had been made to establish such an agency and its members had been chosen. In the controversy over the motu proprio, the Consilium's position was the one approved by the Pope during the audience granted to Cardinal Lercaro on the afternoon of February 15, 1964.

It seems that the Congregation for Rites had overplayed its hand. While its attempt at control created new confusion, it led to a way forward out of the impasse. Not many days later, decisions were being made about the authority and composition of the Consilium. At long last work could begin.

Authority and Composition of the Consilium

B etween the end of February and the beginning of March 1964, the Consilium acquired its character as an international agency for implementing the liturgical reform of the Second Vatican Council. Up to that point the pre-Consilium had been powerless to make even minor decisions. It had also been excluded from the preparation and final redaction of the motu proprio.

However, while this was happening, movement in another direction was taking place that would have great significance for the future. This movement was illustrated by the acceptance of Bugnini's amendments to the motu proprio and the audience given to Cardinal Lercaro on February 15. Nevertheless, the Consilium did not have juridical status as late as the end of February 1964 and was practically nonexistent. The only official references to its existence had been in the motu proprio and in a brief paragraph in *L'Osservatore Romano* of January 31:

> Many of the prescriptions of the Constitution clearly cannot be put into effect in a short period of time, since some of the rites must be first revised

and new liturgical books prepared. In order that this work may be carried out with the wisdom and prudence required, we are setting up a special commission with the principal task of seeing that the prescriptions of the Constitution are put into effect.[19]

As announced in the *Sacram Liturgiam,* the Holy Father has kindly deigned to institute a *Consilium ad exsequendam Constitutionem de sacra Liturgia,* and takes pleasure in counting among its members the Eminent Cardinals Giacomo Lercaro, archbishop of Bologna, Paolo Giobbe, and Arcadio Larraona; and in nominating as secretary Rev. Fr. Annibale Bugnini of the Congregation of the Mission.[20]

Bugnini had not failed to press for a clarification of the authority and responsibilities of the Consilium, which was charged with the interpretation of the Constitution and the implementation of the reform. He had done so in the controversy over article IX of the motu proprio. Cardinal Lercaro, too, was anxious for the situation to be clarified. In a letter dated February 28, he wrote to Bugnini: "Please continue to keep me informed, Father, and do your utmost to see that our commission is publicly announced. . . . I cannot rest until the thing is settled. As I told you, I know the way things can happen."

The institution of the Consilium was finally "settled" with letters on February 29 and March 2. February 29 was the date on which the Secretariat of State sent a letter addressed to Cardinals Lercaro, Larraona, and Gregorio Pietro Agagianian, prefect of the Congregation de Propaganda Fide:

I have the honor of communicating to Your Eminence, in keeping with the directives of Pope Paul VI, the responsibilities of the Consilium for the Carrying out of the Constitution on the Liturgy, of which Your Eminence is President. They are as follows:

a. to suggest the names of the persons charged with forming study groups for the revision of rites and liturgical books;

b. to oversee and coordinate the work of the study groups;

c. to prepare carefully an instruction explaining the practical application of the Motu Proprio *Sacram Liturgiam* and clearly outlining the competence of the territorial ecclesiastical authorities, pending the reform of rites and liturgical books;

---

[19] *Sacram Liturgiam,* Introduction. Latin text: *EDIL* 179; English text: *DOL* 278.
[20] *OR,* January 31, 1964. Editors' translation.

d. to apply, according to the letter and the spirit of the Council, the Constitution it approved, by responding to the proposals of the conferences of bishops and to questions that arise involving the correct application of the Constitution.

Appeals of decisions of the Consilium as well as the solution of particularly sensitive and grave or completely new problems will be referred by the Consilium to the pope.[21]

The Consilium had been entrusted with the implementation of the liturgical reform in its entirety: its organization; the selection of persons for the study groups, as well as its contents; the revision of the rites and liturgical books; the application and interpretation of the Constitution on the Sacred Liturgy; and relations with the bishops' conferences. The intention of the letter was probably to put an end to the situation of uncertainty about the agency responsible for the reform and the prerogatives of that agency, a situation that until then had created no little confusion and difficulty for the Apostolic See.

The letter seemed clear enough in its contents, but no mention at all was made of the Congregation for Rites, and therefore the relations and roles of the two Offices remained uncertain. Moreover, it was only a letter, after all—a document lacking the juridical weight necessary to curb the action of the Congregation for Rites, which was still the Congregation in charge of liturgy in the church. Lastly, it should be pointed out that the text was not published by *L'Osservatore Romano* and certainly not in the *Acta* of the Holy See. It was simply a document filed in the archives until 1975, when it was finally published.

However, apart from these aspects, the February 29 letter did place the Consilium at the head of the reform. In fact, it was the Consilium's legal charter and would later be referred to often in times of controversy and conflict with the Congregation for Rites. Therefore, it marked a most important step in the life of the Consilium. This letter sent to Cardinal Lercaro concerning the Consilium's competencies also appointed him its president.[22]

On March 2 the members of the Consilium were appointed. Thanks to its composition, the forty-two members represented twenty-six nations

---

[21] *EDIL* 191; *DOL* 613.

[22] Lercaro's appointment was communicated to Father Bugnini by a letter from the Secretariat of State, dated March 2, 1964.

from all the continents, and because of the background of its members, the new Consilium was fully able to carry out its task in a competent and experienced manner.

It seemed that the Consilium was to be considered as a self-contained Office, independent of the Roman Curia; it was to report directly to the Pope. In a letter dated March 4, Bugnini wrote to Lercaro that "things have calmed down now, we are beginning to work with more serenity." Unfortunately, that serenity was to be short-lived. Relations with the Congregation for Rites were soon to grow tense once again, especially regarding procedure for formal publication of the revised liturgical texts. However, the important thing for the time being was that work could begin. The Consilium was able to function.

Until that moment, the story of the liturgy of Vatican II had been characterized by what happened outside the Consilium, but from March 1964 onward the implementation of the reform would be determined by events within the Office. Until then, the Consilium's meetings were recalled simply for the record, but from then on its meetings would constitute the milestones of the liturgical reform.

Conclusion

Although the close of 1963 was remarkably calm, that situation would soon change in January to March of 1964, a period characterized by the clamor provoked by certain liturgical publications and events. It was during the first months of 1964 that the important decision was made to establish the Consilium. This decision was the result of the development of the motu proprio *Sacram Liturgiam,* a document born in a polemical context. This was due to the weakness of the preparatory Consilium and the determined action of the Congregation for Rites to take control of the reform. The establishment of the Consilium at the end of February and the beginning of March only temporarily deferred the action of the Congregation for Rites. This preparatory Consilium was dominated by the prefect of the Congregation for Rites, who was not interested in making it work. It held only two meetings, which accomplished little and showed that it was not the right instrument for carrying out the reform.

The weakness of the preparatory Consilium became evident during the preparation of the text of the motu proprio. The draft of this document was in fact prepared, not by the Consilium, but by two other curial Offices: the secretariat of the council and the Congregation for Rites. Even the final corrections of the text, which were to elicit great reaction, were done without the knowledge of this new commission. Confusion reigned regarding which Office was to be responsible for directing the liturgical reform. For the Congregation for Rites, the preparatory Consilium was still an uncomfortable presence. Furthermore, the very fact that the drafting of the first document on the implementation of the conciliar reform had been entrusted to an Office other than the Congregation for Rites must have caused unease and insecurity within that Congregation. That was probably why the Congregation mobilized itself to acquire the direction of the reform. In the meantime, while the Curia busied itself with the preparation of the definitive text for the motu proprio, Lercaro and Bugnini could do no more than keep out of the way.

The text of the motu proprio in *L'Osservatore Romano* included two elements not found in any of the three drafts that had gone before it: the announcement of the institution of a special commission to prepare the reform and the new contents of article IX. The announcement of the institution of the commission was the first evidence of the Pope's intention in this direction. The text of article IX, as it was published in *L'Osservatore Romano,* caused an unexpected series of reactions and made very obvious the division between more conservative circles, especially in the Curia, that wished to curb the scope of the reform and the church outside of Rome, which had placed great hopes for renewal in the Constitution on the Sacred Liturgy.

As we have seen, the most vehement protest came from the French church. In effect, the Roman Curia was accused of attempting to nullify the results of the newly approved Constitution while the bishops who had approved it were still assembled in council. In the face of this reaction, which put the Holy See in an awkward situation, Bugnini was called in, and all the modifications that he proposed for the motu proprio were readily accepted. Thus the controversy was diffused.

However, the episode brought to light several important issues. The various national bishops' commissions were shouldering their responsibility for the liturgy. By acting this way, they confirmed that even during this initial phase of reform, the liturgy was no longer an exclusive preserve of the Roman Curia but belonged to the whole church. Second, during the time between the conciliar decisions and their practical implementation as spelled out in the motu proprio, it became evident that the Curia in general and the Congregation for Rites in particular, which had been formed to implement the Tridentine liturgy, were in no way suited for the implementation of the Vatican II reform. It was likely that the radical nature of the liturgical reform promoted by the Constitution on the Sacred Liturgy was not fully appreciated by the Curia.

Naturally, this served to confirm the need to establish an Office capable of meeting the new requirements. This experience with the motu proprio was one more step forward in the process of the establishment of the Consilium. Since it was Bugnini who supported the idea of the Consilium, he emerged as the one most capable of understanding the needs of the bishops' conferences.

The intention to establish the Consilium was also reflected in the appointments to the preparatory Consilium published in *L'Osservatore Romano* at the end of January. But even with this, the situation remained unchanged. There was the same unease and the same uncertainty that had appeared when the Congregation for Rites and the Consilium jockeyed for position during the last stages of the elaboration of the motu proprio. It was still not known which Office would be responsible for interpreting the Constitution, for examining and approving the decisions made by the bishops' conferences, for answering questions.

The Congregation for Rites was not at all happy with this prolonged state of confusion. It increasingly saw the danger of the reform passing into other hands. This explained the Congregation's attempt to officially classify the Consilium as nothing more than a consultative body of the Congregation for Rites. While the Congregation's move, made public by a document it sent to the bishops of France, increased the confusion, it also spurred the Pope to establish a more autonomous Consilium.

Moreover, while the "new" experts who emerged at the end of 1963 and were named to the preparatory Consilium were excluded from the preparation of the motu proprio, at the moment when the Congregation for Rites felt it had the situation in hand with the publication of the motu proprio in *L'Osservatore Romano*, forces of the liturgical movement appeared on the scene that had placed their hopes in the implementation of the Constitution. These forces made it evident that the Roman Curia's concern for centralization did not correspond to the spirit of the council or the need for reform advocated in the council's documents.

This development brought Bugnini back on the scene. He was successful in mediating the text in *L'Osservatore Romano* and the Constitution's directives, thus giving further support for the idea of the Consilium. Bugnini's return and the confusion regarding the Office charged with implementing the reform impelled the Congregation for Rites to try to consolidate its authority. However, the attempt produced the opposite effect and promoted the establishment of the Consilium. The new Office, the international character of its members, its unique setup, distinguishing it from the other curial Offices, could be considered the first concrete implementation of the Second Vatican Council. The liturgy inspired by the council needed to leave behind Tridentine forms in order to embrace the genuine expression of the faith of the whole church.

Chapter Three

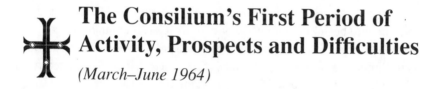

The Consilium's First Period of Activity, Prospects and Difficulties
(March–June 1964)

The First Meetings

The period between October 22, 1963, and March 2, 1964, can be seen as the formative period of the Consilium. The appointments of March 2, 1964, marked the beginning of the actual working phase. It was evident that the Office would need a period of adjustment before it could begin its work in earnest. This initial period of March to June was marked by the new Office's first meetings and by another controversy with the Congregation for Rites.

At the beginning of March, the Consilium's secretariat was made up of just two members: Father Bugnini, secretary, and Father Carlo Braga.[1] In a letter dated March 4 to Cardinal Lercaro, Bugnini wrote, "We are working like 'slaves' on the draft of a general plan for Your Eminence to present to the Holy Father and to prepare the commission for [the plenary meeting of] March 11."

---

[1] The date of Father Braga's appointment to the secretariat of the Consilium was January 16, 1964. He had already worked on the Conciliar Commission on the Sacred Liturgy and had been involved in all the preparatory work for the council. He also collaborated in working on the periodical *Ephemerides Liturgicae*. He was a friend of Bugnini's and, like him, was a Vincentian. He was to become one of the most important resource people at the Consilium.

The first plenary meeting was held at the Palazzo Santa Marta in the Vatican. Attending the meeting, besides the president, Cardinal Lercaro, were Cardinals Gregorio Pietro Agagianian, Paolo Giobbe, Carlo Confalonieri, and Arcadio M. Larraona, Bishops Pericle Felici, Francis Grimshaw (Great Britain), Guilford Young (Australia), Tulio Botero Salazar (Colombia), Clemente Ignazio Mansourati (Lebanon), Carlo Rossi, Emilio Guano (Italy), Juan Hervás y Benet (Spain), Franz Zauner (Austria), Enrique Rau (Argentina), Willem Van Bekkum (Indonesia), Willem Van Zuylen (Belgium), René Boudon, Henri Jenny, and François Kervéadou (France), Hermann Volk (Germany), Monsignor Luigi Valentini, Abbot Benno Gut, O.S.B., Father Ferdinando Antonelli, O.F.M., and Father Giulio Bevilacqua, C.O.

Cardinal Lercaro began by stressing the importance of the reform they were about to begin. Putting the activity of the Consilium in historical perspective, he invoked the memory of those who were charged with carrying out the liturgical reforms of the Council of Trent. He then read the letter from the Secretariat of State, dated February 29, on the tasks assigned to the Consilium. He referred briefly to the work of the pre-Consilium and went on to speak of the challenges awaiting the Consilium according to the Secretariat of State: organizing the work; setting up the study groups of experts; preparing an instruction based on *Sacram Liturgiam;* and ensuring that the conciliar Constitution on the Sacred Liturgy was followed and implemented.

Lercaro concluded his intervention by proposing to the members that Cardinal Confalonieri be elected vice-president. The proposal was unanimously approved. The appointment of a vice-president had previously been arranged with the agreement of the Cardinal Secretary of State. The main reason given to the members of the Consilium for the appointment was that since the president was also archbishop of Bologna, he did not live in Rome. A vice-president permanently residing in the Eternal City would provide a constant point of reference for urgent matters and decisions that could not be postponed.

But in actual fact there was another, more important reason. Lercaro and Bugnini must have spoken more than once about the appointment of a vice-president. Confalonieri's name often came up in letters exchanged by the president and the secretary in the preceding months. And all things considered, it is not out of place to regard the appointment as Bugnini's idea. He had come to realize that the Consilium, as an international agency, was going to be the object of the Roman Curia's opposition. Unlike Lercaro, who was a residential bishop, Confalonieri was an influential curial cardinal with a reputation for being balanced and open-minded and one who could be counted on to "defend" the Consilium—a task he performed on quite a few occasions.

The central part of the first meeting consisted of a report by the secretary on the organization of the work for implementing the Constitution on the Sacred Liturgy. The first item of the report dealt with the revision of six liturgical books: the Missal, the Breviary, the Pontifical, the Ritual, the Martyrology, and the Ceremonial of Bishops. Each book would be divided into several sections according to its proper elements. The Breviary, for example, would be divided into nine sections, the Pontifical into two, the Missal into eight, and so forth. Each section would be assigned to a particular study group, the composition of which was to be made according to the following criteria: expertise, nationality, availability for meetings.

Each study group would consist of five to seven consultors. They were to work following predetermined and approved criteria. Once formed, the study group would prepare a first draft for the particular task assigned to it. The draft would then be sent for examination to a larger group of about thirty to forty experts from different parts of the world, as desired by the council (*SC* 25). The initial draft would be amended according to observations made by the experts and sent out to them once again. This procedure would continue until a text that satisfied at least the majority was produced. This method had already been used in the preparatory work on the conciliar Constitution.

The experts *(periti),* therefore, were to be divided into two categories: the consultors and the advisors. The consultors belonged to one of the study groups and periodically met for the formulation of the drafts. The advisors assisted in examining the drafts but did not ordinarily attend meetings in Rome. The secretary said that it had been decided to publish only the names of the members and not of the consultors to ensure that they were not unduly pressured by outside influences.[2]

The final phase of the work of the study groups was an interdisciplinary review of their drafts by special study groups, purposely formed for this. These study groups considered the texts from the following perspectives:

[2] The names of the consultors and the advisors were actually published at the end of 1964 in a handbook for private use: *Elenchus Membrorum, Consultorum, Consiliariorum, Coetuum a studiis* (Typis Polyglottis Vaticanis, 1st ed., 1964; 2nd ed., 1967); see Appendix II, elenco N. II.

theological, biblical, juridical, historical, stylistic, musical, artistic, and pastoral. However, most of these study groups existed only on paper; the work foreseen for them was in fact carried out by the *periti* and the consultors as they revised the various drafts. It was evident that different study groups working on the reform of one specific liturgical book would have to work in harmony in order to achieve a coordinated whole of the various parts of the book. Once the study groups had completed their work, the draft or drafts would be passed on to a meeting of the plenary group. Only after it had been approved in the plenary group would the schema be sent to the Holy Father for definitive approval.

There were other tasks as well that needed attention, such as revision of the Psalter; an instruction for the implementation of the reform; concelebration and Communion under both species; the examination of the minutes or decisions of the bishops' conferences. A special commission had been formed of those members residing in Rome and some consultors of the Consilium.[3] It was to have met twice a month to deal with the more urgent decisions, but in the end, apart from the opening convocation, the commission was seen as superfluous and never met.

At the end of the first plenary meeting, after several of those present had spoken, Cardinal Lercaro asked the members to take a vote on the following matters: the procedure for implementing the reform presented by the secretary; the preparation of an instruction on the implementation of the reform; the preparation of a draft for concelebration; and Communion under both species. The members voted in favor of all three proposals. The next plenary meeting was scheduled for April 17, 1964.

Included in the material distributed to members of the plenary group were also two papers containing a list of thirty-eight study groups. Actually it was only the index of "The Plan for the Execution of the General Liturgical Reform," dated March 15, 1964. From the beginning of that month, the secretariat of the Consilium had been working on a draft of this document. The basic ideas had already been presented in Project B for the organization

---

[3] Included in the minutes from the meeting was a paper bearing the names of the *periti* who made up the commission: from the secretariat of the Consilium: the secretary and Father Braga; from the Congregation for Rites: Father Antonelli, O.F.M., Monsignor Frutaz; from the Propaganda Fide: Monsignor Paventi, Father Buijs, S.J.; Consilium consultors: Monsignors Bonet, Wagner, Martimort, Fathers McManus, Vagaggini, O.S.B., Neunheuser, O.S.B., Tassi, O.S.B., Dirks, O.P., Schmidt, S.J., Visser, C.Ss.R., Trimeloni, S.D.B.

of the reform, drawn up in late 1963, as well as in the "Draft of the Plan for Execution" of the first meeting of the pre-Consilium.

The ideas previously presented were then amplified so as to give sufficiently exhaustive information about the work to be done, the methods to be used, and the people capable of doing the job. The "plan for execution" consisted of fifty-three typewritten pages. The first four pages were an introduction. This covered roughly the first two points of the secretary's report to the plenary group: the revision of the liturgical books and the composition of the study groups. The remaining pages offered a description of each study group, from number one to number thirty-eight. These included the council's mandate, the criteria to be followed, the particular problems involved, and the composition of the group, naming the *relator,* the secretary, and the members of the group.

This document was to remain the basis for the whole of the Consilium's activity. The "Plan," as it appeared in the draft of March 15, 1964, had been drawn up for presentation to the Holy Father by Cardinal Lercaro following the plenary meeting of March 11. The secretary's report on the organization of the Consilium's activity and on the study groups, approved during the meeting, were part of this presentation. Although the members of the plenary group were not asked to discuss the composition of the individual study groups, they agreed to the general plan put forward by the secretary.

The Consilium's first plenary session marked the end of the preparatory work that Lercaro and Bugnini had carried out patiently and humbly since October 1963 with the Pope's support. The meeting consisted essentially of communicating the results already achieved: the authority of the Consilium, the methodology that the Office would use, and the people who were to be involved in the work of the reform. Subsequent meetings would examine the drafts for the new liturgical books or of new documents. The initial meeting provided the members with a chance to meet one another and to get an idea of the work ahead. However, the unanimous approval given by the members to the president's proposals and to the plan for the execution of the reform presented by the secretary launched the work of the Consilium into the future and marked the official beginning of its activity.

Among the aspects that characterized the first plenary session, one in particular should not be overlooked: the official aspect of the meeting. The pre-Consilium, made up of just four people, was forced to meet informally. The plenary meeting, in contrast, brought together not only the cardinal president and the secretary but also twenty-four members from many nations, the majority of whom were bishops. They met in public to begin one of the greatest liturgical reforms in the history of the Western church. Unlike the reform after Trent, it was all the greater because it also dealt with doctrine. Due emphasis was given to the event in a report written by Bugnini and published in the March 14 edition of *L'Osservatore Romano*.

The Consilium had at last become a reality. There was a secretariat, there were members and experts, and finally a strategy for implementation had emerged. Most of the merit for this success was owed to the efforts of Lercaro and Bugnini. Finally their dream had become reality.[4]

But it would all have been useless if the Pope himself had not chosen their names and had not supported their efforts in the most difficult moments, when the traditional Curia sought to vindicate its right to lead the reform.

Almost as an appendix to the plenary meeting of March 11, two ordinary meetings took place—one on March 20 and the other on April 13.[5] The first

---

[4] Satisfaction for the institution of the Consilium as an international agency, independent of the curial Congregations and in direct contact with the Pope, was high in international circles. Support for the Consilium was especially present in local churches, where the Curia was regarded with suspicion and there were hopes for a profound renewal of the church's structures as a result of the council. An article written by J. Pélissier from this perspective appeared in *La Croix* (March 20, 1964) and was reprinted in *La Documentation Catholique* (April 5, 1964) 440:

> The newly set up Consilium—and not Commission—is an office that is above the Roman Congregations and the Curia. It reports directly to the Pope. It is a first discreet, spontaneous answer from His Holiness Pope Paul VI to the Council Fathers expressing the wish that a senate of bishops be chosen by the Successor of Peter to assist him in his duties and responsibilities for the universal church . . . .
>
> So the dossiers of the Congregation of Rites have been handed over to this Consilium. The Consilium is also examining the proposals and projects of the episcopal conferences, and hence the text of the second disposition issued by the French bishops. The Consilium will hold regular meetings, to be arranged well in advance so that if they judge it to be opportune and possible, all the bishop-members may attend. . . .
>
> Both episcopal and international, this Consilium will have study groups, experts. It alone will be the body that judges and decides, under the authority of the Supreme Pontiff . . . .
>
> Likewise, this is the spirit of collegiality and internationalization which, through a personal decision of the Holy Father, is beginning to penetrate a large area of the central structures of the church, without noise or pointless commotion.

[5] Information on the assembly is taken from the minutes written by the secretary of the Consilium: *Relationes* n. 2: "Acta secundi Coetus Consilii (die 20 martii 1964)."

was prepared by a few experts[6] who had met on March 17. They discussed the more urgent matters concerning the use of the vernacular in the Mass and in the sacraments. After the meeting the material for discussion was prepared. The meeting took place at Santa Marta in the afternoon of March 20. Present were Confalonieri, Agagianian, Giobbe, Bea, Felici, Grimshaw, Young, Rau, Guano, Gut, Mansourati, Valentini, Antonelli, as well as the experts Vagaggini, Schmidt, Dirks, and Neunheuser.

The agenda for this meeting included scheduling meetings for the coming months, communicating information to the presidents of the episcopal conferences and to apostolic nuncios, decisions made by bishops' conferences, the Divine Office for canons and religious. The meetings were scheduled for April, May, and June. Three types of meetings were envisaged: ordinary,[7] plenary, and those of the consultors. The ordinary meetings were set for April 13, May 8, and June 4 and 25. The consultors' meetings were planned for April 14–16 and May 19–20. Among the topics to be taken up at these meetings were the various instructions on the Roman Missal, the Breviary, and concelebration. Two plenary meetings were planned: April 17–20 and May 21–22. These were to examine the material worked on following the consultors' meetings. The schedule was approved, although in actual fact only the dates set for the consultors' meeting and the plenary meeting in the month of April were kept, since during the month of May a recurrence of difficulties with the Congregation for Rites came about.

The most important topic of the March 20 meeting was to draft a circular letter to the apostolic nuncios giving first instructions for the presidents of the episcopal conferences concerning the implementation of the reform. The purpose of the letter was to establish the overall orientation for the ordered implementation of the liturgical reform pending the preparation of a special

---

[6] The experts at that meeting were Bugnini, Braga, Antonelli, Bonet, Dirks, Vagaggini, Schmidt, Neunheuser.

[7] The distinction made by Bugnini between ordinary and plenary meetings caused some perplexity. During the meeting Bugnini gave the following explanation. There was no substantial difference between the two types of assembly. Both the ordinary and the plenary sessions could be attended by all Consilium members who were actually in Rome. The difference consisted in the matters to be discussed. The ordinary would deal with ordinary matters, for example, queries concerning the conciliar Constitution or the arrangement of the work to be done. The plenary, on the other hand, to which every Consilium member was invited, would deal with the more important questions, above all regarding the liturgical reform in general.

instruction that would regulate the matter. The letter indicated the agencies responsible for the reform—the Consilium and the bishops' conferences; the method of procedure—a two-thirds majority vote necessary for adopting decisions, which would then be sent to the Apostolic See for confirmation; the limits to and gradual introduction of the vernacular language and other changes in the rites. The text of the letter was approved on March 24 after the *nihil obstat* was received from the Secretariat of State.[8]

As secretary, Father Bugnini briefly presented the problems posed by decisions made by bishops' conferences concerning various aspects of the liturgical reform: the Mass, the sacraments, sacramentals, the Divine Office.[9] In order to seek confirmation, it was necessary to establish the principles and criteria to be followed.[10]

Given the importance of the problems, all the material concerning decisions by the bishops' conferences was deferred for examination by the plenary meeting planned for the month of April.

Lastly, a brief glance was given to the question concerning the Divine Office for canons and religious. This final problem was raised by the motu proprio *Sacram Liturgiam* concerning the obligation to recite Prime and the Little Hours in private for those who were dispensed from the celebration of these Hours in choir.[11] The problem would have to be studied and presented again at a future meeting.

---

[8] The text of the letter is published in *EDIL* 192–196; *DOL* 79.

[9] The bishops' conferences that had made decisions were the following: Brazil, Caribbean, Chile, Belgium, Tunisia, Australia, South Africa, Thailand.

[10] The secretary's report referred to the text *Quaestiones tractandae,* 1: *Elementi utili per l'esame degli atti delle Conferenze Episcopali* ("Elements useful for the examination of decisions made by bishops' conferences"). The text had five points: (1) There was some explanation of article *SC* 54 on the use of the vernacular and of article *SC* 40 on the meaning of *aptationes* ("adaptations"); (2) a list was given of various formulas of the Mass belonging to the people and those belonging to the president: greetings, acclamations, chants, etc., and also the problems that could arise with their reform; (3) the use of the vernacular was requested for all sacraments; for holy orders the vernacular was requested only for the *allocutiones,* the *admonitiones,* and the *exhortationes;* (4) it was requested that all sacramentals be celebrated in the vernacular; (5) the confirmation of the choice of various translations already completed or in preparation for the Divine Office was requested.

[11] An answer to this query was given in a typewritten page headed *Quaestiones tractandae* 2.

The second ordinary meeting of April 13, held at Santa Marta, was almost a continuation of the first ordinary meeting. Present at the meeting were Lercaro, Agagianian, Giobbe, Confalonieri, Bea, Felici, Mansourati, Rau, Fey, Guano, Valentini, Gut, and Antonelli. A few consultors were also there: Vagaggini, Dirks, Martimort, Schmidt, Bonet, and Wagner.

The agenda items were listed in a folder entitled *Quaestiones tractandae* ("Matters to be treated"): (1) the blessing of spouses; (2) the *admonitio,* or introductory instruction, in marriage outside of Mass; (3) the obligation to recite Prime and the other Little Hours; (4) questions regarding the authority of major superiors of religious communities; (5) the Little Offices. The complete order of the day envisaged three other points that were not included on the agenda: (6) the results of the plenary assemblies of April 17–20; (7) a request from Cardinal Gracias for a concelebrated Mass at the forthcoming Bombay International Eucharistic Congress; (8) and finally, other business.

Regarding the blessing of spouses, it was a matter of interpreting correctly the meaning of the adverb *semper* found in *SC* 78 and in *Sacram Liturgiam* 5, which treated the nuptial blessing. A question had been raised as to the legitimacy of conferring the nuptial blessing in *tempore clauso,* or forbidden times, of the church year: at nuptial Masses and at marriages outside of Mass and in the case of a second marriage. It was decided to give an affirmative answer in all three cases. A question referred to no. 5 of *Sacram Liturgiam:* whether the *brevis admonitio* of which it spoke could be identified as the homily. The answer given was negative.[12]

On the topic of Prime and the Little Hours, there was uncertainty about the obligation of members of a chapter or of a religious community to recite privately Prime and the Little Hours if they had been legitimately dispensed from reciting these in choir. The majority voted against the dispensation. It was then determined that the term "ordinary" used in *SC* 57, 97, 101 and in *Sacram Liturgiam* 6 did indeed refer to major religious superiors. Finally, after a brief discussion Cardinal Lercaro indicated that the texts of the Little Offices or short devotions developed by specific religious communities mentioned in *SC* 98 should be approved by bishops' conferences and confirmed by the Holy See.

---

[12] The query was formulated as follows: "Utrum 'brevis admonitio,' de qua in Motu proprio n.V, qua inchoatur ritus Matrimonii sine Missa, idem sit ac 'brevis sermo' seu sermo qui de more fit in celebratione matrimonii." R. Negative.

On the remaining matters discussion was extremely short. Among the decisions reached was permission to celebrate baptism and confirmation during Mass at the Bombay Eucharistic Congress, subject to the Pope's approval.

The meetings of March 20 and April 13 were the only two assemblies of the ordinary Consilium. The reasons why this group no longer needed to meet were several. Its role had been envisaged as that of treating relatively minor matters that did not need to be dealt with by the plenary group—especially evaluating decisions of bishops' conferences. In effect, the ordinary group served as a special commission for the examination of those decisions. But once the criteria were defined and later clarified further during the consultors' meeting and the plenary meeting in April, it became superfluous to refer to the ordinary group for the examination of the decisions made by the episcopal conferences. Furthermore, it was during that period that the activity of the Consilium's secretariat[13] began to expand. As a consequence, work that had been originally set for the ordinary group was delegated to the secretariat and was attended to as part of the secretariat's normal activity. This move was also favored by the Consilium's president and secretary, who tended to prefer that there be international consultation on such decisions. In contrast, the ordinary group reflected a greater influence of the Curia, since the curial members of this group were a majority. The plenary group, which had fewer curial members, reflected greater international representation—a characteristic of the Consilium.

The Consilium was still in a period of adjustment. But soon all the work would be in the hands of the study groups, the secretariat and the participants at meetings of the consultors, and the plenaries.[14] With the consultors' meeting and the plenary meeting in the month of April, the Consilium really began to forge ahead with its work. From then on, a characteristic of every meeting would be the presentation of drafts for new rites or for new rubrical directives in accordance with the wishes of the council.[15] Moreover, there were to be two types of important meetings: the consultors' meeting and

[13] Besides Father Braga, who had been working in the secretariat since January, Father Gottardo Pasqualetti was hired as archivist on April 9, 1964. During 1964, Doctor Rus Romano and Father Carmelo Garcia del Valle also began working in the secretariat.

[14] Some information about the meetings of April and June was recorded by the secretariat of the Consilium in *Relationes* n. 3: *Notitiae coetus plenarii mensis aprilis et mensis iunii. Criteria et normae ad acta coetuum episcoporum confirmanda. Actuositas coetuum a studiis. Ordo futuri laboris,* July 5, 1964.

[15] See Appendix II, list number VI.

the plenary meeting, closely linked one with the other. On these two types of meetings much of the reform was to depend.

The consultors' meeting began in the afternoon of April 14 in the Vatican. In attendance, beside the president and the secretary, were also the relators and secretaries, as well as several of the most qualified consultors of the Consilium's study groups. They numbered about fifty scholars.[16] The purpose of the meeting was to allow the various people collaborating in the liturgical reform to get to know one another, to present an overall view of the problems, and to begin to plan the work.

The agenda included a general report by the secretary; a first examination of the problems concerning the reform of the Mass and the Office; the examination of the draft on the instruction for the application of *Sacram Liturgiam* and of the Constitution on the Sacred Liturgy; the examination of the schema on concelebration; and finally, the examination of the schema on Communion under both species. At the beginning of the session, the consultors took a solemn oath, and a dossier containing relevant documentation was distributed. After the president's words of welcome, the secretary gave a report, which took up most of the afternoon session.

In a way, the secretary's report marked the official beginning of the consultors' work, just as the general report delivered on March 11 had marked the beginning of the activity of the full members of the Consilium. The secretary was anxious to report the situation of the Consilium and its work to those now directly involved with the reform. It consisted of five points: the Consilium; work to be done; methodology to be adopted; expectations concerning the work; the spirit that should unite all collaborators.

First of all, there was a brief description of the preceding events: the preparatory Consilium; the motu proprio *Sacram Liturgiam;* the letter from the Secretariat of State of February 29; the appointment of the president and of the members; the plenary meeting of March 11; the difference between a plenary meeting and an ordinary meeting; the distinction between consultors and advisors. Then came an outline of the plan already presented during the

---

[16] The consultors present were Agostini, Amore, Balboni, Bonet, Botte, Borella, Cardine, Cuva, De Gaiffier, Diekmann, Dirks, Fallani, Famoso, Fischer, Fontaine, Franquesa, Frutaz, Gherardi, Gy, Hänggi, Hourlier, Jounel, Jungmann, Kleinheyer, Lentini, Martimort, Mazzarello, McManus, Molin, Moneta Caglio, Mundò, Nabuco, Neunheuser, Oñatibia, Pellegrino, Roguet, Rose, Schmidt, Schnitzler, Seumois, Sobrero, Tassi, Vagaggini, Van Doren, Visentin, Volpini, Wagner.

plenary meeting of March 11: the revision of the six base liturgical books, subdivided into various sections; the work of the study groups, composed of a relator, a secretary, and consultors; and the study groups for doctrinal revision.

Furthermore, each study group was invited to draw up criteria for proceeding, which would have to be approved by the plenary group. Indications were also given about how the work was to proceed within the individual study groups. Some indications dealt with relations between the study groups and the secretariat. The whole purpose was to arrange the work over a certain period of time with deadlines, thus ensuring that the work would proceed carefully, but also at a good pace. A brief discussion followed the secretary's report.[17]

The first report of April 15 was on the disputed questions concerning the revision of the Roman Missal given by Johannes Wagner. The report was divided into three parts: preliminary observations; method of inquiry; presentation of the problems. It was not a question of proposing solutions, but simply of grouping together questions regarding the reform of the Mass, for which permission to proceed would have to be obtained from the members during the next plenary meeting. The method proposed was to be faithful to the mandate of the council as expressed in the Constitution on the Sacred Liturgy. There followed a list of questions based on various articles of the Constitution. A comment was made on each one, and some suggestions were made for possible solutions.[18] Wagner's report largely presented the problems without giving definitive answers, which accounted for considerable confusion in the discussion that followed.[19]

In the afternoon session of April 15, two drafts were discussed: *Schema* n. 1: *De concelebratione* 1; *Schema* n. 2: *De Communione sub utraque*

---

[17] Some consultors expressed doubts about the possibility of producing the methodology of their particular group by the set date. Others proposed that the "ordinary" meetings should avoid making decisions that could compromise the work and the freedom of the study groups.

[18] The following articles of the Constitution were considered: 50, 51, 53, 54, 55, 56, 57.

[19] The various interventions touched on a variety of subjects: adaptations in mission territories (the participation of catechumens at Mass); schemas for prayers of the faithful and for the Scripture readings; experiments and optional elements in the new liturgy; acclamations of the people during the Canon; artistic directives for the sanctuary; Gregorian chant and more contemporary liturgical music.

specie 1. Both schemas had been drafted by the relator of the study group, Father Vagaggini, together with the group's secretary, Father Franquesa of Montserrat. The two schemas had been prepared very early on, even before the study groups were definitively formed, and they had been sent out to all the Consilium members on April 2. The reason for moving ahead with these schemas was a widespread desire for permission to concelebrate. The work on the matter had been facilitated by the fact that a fairly good draft prepared in late 1963 was available for reference. Discussion on the two schemas was guided by the following principles: the number of concelebrants; Communion by intinction; the number of prayers to be recited together; concelebration gestures.

The discussion centered on whether or not the number of concelebrants should be limited and whether the rite of Communion by intinction should be introduced. With regard to the number of concelebrants, it was decided that the judgment of the local ordinary would suffice. But on the questions of Communion by intinction and the prayers of the Canon to be recited together by all the concelebrants, there was a considerable difference of opinion.[20] Eventually the participants came to the conclusion that it would be necessary to experiment to see in practice which would be the best solution.

The next morning, April 16, Father Vagaggini presented the draft of the proposed instruction for discussion. This document was meant to implement what had been recommended by the first plenary session and the Secretary of State. It was based on a previous version drafted in March.[21] The material had been divided into four sections. The pastoral section dealt with the pastoral

---

[20] Some were against intinction because the *veritas signi* was missing from the rite. Others were in favor. In the West there had been some aversion to intinction because of the reminder of Judas' "communion" at the Last Supper. But the rite presented some hygienic advantages. On the prayers to be said together, the discussion considered whether they should be said from the *Hanc igitur* or from the *Quam oblationem* or from the *Qui pridie*. Some even considered the possibility of reciting together the whole of the Canon, at least on solemnities.

[21] Toward the middle of March, the first draft was sent for examination to some fifteen consultors. The observations received by the secretariat advised a complete rewriting of the document, broadening its scope, dividing it into four sections: the first was entrusted to Bishops Jenny and Volk; the second, to Father Vagaggini; the third was based on the *Primitiae* project; the fourth was entrusted to Monsignor Famoso. The instruction (fourth draft) at that time really only consisted of the second and third parts; the other two were still draft proofs.

character of the Constitution as a whole. The normative section interpreted some articles of the Constitution and offered directives. The section on implementation indicated those parts of the reform that could be put into effect immediately. Finally, the rubrical section described some innovation in the rites. Discussion on the normative section was quite problematic,[22] while discussion on the section dealing with implementation was easier.

During the final afternoon of the meeting, the Divine Office was discussed. Canon Martimort was the group secretary and presented the draft on the Breviary. He posed nine questions regarding the new Divine Office to the consultors: (1) the structure of the Breviary—whether or not there would be two forms of celebration, one for those bound to pray the Office in common and those who were not; (2) the structure of the individual Hours, with special attention to Lauds and Vespers; (3) the distribution of the psalms; 4) the scriptural and patristic readings; (5) the saints' days and the calendar in the Office; (6) the other parts of the Office; (7) singing and reciting the Office; (8) combining the Divine Office with other liturgies; (9) further questions. The discussion did not go beyond the agenda. The participants limited themselves to commenting on the points listed in the draft and to making a few suggestions. All questions were referred to the Breviary study group.

Thus this first consultors' meeting ended after discussing drafts 1, 2, and 4 on the rite of concelebration, of Communion under both kinds, and on the preparation of the new instruction. The reports on the two major questions of the Missal and the Breviary were still only in the preliminary stage of establishing principles. Bugnini was pragmatic in his approach and would have preferred to have had the practical questions of the Mass and the Office tackled during that meeting. More than once during the discussion, when the need for experimentation was raised, he insisted on a more rapid procedure, given the fact that the whole church was waiting for the new rites. He had prepared two papers himself, both dated April 15, urging that the process of the revision of the Missal and the Breviary be more rapid. However, the two

---

[22] The participants sought to distinguish between what was necessary and what was superfluous or not in keeping with the style of an instruction. They made every effort to reach a balance between the document's juridical, pastoral, and ritual aspects. The instruction was to give practical modes for implementation but at the same time it was to allow the necessary freedom for pastoral activity. Another difficulty was the need to avoid giving directions which would be changed during the course of the reform.

papers were not presented at the meeting. After the two group secretaries had delivered their reports, it seemed better not to intervene. But this was one of the symptoms of the increased activity of the secretariat, which soon was not only to assume the work of the ordinary group but also to exert considerable influence over the progress and the orientations of the reform.

The second plenary meeting was held at Santa Marta on April 17, 18, and 20, 1964.[23] In addition to Cardinal Lercaro and Father Bugnini, in attendance were Cardinals Giobbe, Confalonieri, Ritter, Silva Henríques, Bea; Bishops Felici, Grimshaw, Mansourati, Rossi, Jop, Hervás y Benet, Fey, Schneider, Van Zuylen, Spuelbeck, Bekkers, Boudon, Nagae, Jenny, Malula, Pichler, Isnard, Volk, Guano, Kervéadou, Monsignor Valentini, and Fathers Gut, Antonelli, and Bevilacqua. The agenda for the meeting included the following matters: (1) establishing criteria and norms for the Holy See's confirmation of decisions made by bishops' conferences;[24] (2) a report on the reform of the Mass and the Divine Office;[25] (3) a report on the instruction for the implementation of the motu proprio *Sacram Liturgiam*;[26] (4) an examination of the first drafts of the documents on concelebration and Communion under both species.[27]

The first item on the agenda was establishing criteria for confirming decisions made by bishops' conferences. This was actually a new draft of the report the secretary had presented at the ordinary meeting of March 20. The "Matters to Be Treated, n. 3" contained a clear explanation of the problems concerning the rite of the Mass, the sacraments and sacramentals, and the Divine Office, problems that resulted from the legislation then in force, with particular reference to the Constitution on the Sacred Liturgy. Twenty questions were formulated relative to each issue presented. On the whole, the questions regarded the use of the vernacular. For the Mass, a number of ritual improvements were also envisaged—the possibility of omitting the prayers at the foot of the altar and those at the end of Mass, including the last gospel, and the possibility of using a new formula for the distribution of Communion.

[23] See *OR*, April 22, 1964.

[24] This referred to the *Quaestiones tractandae*, n. 3, headed: *Elementa quae proponuntur ad statuenda criteria seu normas in examina actorum Coetuum Episcoporum nationalium, de quibus in Motu proprio* Sacram Liturgiam *diei 25 ianuarii 1964*, n. X.

[25] See *Schema* no. 7: *De Missali*, 1; *Schema* no. 6: *De Breviario*, 2.

[26] See *Schema* no. 4: *De instructione*, 2.

[27] See *Schema* no. 1: *De concelebratione*, 1; *Schema* no. 2: De *Communione sub utraque specie*, 1.

Discussion on the twenty questions continued throughout April 17 and ended in the afternoon of April 18. All the questions were approved.

With the approval of the questions, the Consilium produced its first concrete accomplishment since being mandated by the ordinary meeting on March 25. Because the question of the introduction of the vernacular was dropped, the decisions on the remaining nineteen questions in the document *Quaestiones tractandae, n. 3*[28] constituted a reference that would be employed when confirming the decisions made by the episcopal conferences. The instruction being prepared would have to be adapted from these documents.

The reports by Martimort on the Breviary and Wagner on the Mass given on April 18 were enthusiastically welcomed by the members of the plenary group and marked a practical starting point for the process of reform. It was decided that the members were to submit their observations on these two reports no later than May 10 so that the texts could be corrected for the plenary meeting set for mid-June.

The morning session of April 20 opened with a brief presentation by Cardinal Lercaro of the three remaining drafts on the agenda: the instruction, concelebration, and Communion under both species. He reviewed the origin and precedents for the text of the instruction, which was only fully developed in its second and third parts. The text still needed to be revised and integrated on the basis of the consultors' observations and particularly on the basis of the decisions reached by the Consilium a few days earlier, when it approved the nineteen questions contained in the *Quaestiones tractandae n. 3* on various parts of the liturgy.

The same procedure was indicated for the other two schemas on the agenda. When the president had finished his introduction, Vagaggini presented the draft on the instruction. In order to guide the discussion of such a complicated topic, Vagaggini had prepared seven questions to clarify the Consilium's opinion on certain basic issues. With a few slight alterations these questions were approved. This allowed the study group to confidently carry on its work.

There was some interesting discussion on the first question, which dealt with practical norms to be proposed, concessions, and ritual changes to be made. A question was raised as to the Consilium's competence and its authority over the implementation of the reform. The letter of February 29 was read out once again. Some, particularly those belonging to the Curia,

---

[28] See Appendix I, Document N. IV.

were inclined to limit the Consilium's competence and authority. Others held that the Congregation's competence went beyond the instruction, because it was the Consilium that was to oversee the implementation of the reform. This was a new indication that there would be trouble ahead between the Consilium and the Congregation for Rites, which were jointly responsible for safeguarding the rites.

The afternoon of April 20 was devoted to a discussion on the drafts for Communion under both species and concelebration. Vagaggini informed the members of the observations and changes suggested by the consultors. As before, he prepared seven focus questions regarding, among other things, the number of concelebrants, the manner of receiving the Blood of Christ from the chalice, the prayers to be recited together during concelebration, vestments, and the placement of the concelebrants. On the whole, the drafts were seen to be satisfactory.

The plenary meeting concluded with an examination of three other matters that led to decisions: those clerics bound to the Divine Office would have a choice to use either the Latin or a bilingual version; the approval of the use of the phrase *Ite, missa est* after the final blessing at Mass; the delegation to the president of the Consilium authority to confirm decisions made by bishops' conferences when these decisions were in conformity with the approved principles and did not contain other requests. This decision marked a turning point between the end of the ordinary group's activity and the beginning of the secretariat's increased responsibility.

The second plenary session and the related consultors' meeting were the first concrete experience of coordination between the Consilium's departments: secretariat, consultors' meeting, and plenary session. The experience of April 1964 demonstrated that the consultors' meeting could not be held too close to the plenary session because there was not sufficient time to correct the various drafts presented. The secretariat was fast becoming a dynamic catalyst for the reform, stimulating the work of the study groups and prioritizing decisions regarding the work schedule. Moreover, having received delegation from the plenary members to confirm decisions made by the bishops' conferences, it had received an extraordinary amount of authority for directing the reform in each country. Nevertheless, the efforts of the secretariat were by no means unobstructed. It was all too evident from the discussion during the meeting held on the morning of April 20 that the problem of the relationship between the Consilium and the Congregation for Rites had yet to be resolved.

Despite the fact that the organizing meeting on March 20 had scheduled several meetings during the month of May, none was held. There were various reasons for this. First, the ordinary meetings had outlived their usefulness, while the plenary session and its related consultors' meeting were judged to be unnecessary, since the time was insufficient to garner the responses from a larger group of experts. Nevertheless, the month of May was not lacking in excitement, for another battle with the Congregation for Rites was brewing.[29]

In the discussion during the second plenary session of the Consilium, someone had already indirectly claimed that the Congregation for Rites had the right to issue directives of a general nature and that the Consilum's task was to follow and coordinate the work of the reform and to see that the Constitution on the Sacred Liturgy was implemented. It should be noted that the prefect of the Congregation for Rites, as a member of the Consilium, attended only the first plenary session and then failed to participate in any of the other meetings of the Consilium. In practice, the only connection between the Consilium and the Congregation for Rites was constituted by two leading officials of the Congregation who were part of the new agency: Father Antonelli and Monsignor Frutaz.

A Controversy Between the Congregation for Rites and the Consilium

The letter of February 29 that had permitted the Consilium to begin its work had not posed the problem of relations with the Congregation for Rites, and still less the question of which Office was to give canonical status to the changes demanded by the reform. This problem arose after the Consilium had drawn up its first resolutions. At the end of the second plenary meeting, during the papal audience on April 21, Cardinal Lercaro submitted to the Pope the decisions made at the ordinary meeting of April 13 as well as those made by the plenary session. The Pope approved all the decisions reached by the Consilium.

---

[29] The May 1964 controversy between the Congregation for Rites and the Consilium was limited to those in charge of the two Offices. They were the ones who prepared the various drafts for general discussion. That is why news of the controversy was kept within the secretariat of the Consilium and was not reported in the *Relationes* papers, which, beginning in March, were sent out regularly to members and consultors.

The resolutions published were the following: matters concerning the blessing of spouses; the form for marriage outside of Mass; the approval of the Little Offices; the versions of the Divine Office and the Little Offices to be used in public celebration; the question of the canonical term "ordinary" for a religious superior; the obligation of praying the Hour of Prime and the other Little Hours outside of choir; the publication of the Breviary in Latin or in bilingual editions for clerics.

During the audience the tension between the Consilium and the Congregation for Rites regarding the publication of the decrees on the reform was also discussed. It fell exclusively to the Consilium to confirm the decisions made by the bishops' conferences. For general decisions concerning the universal church, it would be necessary to consider the possibility of issuing the decrees jointly with the Congregation, signed by both the prefect of the Congregation and the president of the Consilium. The ultimate solution to the tension between the Consilium and the Congregation was already in sight, but it would not be easily reached.

In this ambiguous situation, as had already happened in February with the rescript to the French bishops, the Congregation for Rites took the initiative and published a decree on the new formula for the distribution of Communion.[30] This was an obvious attempt to reassert its right to issue general liturgical directives. The decree was issued April 25, a few days after the conclusion of the Consilium's second plenary session.

The fact that this move on the part of the Congregation was made while the Consilium was working on an instruction regarding the general reform of the liturgy could only be interpreted as a way to assert control. Even though the members of the Congregation for Rites who were also members of the Consilium had already received the draft of the instruction proposed by the Consilium on April 2, the Congregation went ahead with its own version of the Communion formula and other points requested of the Consilium by the Pope.

Father Bugnini expressed his dismay over this development in a letter to the Secretary of State, dated May 5, 1964. A similar opinion was expressed by Cardinal Lercaro to the Secretary of State in his letter of May 22:

> Perhaps the publication of the decree on the formula for the distribution
> of Holy Communion could have been postponed in order to include it in

---

[30] See *EDIL* 197; *DOL* 252.

a wider framework with the other reforms; in any case, before its publication, even in advance, more study and a little experiment would have
been necessary; some of the queries which have now arisen could have
been avoided.

Furthermore, in both letters Lercaro and Bugnini explicitly requested
that no decision of a general nature touching the liturgical reform coming
under the competence of the Consilium be made without the Consilium's
being duly consulted.

Given the Congregation's attempt to gain control of the reform, as well
as the reaction and resolutions of the Consilium, it was evident that there
was a need to clarify how the decrees of reform were to be published. It
was a matter of finding a formula of compromise between the Consilium
and the Congregation for Rites. This was all the more necessary, since by
order of the Pope, the Consilium was preparing the implementation of the
conciliar liturgy. This action seemed to those at the Congregation for Rites to
be contrary to the Congregation's centuries-old, never-repealed prerogative
of responsibility for the church's liturgy.

The drafting of a decree clarifying the corresponding responsibilities
of the Consilium and the Congregation for Rites for the liturgical reform
continued for the whole of May. This text underwent nine drafts. It was
obvious that the principal issue was the problem of defining the role of the
Congregation for Rites in approving resolutions made by the Consilium. In
other words, the very autonomy of the Consilium was at stake.

The text of the ninth and final draft of the decree of compromise was
approved by the Pope and officially communicated to the Consilium and to
the Congregation for Rites on May 28, 1964.[31] It established that the Congregation for Rites would grant juridical approval to the reforms proposed
by the Consilium. This did not, however, solve the problem, and in practice
both sides would be unhappy with the compromise. The Consilium, which
was to carry out all the work of the reform, lacked the faculty to give juridical
weight to its decisions. The Congregation for Rites was ill-equipped by its
traditional structure to involve itself directly in the liturgical reforms of the
council, but it was attached to its juridical prerogatives and always ready to
affirm its authority over the Consilium.

---

[31] See Appendix I, Document N. V.

While the February compromise had been more favorable to the Consilium, the one worked out in May was less so. It was accepted by Lercaro owing to his trust in the Pope's support of the Consilium and in order that the work could continue.

The Third Plenary Meeting

The May meetings having been canceled, the secretariat of the Consilium retained only the June plenary session, which was held June 18–20.[32] As usual, meetings took place at Santa Marta, with twenty-seven members and several consultors in attendance.[33] The presence of consultors at a members' assembly was one of the characteristic aspects of the third plenary meeting. This was a change in procedure, since at the two previous plenary sessions consultors were present only to discuss their particular documents. Their participation was expanded at this point, since the ordinary meetings at which they would have been present in May and June had been canceled. It was also thought that their presence would be useful at the discussion of the drafts of some important topics. This proved to be a wise decision. Beginning with this third plenary meeting, the presence of the consultors was indeed one of the most important elements of subsequent meetings.

The agenda of this third plenary meeting included a report from the secretary, a review of the instruction, and the drafts on concelebration, Communion under both species, and a report of the reform of the structure of the Mass. The agenda also envisaged two events during the session dealing with the new rite of concelebration. One, on June 18, was the showing of a film at the Catholic Cinema Center on the Via della Conciliazione of a concelebration in Bologna on the occasion of Cardinal Lercaro's fiftieth anniversary of priestly ordination. The following morning the group attended

---

[32] The documentation in the archives of the third plenary session is in some points incomplete. Therefore, it is impossible to give an exact list of the participants. The report on the discussion is also very brief. Some information about the assembly has been taken from the *Relationes* n. 32 (5 July 1964): *Notitiae Coetus Plenarii mensis aprilis et mensis iunii—Criteria et normae ad acta coetuum episcoporum confirmanda Actuositas Coetuum a studiis—Ordo futuri laboris. L'Osservatore Romano* did not publish the usual report on the meeting.

[33] The consultors present on the morning of June 18 were the following: Wagner, Neunheuser, Dirks, Buys, Franquesa, Bonet, Vagaggini, Tassi, Schmidt, Trimeloni.

an experimental concelebration on the Aventine by the Benedictine monks of Sant'Anselmo.

In his report on June 18, the secretary outlined the activity of the Consilium since the previous plenary meeting on April 21. He reported on the work of the secretariat as well as that of the study groups. Forty-two decisions made by the bishops' conferences had been received by the secretariat, and of these, nineteen had already been confirmed, while the others were being examined. Furthermore, the secretariat had been busy establishing the final membership of the Consilium. It was composed of 41 members, 132 consultors, 30 advisors, and 3 in the secretariat. Altogether 206 people were engaged in the work of the 40 study groups.[34] The second part of the secretary's report dealt with the work already well underway in the study groups. In addition to the drafts on the instruction, on concelebration, and on Communion under both species, the assembly was also informed about the work of other study groups.

The discussion of draft number 4 of the instruction, a copy of which had been handed to the members and consultors, began with a reading of the presentation written by Carlo Braga outlining the process followed in drafting the various schemas. The second schema on the instruction, after being presented to the plenary session held April 17–20, had been amended according to the comments received. The observations judged that this draft was good, but overly detailed. Because it was to be an instruction, and therefore a pastoral decree, the doctrinal part would have to be limited to a few principal elements. The third draft was the result of a revision carried out by the secretariat on the basis of the observations already mentioned. The new schema had been sent on May 22 to all the members and to forty consultors. Before the June plenary assembly, the secretariat had received the observations of eight members and thirty-two consultors. This made it possible to draft the new text, the fourth draft, for the plenary meeting of June 17, 1964. Discussion on this fourth draft of the instruction took up most of the meeting and dealt with every part of the schema.

Regarding the introduction, which gave some doctrinal principles and explained the nature of the instruction, almost everyone agreed that the dogmatic-liturgical part should be reduced to a minimum to avoid duplicat-

---

[34] On May 10 the sixth list of consultors had been sent to the secretariat, and on May 17, 20, and 22 the letters of official nomination, which also indicated the study group to which they were assigned, were sent out to those concerned.

ing what had already been amply covered in the Constitution on the Sacred Liturgy and to avoid the disputed theological issues.

It was decided that following the introduction, instead of the four parts, as was proposed in the second draft, there would be five chapters in the same order as that of the Constitution. Some chapters had been drawn up in collaboration with other Vatican dicasteries. The sections of the document dealing with the formation of students in seminaries and religious formation houses had been drafted by a mixed commission that met on June 2 and was comprised of the Consilium, the Congregation for Seminaries, and the Congregation for Religious. The articles on the Divine Office were the work of another mixed commission—the Consilium and the Congregation for Religious, whereas the text concerning the Divine Office in the missions was based on recommendations by the Propaganda Fide.[35] The articles cited are those of the text of the instruction as published and do not correspond to those of the schema discussed during the third plenary session. The contents, however, are identical. With the observations made during the plenary meeting, the schema on the instruction was on its way to completion, and the fifth draft, dated June 21, was essentially the definitive version.

Following the draft of the instruction, the other two schemas on the agenda were examined: concelebration and Communion under both kinds. The basis for the work of reform had been the pontifical Mass, which remained the norm for the other, less solemn celebrations. As in the case of the instruction, the more abstract theological sections were removed. The members all agreed that the draft should contain only the rite and that doctrinal elements should be reserved for a future instruction. Other observations were made by the members about restricting the number of concelebrants, the liturgical vestments, etc. Finally, they thought it worthwhile to set a period of experimentation both for concelebration and Communion under both species before arriving at a definitive rite.

The report on the structure of the Mass was given by Johannes Wagner during the morning session on June 20. He presented the various parts of the Order of Mass, highlighting the problems and suggesting some solutions. The work was the result of the two meetings that Group X had held, May 8–10 at Trier, and June 5–7 at the Abbey of Einsiedeln in Switzerland,

---

[35] It was a question of the following numbers of the instruction: *EDIL* 209–215 = *DOL* 303–309; *EDIL* 276–287 = *DOL* 370–381; *EDIL* 276 = *DOL* 370.

at which Bugnini was present. This was more an informative report than a text for discussion.

The third plenary gathering concluded with positive results. First, the presence of the consultors was a positive development, underlining the scholarly aspect of the work of reform. Second, the drafts of three documents dealing with substantive matters had been brought to the final version: the instruction on the Roman Missal, concelebration, and Communion under both species (Schemas 17, 18, 19). The secretariat had become an efficient organization for developing constantly improved drafts of the documents of liturgical reform.

The new drafts, fruits of the third plenary session, were presented to the Pope by Cardinal Lercaro in an audience on June 26. During the audience Pope Paul gave permission for concelebration "ad experimentum" in a few centers, in view of a definitive redaction of the rite.[36] The faculty to allow concelebration and Communion under both species was communicated to the president of the Consilium on July 3, 1964, by a letter from the Secretariat of State. Moreover, it is important to note the various contacts that the Consilium had during this period with the other curial congregations in the development of the various parts of the instruction of the Roman Missal. In effect, the Consilium had become the point of convergence for the work of various Vatican offices in matters liturgical.

It really seemed that after the initiative taken on April 26 and the controversy during the month of May the Congregation for Rites was at last resigned to relinquishing oversight of the reform into the hands of the newly formed Consilium. The Consilium had indeed become an efficient Office, directing the work of its study groups being carried out in various parts of the world.[37] The secretary planned that from September to October, the Consilium would approve the norms to be followed by the individual study groups in their work. In June 1965 the Consilium would examine the greater part of the

[36] The centers to which the faculty of concelebration "ad experimentum" was conceded were the following: the abbeys of Montserrat (Spain); En-Calcat (France); Maria Laach (Germany); St. John's, Collegeville, Minn. (U.S.A.); Maredsous (Belgium); Sant' Anselmo (Italy); and the Dominican Maison d'Etudes du Saulchoir (France). During an audience on June 26, the Pope also approved concelebration for the Eucharistic Congress of Bombay and the possibility to apply the instruction at least one month before the Congress so that the people could be prepared for the small changes in the rite.

[37] In the month of June more consultors were appointed, and they immediately joined the various study groups.

groups' work. The review of these drafts would be more or less completed by the end of November 1965.

This plan had already been presented to the Pope. Although highly optimistic, it reflected Bugnini's frame of mind in continually seeking to expedite the work of the reform. The practical reason for this was obvious—to take advantage of the presence in Rome of the members and consultors who were participating in the council in order to facilitate the liturgical reforms. However, it is not unlikely that in the absence of clear juridical lines of authority, the secretariat of the Consilium believed that it was necessary to accomplish as much as possible during the time that the council was in session. It was feared that with the end of the council, set for December 1965, there would be a return to the traditional spirit of the Curia, which could not only impede the reform but even thwart it.

Conclusion

March 1964 saw the beginning of a new period in the story of the Consilium. The critical attention that had been directed to events leading to the birth of the Office was now diverted to the Office's actual activity, which was finally focused on the concrete implementation of the reform. From then on, the reform's most significant points of reference would be the meetings and the decisions of the Consilium. The new period began with the Consilium's adjusting its own internal organization. This phase characterized the first few months of the Consilium's life, beginning in March until the end of June 1964. Two key events shaped this period: the first meetings of the Office and the struggle with the Congregation for Rites. This twofold series of events helped the Consilium to mature.

The first meetings held during this period were concerned with both internal organization and external relations. They afforded an opportunity for the members to meet, to get to know one another and exchange first impressions. Moreover, these meetings provided an opportunity for the secretary to present an overview of the responsibilities of the Office and its work schedule. Particularly significant was the appointment of a vice-president, who happened to be a curial cardinal, since the members of the Consilium were aware that as an international body they needed allies in the Roman Curia.

The Consilium members resident in Rome, called "the ordinary," held two meetings—one in mid-March and the other in mid-April. The first meeting was significant in that it approved a draft of a letter addressed to nuncios that outlined the procedure to be used by bishops' conferences in requesting approval and confirmation of their decisions in liturgical matters by the Holy See. That letter was the first official contact between the Consilium and bishops' conferences.

Thanks to decisions of the second plenary meeting, the secretariat of the Consilium grew in importance, as evidenced in its being delegated, for example, to examine the decisions of the bishops' conferences. From then on, it would be the center of the reform under the secretary's guidance. It also became the place where priorities for the work were established and encouragement given to the various study groups as well as for the implementation of the reform internationally.

Chapter Four

The Instruction *Inter Oecumenici*, a Decisive Turning Point
(July–October 1964)

The Sacred Congregation for Rites' Position on the Instruction

The May compromise over the juridical formula for the publication of general decisions had left unresolved the problem of relations between the Consilium and the Sacred Congregation for Rites. The difficulties encountered in searching for a satisfactory solution were due not so much to questions of procedure but to the definition of the role of the two Offices in the implementation of the reform. The Consilium's position was supported by the motu proprio *Sacram Liturgiam* as well as by the letter of February 29, which recognized both its authority and the representative nature of its members and consultors. It therefore considered the role of the Congregation for Rites as basically procedural: the Congregation was to limit itself to authorizing the resolutions of the Consilium. The Consilium, however, was deputed exclusively to carry out the reform. On the other hand, the Congregation for Rites regarded the Consilium as a group dependent on the Congregation. It maintained that its duty was not only to give juridical force to the work of the Consilium but to both modify and be the ultimate judge of its resolutions before they were published.

This impasse, which had dragged on ever since the birth of the Consilium, surfaced again when the instruction *Inter oecumenici* was being prepared. The fifth draft of the instruction was presented to the Pope after the plenary meeting on June 21, together with drafts on concelebration and Communion under both species. During an audience on July 1, the Pope gave all three documents to Cardinal Larraona, the prefect of the Congregation. The Consilium's text was certainly not new to the Congregation for Rites. Father Antonelli and Monsignor Frutaz, officials with leading positions in the Congregation,[1] were also working with the Consilium as member and consultor, respectively. The Congregation for Rites, however, had not intervened during the preparation of the document. Evidently it was waiting to examine the text when the time came for its approval. The draft on the instruction drawn up by the Consilium was examined by a few leading officials of the Congregation for Rites.

On July 23 the Congregation for Rites' observations, entitled "Observations on the Instruction," were presented to the Pope. They took the form of thirty-two typed pages and were divided into three categories. The first and longest category was comprised of observations of a stylistic and juridical nature. The second category contained observations regarding the interpretation of the texts of the Constitution on the Sacred Liturgy and *Sacram Liturgiam.* The third category was made up of observations of a general character.

The stylistic and juridical observations were almost insignificant. They were slight alterations, many of which were later accepted by the Consilium. More serious, though, because of the possible consequences, were those observations concerning the interpretation of the Constitution on the Sacred Liturgy and those that undermined the essence of the instruction. Among the observations regarding the interpretation of the Constitution, the strongest attack was precisely on the use of the vernacular language. The instruction, it was said, went beyond the spirit and maybe even the letter of the Constitution.

This seemed to be a return to the polemic of February, when an attempt had been made to deny the bishops' conferences the right to approve vernacular texts. Now the intention was to limit as far as possible the extent of the vernacular in the Mass. The articles of the instruction that, according to the Congregation for Rites, exceeded or perhaps even went against the Constitution were articles 55 and 59. Both of these articles dealt with the use of the vernacular: the first in the Mass and the second in the celebration of the sacraments.

---

[1] Father Ferdinando Antonelli was later appointed secretary of the Congregation for Rites (January 27, 1965), and Monsignor Pietro Amato Frutaz was named undersecretary of the same Congregation.

Basing its critique on *SC* 36 and 54, it was said that article 55 of the draft instruction promoted a use of the vernacular that went beyond the limits set by the two aforementioned numbers of the Constitution on the Sacred Liturgy. The Holy See, then, would be favoring the ever wider use of the vernacular in the Mass, "and this is contrary to the spirit and letter of §1 of *SC* 36." This article presupposed the preservation of Latin as the liturgical language. Consequently, if article 55 were approved as proposed, it would directly violate a fundamental principle of *SC* 36 and lead to the paradox of Latin taking a secondary place to the vernacular in liturgical celebration.

It was proposed then that the vernacular should only be accepted for the epistle, the gospel, and the prayers of the faithful. On the other hand, it was seen to be inopportune and premature to admit the use of the vernacular in other parts of the Ordinary of the Mass, for example in the *Kyrie, Gloria, Credo, Agnus Dei,* and also the introit, offertory, and communion antiphons.

The Congregation for Rites also said that article 59 of the Consilium's draft of the instruction violated the Constitution. The reasons were essentially the same as those raised for article 55. It was maintained that article 59 exceeded the spirit and the letter of the Constitution in going beyond the provision of *SC* 63, which only provided for "more space" for the vernacular in the celebration of the sacraments and sacramentals, not a total change to the vernacular. Therefore, this proposed article 59 seemed to be giving the erroneous impression that the Holy See was in favor of a total elimination of Latin from the liturgy. It was for this reason that the Congregation for Rites argued that it was not opportune to approve this part of the instruction—all the more so since almost every country had an already approved bilingual Ritual, which provided for an ample use of the vernacular in the celebration of the sacraments, sacramentals, and funeral rites. If any nation still lacked a bilingual Ritual, it would be conceded on request.

Once again the vernacular was at the heart of the disagreement, as was the interpretation of the Constitution. It is not surprising that the Congregation for Divine Worship, established four hundred years earlier to safeguard the Tridentine liturgy, was in support of a more restrictive interpretation of the Constitution and limiting the use of the vernacular.[2]

---

[2] G. Landotti, *Le traduzioni del Messale in lingua italiana. Anteriori al movimento liturgico moderno. Studio storico.* (Rome: Edizioni Liturgiche, 1975) 90–93.

The third group of observations regarded the text of the instruction in general. The Congregation urged that the document be reworked to take a more cautious position vis-à-vis implementing the reforms, favoring a more gradual approach and one that would prioritize implementing the more simple reforms. This group of objections undermined the general plan of the whole project of an instruction.

Collectively, then, the Congregation for Rites' observations were intended to throw doubt on all that the Consilium had accomplished, including the resolutions concerning the use of the vernacular already submitted to the Pope and confirmed by him in an audience on April 21. This attack on the Consilium came to a logical conclusion in a proposal for a new procedure to be used in promulgating documents that reaffirmed the customary power of the Congregation for Rites as the Office responsible *"nomine Summi Pontificis"* for the liturgy. The Consilium was regarded in the document as a mere commission dependent on the Congregation. This critique of the instruction was actually a veiled attack on the Consilium. Once again this was an attempt to restrain the Consilium in order to limit the reform.

The Reaction of the Consilium

The observations made by the Congregation for Rites caused a strong reaction among the members of the Consilium. The observations of the Congregation elicited much the same reaction as the controversy in February over article IX of *Sacram Liturgiam*. It was said quite openly that this was another attack on the Consilium by the Curia, which had never shown enthusiasm for carrying out the mandates of the council.

A good example illustrating the reaction of some members of the Consilium to the observations of the Congregation for Rites was that of Bishop Emilio Guano of Livorno, who expressed his concerns in a memo addressed to the Pope in August 1964. He began by stating that he was writing out of a sincere desire to collaborate in the best way possible with the Congregation for Rites in order to fruitfully implement the Constitution on the Sacred Liturgy.[3] While not judging the intentions of the Congregation, he noted that even a mere glance at the document immediately revealed a spirit of criticism and opposition, not only against the draft instruction but more importantly against the Constitution on the Sacred Liturgy itself. He also noted that all the polemics

---

[3] Congregation for Rites, "Observations," 4.

at the time of the council debates reappeared in these critiques—a tenacious return to preconciliar positions, such as an uninterrupted tendency to mistrust the episcopate and its genuine loyalty to the Holy See, an obsessive concern to return to the previous centralization of all liturgical authority, a tendency to see danger in any practical attempt at *aggiornamento*. But, above all, he continued, there appeared to be obvious misunderstanding of the twofold character of the Second Vatican Council: a council dominated by pastoral concerns and anxious to return to the biblical sources of the liturgy.

Bishop Guano supported his comments by noting that many of the Congregation's observations stemmed from a mentality in open conflict with the spirit of the council. This was clearly seen in the diffidence shown toward biblical celebrations on the eve of solemnities and principal feast days—vigils suspected of promoting a Protestantizing of the Roman liturgy. Even more astounding was the proposal that Benediction of the Blessed Sacrament be imposed on these biblical celebrations to render them more "Catholic." This proposal, the bishop said, gave the impression that the Congregation believed that in order for them to be rendered sufficiently orthodox, services such as Matins or Vespers should always conclude with eucharistic Benediction.

Bishop Guano concluded his comments by criticizing the Congregation's proposal for approving liturgical texts. He maintained that such a proposal would reduce the Consilium to a consultative subcommission of the Congregation for Rites. The bishop members who had been directly appointed by the Pope and by the council would feel humiliated and limited in their ability to implement the letter and spirit of the Constitution's mandate. As a consequence, all the other postconciliar commissions would begin to fear that the final implementation of the council would be carried out by the Roman Curia, which had never shown any enthusiasm for it. Thus the rift between the church and the Curia would become more profound and more irreparable.

On September 2 the Consilium presented the Pope with a document entitled "Response to the Observations Made by the Sacred Congregation of Rites," [4] together with the text of the instruction, revised in light of these Observations (*Schema* no. 27, *De instructione,* 6). The Consilium's response dealt with each observation made by the Congregation for Rites, with the intention of giving "an exhaustive and non-confrontational reply, based on

---

[4] See Appendix I, Document N. VI, C (37 typescript pages, dated August 31, 1964).

a careful study of the council minutes, the purpose of the document, its psychological and circumstantial setting, and a systematic overview of the work being done by the Consilium." The observations of the Congregation that were of a stylistic and juridical character were accepted without difficulty. In fact, some of these observations had already been included in the draft *De instructione,* 6.

Much more space, however, was given to answering the other observations. Replying to the concern that the Consilium proceed more slowly and carefully, the response maintained that this posture was always kept in mind. The document continued:

> However, we think it also necessary to avoid the obstacle dictated by excessive caution, which only leads to undue immobility. Up to now the response to proposals or requests for reforms has always been a postponement pending a statement from the Council. Now that the Council has spoken, and spoken clearly, we see no reason to further defer the reform awaited and desired by all. To act otherwise would be to humiliate all those, who with good will and honest intentions, intend to carry out the Council's resolutions.

Lastly, it was pointed out that many of the norms that officially regulated the liturgical action of the church had, for some time, been held in question. Regarding the fear that some points of the reform would interfere with the future general reform, the response said:

> The reforms dealt with in the instruction are solidly supported by scholarship, the review of the various study groups, and the drafts written since the time of the Preparatory Commission. These reforms are accepted by all liturgists and experts in pastoral liturgy because they are doctrinally and historically grounded and provide the basis for promoting the active participation of the faithful. Therefore, if they are introduced now, they will not be touched again in the definitive reform.

Furthermore, the Congregation's insistence on allowing only a gradual reform was answered in the response:

> We can see no reason to doubt the need for the principle of gradualness. . . . Now, at long last, a systematic plan of revision is beginning to emerge. It will take time, but it already fits into the context of the entire reform desired by the Council. Therefore it is definitive. If there were

complaints when *Sacram Liturgiam* was published, it was due to the disappointment of seeing the implementation of the reform further delayed.

The most trenchant part of the Consilium's response was certainly that on the use of the vernacular, regarding articles 55 and 59 of the draft. Most basically it defended the correct interpretation of the Constitution and at the same time the validity of the work achieved by the Consilium. "Article 36 §1 of the Constitution," said the response, "should, in our opinion, be interpreted together with §2 of the same article: extending the limits of the use of the vernacular . . . according to the regulations of this matter to be laid down for each case in subsequent chapters."

In the chapter on the Mass, article 54 indicates the parts where the use of the vernacular is to be conceded: "This is to apply in the first place to the readings and 'the universal prayer,' but also, as local conditions may warrant, to those parts belonging to the people." The explanation was then carried further with a commentary on two texts: "The report delivered during the Council before the vote" and the phrase "to those parts belonging to the people." With regard to the report, it was said: "Even without being an ardent promoter of the vernacular, one cannot fail to notice in the official report the phrase 'for those various parts of the Mass that may be said in the vernacular and we do not purposely exclude any part of the Mass, although there may be good reasons why some Council Fathers wish to exclude the Canon of the Mass.'" Regarding the phrase "those various parts," it was pointed out that the text was derived from the Instruction on Sacred Music and Sacred Liturgy of 1958 (no. 14b), which indicated "the parts which belong to the people," a phrase repeated in article 54 of the Constitution on the Sacred Liturgy envisioning the possible use of the vernacular.

Likewise, the Consilium's answer to the Congregation for Rites' objection to article 59 concerning the use of the vernacular for the sacraments was based essentially on a clarification of the Constitution on the Sacred Liturgy. First of all, in answer to the Congregation for Rites' objection to the use of the vernacular in sacramental formulas, the Consilium defended its interpretation by pointing out that the council had voted 1848 to 335 to authorize the use of the vernacular in the celebration of the sacraments in their session of November 21, 1963. The Congregation for Rites further objected that the use of the vernacular implied by article 59 of the Constitution was not to be accepted because most countries had already been provided with a bilingual Ritual, and therefore it was not necessary to broaden the legislation.

In its reply the Consilium emphasized that it had been precisely those bishops whose countries were using the bilingual Ritual who had approved giving "greater place" to the vernacular in the administration of the sacraments. This approval obviously extended to the sacramental formulas, which until that time had to be proclaimed in Latin. Lastly, it was pointed out that article 63b of the Constitution gave the bishops the right to prepare their own Rituals. The Consilium's response concluded with a proposal for a new version of the document governing the process of approving liturgical texts that would give greater leeway to the Consilium in the process.

The Consilium's response was delivered to the Pope on September 2. Exactly two weeks later, on September 15, during a private audience granted by the Pope to Cardinal Lercaro, the instruction's future was determined.[5] Three days later the Secretary of State informed the Consilium of the Pope's wish to publish the instruction as soon as possible. Controversial points were to be resolved together with the Congregation for Rites. That reply, given three days after Lercaro's audience, was in actual fact a sign that although he was anxious to avoid disturbing the Congregation for Rites, the Pope had accepted the Consilium's schema.

The Consilium's Position Adopted

On September 22 a meeting was held at Cardinal Larraona's apartment between officials of the Congregation for Rites and the secretariat of the Consilium.[6] There was unanimous agreement on all the questions discussed. The atmosphere of the meeting was very relaxed. Here, too, as in the meetings of the preparatory Consilium, everyone was convinced that

[5] During this meeting the Pope also approved the formula of promulgation proposed by the Consilium, which was then published at the end of the instruction. Mention was made of this audience by Lercaro in a letter dated September 15, 1964. See *Lettere dal Concilio 1962–1965*, ed. Giuseppe Battelli (Bologna: Dehoniane, 1980) 256–57.

[6] Present at the meeting were: for the Congregation for Rites: Larraona, Dante, Antonelli, and Frutaz; for the Consilium: Lercaro, Bugnini, and Braga. It is interesting to note what Lercaro says about the meeting in a letter dated September 22: "In the afternoon I fought another battle . . . it was a matter of the Consilium and the Congregation for Rites reaching an agreement over the remaining disagreements over the 'instruction,' which was already in the process of being printed. There were seven of us present (four from the Congregation and three from the Consilium). The meeting lasted two and a quarter hours, and the Consilium's position prevailed."

the essential matters had been decided outside the actual meeting. Cardinal Larraona and the representatives of the Congregation for Rites realized that the Pope had already taken the side of the Consilium.

The results of this meeting were presented by Lercaro to the Pope on September 24.[7] In the meantime, because the secretariat of the Consilium was certain of the Holy Father's agreement, the text of the instruction had been sent to the printers. Following the meeting on September 22, all the problems had been ironed out, and all that was needed were the signatures of Lercaro, Larraona, and Dante. This was the very first time that the prefect of the Congregation for Rites put his signature to a document of the conciliar reform. From that point forward he would be forced to sign documents prepared by the very group that he had consistently opposed.

The instruction was again mentioned in an audience that Cardinal Lercaro had with the Pope on October 1.[8] Since the instruction appeared to be published by the Congregation for Rites, it seemed opportune, in order to avoid confusion, to make it clear that it fell to the Consilium to answer any queries. The final go-ahead for publication was sent by the Secretariat of State to the Congregation for Rites on October 8. The first copy of the instruction was submitted by Bugnini to Lercaro on October 14, 1964. On October 15 a copy of the instruction was presented by Lercaro to the Pope, and the following day to the Council Fathers.[9] Two days later the text was published on the front page of *L'Osservatore Romano*. It was decided that the instruction would take effect on March 7, 1965, the First Sunday of Lent.[10]

The instruction *Inter oecumenici* of September 26, 1964, was an event of fundamental importance for the Consilium, not to mention the liturgy of the church in the West and for the liturgical reform of Vatican II. It was the

---

[7] See ibid., 270.

[8] Ibid., 276.

[9] Ibid., 293, 294, 295.

[10] Previously the Consilium had indicated that the instruction was to take effect on the First Sunday of Advent. But that date became impossible because of the difficulties raised by the Congregation for Rites. The Congregation itself had proposed in its "Observations" of July 23 that the instruction take effect on March 7, 1965—the First Sunday of Lent, marking the first anniversary that *Sacram Liturgiam* took effect. In its response of August 31, the Consilium proposed the date of January 1, which was included in the draft of promulgation. In the end, however, the position of the Congregation for Rites prevailed. This was truly providential, because it allowed time for the publication of the various liturgical texts revised on the basis of the instruction.

first fundamental set of practical guidelines for a liturgical reform since the promulgation of the Tridentine liturgical books in the late sixteenth century. The guidelines contained in this document were to guide the whole future reform. Just as the Constitution on the Sacred Liturgy of the Second Vatican Council was the Magna Carta of the liturgical reform, so *Inter oecumenici* was the foundational document for its practical implementation. The Consilium and the Congregation for Rites, however, championed two different perspectives. The Consilium remained true to its mission in support of a liturgy open to renewal. The Congregation for Rites was still firmly anchored to a limited tradition since the Council of Trent and not in favor of the broad innovations desired by the council.

While the publication of the instruction was a triumph for the Consilium, it also heralded the beginning of a year of adjustment and difficulties. The document was drawn up during the early days of the Consilium, when the elements of its structure were still undefined and the Office was still in search of its own particular juridical identity within the Curia, especially its relationship to the Congregation for Rites. The publication of the instruction also marked the resolution of the serious problem of the interference of the Congregation for Rites in the implementation of the reform.

Conclusion

The May resolution of the controversy between the Congregation for Rites and the Consilium was achieved more because of the weariness of the contending sides than because of an agreement on a formula of compromise. Each side maintained that it should direct the conciliar liturgical reform. Therefore it was quite predictable that tensions would flare up again at the first opportunity. This indeed happened with the publication of the instruction *Inter oecumenici,* which had been prepared by the Consilium after authorization from the Secretariat of State. After going through several drafts, the text was approved in its substance by the June plenary session and then presented to the Pope for final approval. The text was then passed on to the Congregation for Rites. The approval of this document occasioned the definitive solution concerning the nature of the Congregation for Rites' authority in the implementation of the reform.

All the difficulties in relations between the Consilium and the Congregation for Rites came immediately to the surface. According to the Congregation for Rites, the Consilium's version of the instruction (arts. 55 and 59) was too broad in its interpretation of the Constitution's favoring the use of the vernacular in the Mass and the sacraments, going well beyond the limits laid down by the conciliar document.

For the Mass, the Congregation for Rites proposed to limit the use of the vernacular to the readings and the prayers of the faithful. As for the sacraments, it recommended that no innovation be made in the practice prior to the council. It was clear that the position of the Congregation for Rites was fairly extreme. In support of this restrictive position, the Congregation referred to articles of the liturgy Constitution (*SC* 36, 63). In restricting room for the vernacular, the position of the Congregation for Rites indirectly limited the role of the bishops' conferences. Many of the prerogatives belonging to the bishops, for example, the right to determine the extent of the use of the vernacular and to indicate adaptations judged to be opportune, were withdrawn or at least limited owing to the rigid position taken by the Congregation for Rites. That is why the "Observations" document of the Congregation for Rites provoked the same reaction in the Consilium that article IX of the motu proprio *Sacram Liturgiam* had caused a few months earlier. Once again the point of controversy was the question of the vernacular.

The Consilium's "Response to the Observations Made by the Sacred Congregation of Rites" argued for the original meaning of the conciliar text and therefore defended the authentic interpretation given to it by the instruction. The document examined the evolution of the conciliar texts in question, especially the background conciliar discussion of *SC* 54 and 63 before they were voted on. The meaning of the texts that were approved by a large majority was quite clear. Moreover, the incongruity of the position of the Congregation for Rites on the celebration of the sacraments in the vernacular was exposed, since the council had voted for more flexibility, not the maintenance of the status quo. In addition to being a defense of the authentic meaning of the Constitution and of the Office's work, the response given by the Consilium was also a vindication of the rights of the bishops' conferences. The council had solemnly authorized the right of bishops' conferences to determine the extent of the use of the vernacular. Therefore it fell to the Apostolic See simply to confirm the determination of the bishops' conferences regarding the extent of the use of the vernacular.

This new approach to liturgical renewal was entirely foreign to the spirit of the Council of Trent. It is hardly surprising, therefore, that the Congregation that had been instituted four hundred years earlier by the Council of Trent to safeguard a uniformity of practice in the celebration of the Roman

Rite should argue against the right of the bishops' conferences to make such determinations.

The Congregation for Rites and the Consilium also had very different conceptions of how the Holy See was to lead the reform. The Congregation maintained that Rome was to be cautious in implementing the reform in order to avoid mistakes that would compromise its future. It was also of the opinion that partial reforms should be avoided, since these would tend to weary the faithful and the priests. It is clear that the Congregation's position was essentially defensive. Those in charge of the liturgical reform were to be on guard against potential dangers. This position was illustrated in the Congregation's reticence to allow a freer hand in the use of the vernacular in the celebration of the sacraments.

The Consilium's position was completely the opposite. Not fear, but scholarly rigor and pastoral concern for the faithful's active participation were to guide the Office charged with the reform. Foot-dragging in the areas of the reform that had already been approved would lead to mistrust of, and disappointment with, the Holy See, or even to accusations of betraying the Constitution on the Sacred Liturgy. Furthermore, the concept of a static reform similar to that instituted after the Council of Trent was considered un-realistic by the Consilium. Just as clergy and laity needed time to assimilate the other reforms of Vatican II, so their acceptance of the liturgical renewal would need to be gradual. Since the Consilium advocated a more decentral-ized approach to the reform, leaving significant aspects in its implementation to bishops' conferences, it was opposed by the Congregation for Rites, which wanted to maintain its monopoly over approving the details of the renewal mandated by the Second Vatican Council. The Consilium, however, did need the Congregation's power to officially approve the new liturgy. In its view, though, the Congregation's role should have been only to confirm what had been prepared by the Consilium and approved by the Pope.

The instruction *Inter oecumenici* marked the victory of the more open view of the implementation of the Vatican II liturgy advocated by the Consil-ium, in which the bishops' conferences would be associated with the respon-sibility of the Holy See. It also marked the end of the Tridentine mentality, which had considered the liturgy as an unchangeable reality reserved solely to the Congregation for Rites. It also marked an important change in the life of the Consilium itself, which then emerged as the principal Office respon-sible for the liturgical reform, while the Congregation for Rites was relegated to a secondary role. The Congregation was practically forced to accept the

Consilium's work, although the appearance of consensus between the two Offices was maintained by means of joint meetings. These meetings, though, were not entirely foolproof. With its conservative mindset, the Congregation would still be able to oppose or at least modify the Consilium's texts at the last minute. Only in practice would it become clear if, with the instruction, the Consilium had opened the door to reform fully or only halfway.

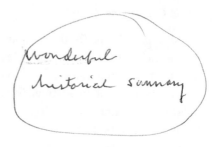

Wonderful
historical summary

Chapter Five

✠ The Consilium Engages the Reform
(October 1964–March 1965)

Meeting in the Wake of the Instruction *Inter Oecumenici*

The publication of *Inter oecumenici* marked a victory for the Consilium's approach to liturgical reform. At the end of yet another battle with the Congregation for Rites, the Consilium had come out stronger than ever before. Not only had its version of this instruction been accepted without any major changes, but in the promulgation itself, found at the end of the document, the role of the Consilium and its president in the implementation of the liturgy was given official recognition. Furthermore, the role of the Congregation for Rites had now been limited to offering some suggestions to the Pope before the final approval of the new liturgical books. The atmosphere in the offices of the Consilium had become much more positive, but it would be necessary to wait to see if the problem of the attempts by the Congregation for Rites to impede the work of the Consilium had indeed been settled. There was hope at this point among the members of the Consilium that they would be able to continue their work without further interference.

The fourth plenary meeting of the Consilium[1] took place over a three-month period in the fall of 1964 (September–November). The presence of

---

[1] Some information on the fourth plenary session and on the events of October–November 1964 was given in *Relationes,* n. 4: *Notitiae:* labores de singulis libris liturgicis. Concelebratio. Coetus particulares. "Kyriale simplex" et "Cantus." "Audientia." "Omina natalicia," (4 decembris 1964) 6.

the bishops in Rome for the sessions of the Ecumenical Council facilitated the meetings of the Consilium's plenary meetings. There were thirty-three members present at the meetings of the fourth plenary: Lercaro, Giobbe, Confalonieri, Rugambwa, Ritter, Silva Henríquez, Grimshaw, Young, Botero Salazar, Mansourati, Rossi, Jop, Hervás y Benet, Zauner, Martin, Rau, Fey Schneider, Lópes de Moura, Van Zuylen, Spuelbeck, Bekkers, Boudon, Nagae, Jenny, Pichler, Isnard, Volk, Guano, Kervéadou, and Fathers Gut, Antonelli, Bevilacqua, and Bugnini, who continued to serve as secretary. The agenda included reports on the Divine Office, the Mass, the Roman Ritual, prayers of the faithful, and the preface of the Eucharistic Prayer in the vernacular.

In his introduction to the afternoon meeting on September 28, the secretary omitted the customary review of the Consilium's activity since the previous plenary meeting[2] in order to report on the progress of the three schemas approved at that meeting, which was held June 18–20, 1964, and presented to Pope Paul on June 28. After some information on the conclusive phases of revision of the draft of *Inter oecumenici,* the secretary explained that a few minor but helpful changes had been added to the final version presented to the Pope on September 24. The text as a whole, however, remained the one approved by the Consilium in June. The secretary then reported that on July 3 the Holy Father granted permission for experimental use for two of the schemas presented: concelebration and Communion under both species. Since this concession was granted, full reports had been drawn up regarding these experiments of concelebration and sent to the Holy Father on September 24 along with the text of the instruction.

A general report on the reform of the Breviary was given by Canon Martimort. This was the result of work done by the various study groups on the Breviary at a series of meetings held from April to August. Much of the future work on the Breviary depended on the response that the members would give to the points for clarification in Martimort's report. The report was divided into five sections, corresponding to the principal celebrations of the Hours: Lauds, Vespers, Compline, Terce, Sext, None, and the Office of Readings. Discussion was lively, because the future structure of the

---

[2] A lengthy report on the activity of the Consilium was published in *L'Osservatore Romano* on September 23, 1964. The article, by Bugnini, was called "Six months of the Consilium's activity."

Breviary was at stake.[3] When the session came to an end, only the first four sections had been discussed and put to a vote. The fifth section was taken up in the afternoon meeting on September 30, which concluded with discussion and voting on the first thirteen questions for clarification put forward in Martimort's general report.

The afternoon of October 1 opened with a report by Monsignor Pascher on the distribution of the psalms. The debate was mainly whether it would be advisable to use all the psalms in the ordinary *cursus,* or course, of the Breviary, including the so-called imprecatory or cursing psalms. After Pascher's brief report, voting resumed on the points of clarification in Martimort's general report. Then Monsignor Pellegrino gave a report on the patristic readings, after which the choice of authors to be included in the Breviary was approved.[4] The next presentation was a brief report on the historical readings and texts for the Office of Readings.

At the beginning of the afternoon working session of October 5, the secretary made an important statement regarding the results of votes taken by the plenary group. The decisions reached were not considered definitive but were to be taken more as guidelines for the work of the study groups.

The group thought that it was especially important that no final decisions be made regarding the reform of the Mass, since it was impossible to form a definitive opinion on many of the aspects of the reform without having experimented with the rite. Monsignor Wagner began his report by giving a summary of the study group's work. He then went through the various parts of the Mass, describing the problematic issues. He, too, stressed that

[3] The fundamental problem was one of considerable importance because it concerned the actual structure of the Hours of the Office, namely, if only one schema for the Divine Office was to be prepared or two: one for celebration with the people and the other for celebration without the people. The discussion was particularly animated between those in favor of three psalms for Lauds, especially for pastoral reasons, and the majority, who did not think that the prayers should be shortened. Of the 29 present, 23 voted for five psalms, which could, however, be reduced to three in celebrations with the people.

Reference to the differences of opinion among the members at that meeting is found in a letter written by Lercaro on September 28. See *Lettere dal Concilio 1962–1965,* ed. Giuseppe Battelli (Bologna: Dehoniane, 1980) 269.

[4] The various reports on the Breviary given during the fourth plenary session were collected together with the queries and results of the members' votes in *Schema* no. 50: *De Breviario,* 14, and successively entered in the *Res Secretariae,* n. 19, pars II. See Appendix 1, Document N. VIII.

no decisions should be made in haste and without being mindful of the overall reform of the Mass.

The were nine issues for clarification, and they were all approved by the members on October 5 and 6, after Wagner concluded his report.[5] On October 6 there were brief reports from Father Schmidt on votive Masses, Father Diekmann on the Scripture readings at Mass, and Father Cardine on hymnody in the Mass. All the issues for clarification presented in these reports received the members' approval.

The next session was held in the afternoon of October 9 in the Apostolic Palace.[6] The subject was the reform of the Roman Ritual; the report was delivered by Professor Fischer. Again, for this part of the reform it was a matter of the members' giving some general guidelines. And once more, these guidelines were based on the acceptance of eight issues for clarification presented in the report.

The last meeting of the fourth plenary session was held in the afternoon of Monday, November 16, at the General Curia of the Salvatorians. There were three items on the agenda: the report on the prayers of the faithful; permission to say the preface in the vernacular; a general résumé of the work completed by the Consilium and future directions.

The report on the prayers of the faithful was given by Father Roguet, reporter for Study Group XII. The second part of the text (Schema 47) also included several models for these prayers. After the report there was a discussion on four points of clarification presented in the report, all of which were approved. But the major item discussed at this session was the vernacular. A paper on the preface of the Eucharistic Prayer in the vernacular had been distributed among the members. The problem was then presented. Several episcopal conferences had requested permission to pray the preface in the vernacular. The Consilium had considered the matter in April, during the second plenary meeting, when it approved the nineteen principles on the introduction of the vernacular. At that time it was agreed that the preface should remain in Latin, not only because it was part of the Roman Canon but also because its Gregorian melody required the Latin text.

Now the problem was put to the members once again. Since it had been decided that both the initial dialogue and the *Sanctus* would be in the vernacular, praying the preface in Latin seemed out of place, since it was in-

---

[5] See Lercaro, *Lettere dal Concilio,* 277, 279.
[6] See ibid., 284.

troduced and concluded by texts in the vernacular. Moreover, the preface in the vernacular could still be sung using the Gregorian plainchant. Having discussed the possibility of allowing the preface in the vernacular, the members voted 21 in favor and 4 opposed.

However, the problem of the preface was more important than it would initially appear. By weighing in on this issue, the Consilium, and especially its secretary, once again became a kind of spokesperson for the episcopal conferences. To propose the same subject to the plenary assembly six months later was certainly an act of courage, but it was also a sign that the Consilium's situation had become stronger.

The Pope's Strategic Support of the Consilium

Three events need to be kept in mind in order to understand the Consilium's changed situation, namely, the audience granted by Pope Paul VI to the Consilium on October 29, the meetings arranged for the presidents of national liturgical commissions, and the meetings for directors of liturgical publications.[7] At the audience the Pope had actually endorsed the line of reform being followed by the Consilium and had therefore given new authority and vigor to the organization's activity. Furthermore, the various meetings of the working groups were a confirmation of the support the Consilium had gained outside the Curia.

The organization was beginning to feel more secure and more than ever an advocate for the renewal desired by the various national episcopal conferences and dioceses. By that time there was great confidence in the Consilium. All those who desired a liturgical reform that would be above all pastoral placed their hopes on this organization. For all of these reasons, the secretary thought that the time was right to present the matter of the preface to the plenary again.

As he closed the session on the preface, the secretary referred briefly to the meetings of the presidents of liturgical commissions and of directors of liturgical publications in a report containing a summary of the work and future directions of the Consilium. The central part of the report gave significant attention to experimenting with concelebration.

---

[7] All three are described on the following pages, where, for systematic reasons, they have been put together with other particularly significant facts.

On November 11, several days before the last plenary session, a meeting took place between a few of the Consilium's *periti* and some officials of the Congregation for Rites in order to deal with a number of difficulties with the rite of concelebration and to agree on a definitive text to submit to the Pope. The secretary made it clear that until the experiments had been concluded, the agreed upon rubrics were to be followed, and debate about the rite of concelebration could not be indiscriminately extended.

Bugnini then indicated the three phases necessary for the approval of every new rite: reform of the rite and an appropriate period of experimentation; examination and approval of the definitive rite by the experts of the Consilium and the Congregation for Rites; final approval by the Pope and subsequent publication by the Congregation for Rites. The secretary made this intervention in light of the Congregation for Rites' written negative reaction to the instruction and to the proposed rite of concelebration and Communion under both species. With the approval and publication of the instruction, the Consilium had overcome the greatest obstacle, but the rite of concelebration and Communion under both species were still not yet approved.

Therefore Bugnini sought to avoid further difficulties. In his talk he emphasized the role of the Congregation for Rites in examining and approving the texts. While it was true that the Congregation for Rites was not allowed to make any substantial modifications in the instruction, nonetheless its presence in the process at this moment had to be accepted. On no account was the work of the Consilium to be compromised. Although many drawbacks had been surmounted, the greater part of the task had yet to be accomplished. There were to be no detours if they were to continue along the road that had at last been opened. One week later, on November 24, Bugnini was received by the Holy Father in audience and was able to inform him of the Consilium's actual situation and of its future prospects.

In the interval between the publication of the instruction *Inter oecumenici* and its taking effect, a few events came about that were particularly indicative of the positive change taking place in favor of the Consilium. While these events might seem unimportant, they need to be considered in context to appreciate how they clearly indicate the new positive attitude that had developed concerning the Consilium.

The success obtained by the Consilium as 1964 drew to a close, both in curial and international circles, would never have come about without the support of the Pope. The existence of this support was clearly evident in the audience granted by the Holy Father on October 29 to the members and consultors of the Consilium. The Pope's speech was mainly on the task of implementing the conciliar Constitution, which was the responsibility of the Consilium:

> You are well aware of our great esteem and constant concern to follow your work, which—and rightly so—we regard as so important. For yours is the task, along with the Congregation of Rites, of carrying out the norms of the Constitution on the Liturgy, so happily promulgated by the Vatican Council II. Clearly, then, the most welcome results, which we are sure will benefit the Church, largely depend on your work. Through your activity especially, the wise prescriptions of the Council will be received gladly and daily be more appreciated; little by little the Christian people will shape their lives according to that model.

The Pope then referred in particular to the work of revision of the liturgical books:

> The portion of the work particularly entrusted to you involves taking up the revision of the liturgical books. That, it need hardly be said, is a work of immense importance and entails the most serious difficulties. Formulation of the prayers of the liturgy is the issue. To evaluate them, to revise them or to compose new ones, you need not only the highest wisdom and perspicacity, but also an accurate sense of contemporary needs combined with a full understanding of the traditional liturgical heritage handed on to us.[8]

The Holy Father went on to indicate some of the norms the Consilium would have to follow while working on the reform: faithful expression of Catholic teaching; the highest form of art; brevity and simplicity; the liturgy must be a school for the Christian people; a blend of new and old. At the end of his speech the Pope returned to the subject of the Consilium's task as a whole:

> As you see, you have a long, rough trek ahead. Your application, however, has already produced the most welcome results—an outstanding example of which is the Instruction on the Liturgy *(Inter oecumenici)* promulgated recently by the Congregation of Rites. Our high hopes, then, for your future work are well-founded. Meanwhile, be mindful that not only we ourself but the whole Church look to you with anxious anticipation. Remember always that it is a magnificent task to offer to the praying Church a voice

[8] *DOL* 621–24.

and, so to speak, an instrument with which to celebrate the praises of God
and to offer him the petitions of his children.

It was quite clear that the Pope was of the opinion that the whole work
of the reform, that is, the implementation of all the conciliar mandates, was
to be carried out by the Consilium. The Congregation for Rites was mentioned twice: at the beginning, when the Pope seemed to wish to associate
the Congregation for Rites with the task of applying the conciliar norms, and
toward the end, when he recalled its juridical participation in the promulgation of the instruction.

But it was quite obvious that both references to the Congregation were
merely two parentheses inserted into a logical discourse centered entirely
on the Consilium's complete responsibility, only because of the extreme
courtesy of Pope Paul, who had no desire to embarrass the Congregation for
Rites. In short, the words of the Pope endorsed the fact that the Consilium
had earned the credibility necessary for carrying forward the work of the
reform on its own. So on October 29 the Pope himself confirmed that state
of affairs which the publication of the instruction had brought about by the
authority of his own words. The Consilium's duty was to do the work of
reform; the Congregation for Rites' was to give it formal confirmation.

In the final analysis, it was a triumph for Cardinal Lercaro and Father
Bugnini, who, sustained by faith in the value of the reform, had worked
tenaciously for more than a year for the realization of the Consilium. But
the greater part of the Consilium's success was due to the efforts of the
secretary, who was an expert on the subtle maneuvers of the Curia, having
suffered at its hands himself, and was able to make use of his considerable
experience. This personal success of the secretary was endorsed when Pope
Paul VI received him in audience on November 24. During the audience the
Pope and Bugnini had a long discussion about the Consilium, its work, and
the various problems and difficulties.

In the new atmosphere that had been created with the publication of
the instruction, the Consilium took the initiative of organizing two meetings—one for presidents of national liturgical commissions and another
for editors of liturgical-pastoral periodicals. This was something new for
the Roman Curia. The Consilium was an innovation in the administrative
structure of the Curia. It had a special juridical "status" that prevented it
from giving legal weight to its decisions. Its members and consultors were
much more international than the rest of the Curia. The role of the Consilium
was also novel in that it was not only to execute the wishes of the Pope, but

it was also to reflect the hopes and needs of local churches throughout the world—considered the "periphery" by many in the Curia.

Meetings for Presidents of National Liturgical
Commissions and Editors of Liturgical Periodicals

B ecause its new role did not correspond to traditional curial arrangements, the secretary of the Consilium was anxious to secure the widest possible support for the liturgical reform it was promoting. In order to renew the liturgy, it was not enough to issue new directives; it was also necessary to change the attitudes of both the clergy and the lay faithful to enable them to grasp the purpose of the reform. Since communication was so crucial to the process of reform, the secretary wasted no time in organizing meetings in Rome with those who would present the reform to the local churches and with publishers.

The meeting with the presidents of national liturgical commissions was held in the afternoon of Monday, October 26, at Santa Marta, where the Consilium had its offices.[9] The agenda was quite straightforward: a welcome by Cardinal Lercaro; a report on the Consilium's activity by the secretary; an explanation of the nature and importance of the instruction *Inter oecumenici* by Father Carlo Braga; and a discussion of the duties of the bishops' conferences in implementing the reform.

The purpose of the meeting was indicated clearly by Cardinal Lercaro: the implementation of the liturgical reform was to be based on close collaboration between the Consilium and the liturgical commissions, that is, between Rome and the local churches. The dialogue that had been initiated with the letter sent to the nuncios and apostolic delegates on March 25 would continue. Another letter by Cardinal Lercaro, dated October 16, addressed to the presidents of episcopal conferences, dealt with the topic of uniform translations in a language common to several nations.[10]

The secretary's report contained information on the activity of the Consilium,[11] the problems to be faced, and future prospects. Afterwards Father Braga emphasized those aspects of the instruction *Inter oecumenici* that directly concerned the work of the national liturgical commissions.[12]

[9] See Lercaro, *Lettere dal Concilio*, 307.
[10] See *EDIL* 298; *DOL* 108.
[11] *Res Secretariae* 12 (Oct. 26, 1964) 4.
[12] *Res Secretariae* 11 (Oct. 26, 1964) 10.

The meeting of the presidents of the national liturgical commissions provided the Consilium and the national liturgical commissions an opportunity to come together. The implementation of the reform would count on this collaboration. This was certainly quite a different approach than the one usually followed by the Curia.

The second initiative, undertaken by the secretary of the Consilium at the end of 1964, was a meeting with the editors of liturgical and pastoral publications. The meeting had been planned since the beginning of September, and considerable care had been taken in its preparation. The Pontifical Commission for Social Communications was asked for input, and national churches were consulted in order to compile a list of the names and addresses useful for the meeting. The gathering, which was held at Santa Marta on November 13 and 14,[13] was attended by more than one hundred directors of liturgical-pastoral publications from many different nations.

The agenda began with a report on the activity of the Consilium given by the secretary.[14] Father Schmidt then spoke of those responsible for the reform.[15] Father Braga then offered an exposition on the nature of the liturgical reform.[16] Father Godfrey Diekmann spoke of the role of social communications in promoting the implementation of the reform.[17]

In addition to the information on the Consilium's activity and the spirit and contents of the new instruction, some interesting points were highlighted, for example, the importance of the means of social communication in promoting the new spirit of the liturgical reform, in circulating documents, in offering a complete and accurate presentation of the reform, and in preparing the faithful to welcome the reform.

One of the most outstanding results of the meeting was a unanimous request on the part of the editors for more information on the activity of the Consilium and on the progress of the reform. This desire for ongoing information led to a publication that would later be called *Notitiae,* which began as an in-house journal for the members and consultors called *Relationes.* In 1965 *Notitiae* became the Consilium's regular monthly publication.

---

[13] See Lercaro, *Lettere dal Concilio,* 331, 333.

[14] See *Res Secretariae* 13 (Nov. 13, 1964) 8. The secretary's report was along the same lines as that given at the meeting of the presidents of the liturgical commissions.

[15] See *Res Secretariae* 14 (Nov. 13, 1964) 7.

[16] See *Res Secretariae* 15 (Nov. 14, 1964) 13.

[17] See *Res Secretariae* 16 (Nov. 14, 1964) 3.

The meetings held with the presidents of the liturgical commission and with the editors of liturgical publications were a most timely initiative. In fact, they served to involve all levels of the church, empowering them to promote the conciliar reform. After these two meetings the secretariat of the Consilium felt a great deal more secure, knowing that it could count on far wider support.

The Pope's Continuing Support; Appointment of Bugnini as Undersecretary of the Congregation for Rites

It was not long after these meetings that the Pope exhibited trust in the Consilium in its relationship with the Congregation for Rites. In a letter dated November 30, 1964, the prefect of the Congregation for Rites attempted to clarify the respective competence of the Consilium and the Congregation for Rites. The Secretariat of State replied on January 7 with a letter in which the roles of both the Consilium and of the Congregation for Rites were defined. A copy of the letter was also sent to the president of the Consilium. The most significant part of the letter read as follows:

> . . . to the Consilium will fall attention either to issues or to liturgical texts that application of the Constitution on the Liturgy now requires. To the Congregation of Rites will fall, with consultation of the Consilium, promulgation of the documents that will put into effect norms and liturgical texts as they become available. It seems advisable to reserve to the critical evaluation of the Consilium those conditions required for the applications of the Constitution now in the process of testing. The Consilium will thus have a basis for deciding what forms may be best for definitive and authoritative approval by the Congregation of Rites.
>
> Promulgation of liturgical books of an official, permanent, and universal character will naturally be reserved to the same Congregation. At the same time, it is clearly appropriate that the decree of promulgation also bear the signature of the Cardinal President of the Consilium, as was the case with publication of the recent Instruction.[18]

This was a reminder to the Congregation for Rites not to impede the activity of the Consilium. The role that fell to the Congregation for Rites was purely formal. The letter, however, also sought to avoid misinterpretations,

---

[18] *EDIL* 379; *DOL* 82.

and so the role assigned to the Congregation for Rites was curtailed by the role assigned to the Consilium. It is evident that not even in matters of legal effect was the Congregation for Rites to be fully autonomous. In fact, the promulgation of the documents was to be done with the Consilium, and the decrees were to also bear the signature of the Cardinal President of the Consilium.

This letter dealing with the respective responsibilities and authority of the Consilium and the Congregation for Rites can take its place alongside two other documents that provided the Consilium with its juridical basis: the motu proprio *Sacram Liturgiam* and the letter from the Secretariat of State of February 29, 1964. It could not yet be said that all the difficulties concerning the relationship between the Consilium and the Congregation for Rites had been resolved, but this most recent letter of the Secretariat of State sufficiently clarified the situation in order to expedite the publication of the documents and the liturgical books.[19] The Consilium, and especially its secretary, could rely on the full support of the Pope.

Two appointments appeared in *L'Osservatore Romano* on January 27, 1965: that of Monsignor Frutaz as undersecretary of the section of the Congregation for Rites that dealt with beatification and canonization and that of Father Bugnini as undersecretary of the liturgy section of the same Congregation. It is not clear how Bugnini, the secretary of the Consilium, came to be appointed to this post. Members and consultors of the Consilium were apprehensive over this appointment, because they had long been suspicious

---

[19] As was said earlier, the initiative to clarify the competencies of the two Offices was taken by the prefect of the Congregation for Rites. The concrete occasion arose when a Roman Missal and a Roman Breviary in English were published by Benziger Brothers of New York. Until then, official editions of liturgical books had always been prepared by pontifical publishers. Now, with the wide-scale introduction of the vernacular in the liturgy, here was another problem that had to be solved.

With regard to the problem and following the letter on January 7, 1965, a meeting organized by Bugnini with the consent of the competent authorities was held for pontifical publishers (Libreria Editrice Vaticana, Pustet, Mâme, Desclée, Marietti, Daverio, Gili, Benziger, Dessain) at the Santa Marta on January 12.

As soon as possible an *Ordinatio* would have to be prepared and published so that editions of liturgical books would comply with the requirements of the Constitution and the instruction. The norms would have to be agreed on with the bishops' conferences of every nation. The copyright of the Latin text would still be reserved to Libreria Editrice Vaticana.

of anything connected with the Congregation for Rites. The Consilium soon began to receive numerous requests to explain Bugnini's new role. Some even feared that this appointment was a maneuver to place the Consilium under the control of the Congregation for Rites.

Bugnini felt obliged to respond to these requests with a public explanation, which appeared on the front page of *Notitiae,* dated March 15, 1965. He noted that this appointment was in fact a positive move to assist the Consilium in its work of implementing the reform rather than an attempt to control or limit its mission.

The secretary's positive interpretation was fundamentally correct, at least in theory. In actual fact, two different interpretations were possible. First, that the Consilium was to be more similar in its action to the Congregation for Rites. Second, that Bugnini, while still secretary of the Consilium, would have a greater voice within that Congregation. Probably these two points of view were those of the Congregation for Rites and the Consilium's secretariat, respectively.

It would seem that Bugnini's opinion corresponded best to the reality of the moment. He had no intention of reducing his commitment to the Consilium or of becoming in any way part of the structure and bureaucracy of the Congregation. In practice, the appointment changed nothing and brought no improvement in the relationship between the two Offices. It was an appointment that existed only on paper and was probably the fruit of a good intention. As such, it could be considered one of the many positive developments that came about for the Consilium at the end of 1964.

The Birth of *Notitiae*

The publication to provide information about the activity of the Consilium, begun in the early months of 1965, constituted one of the many positive accomplishments that the Consilium was able to achieve because of the support it enjoyed following the publication of the instruction *Inter oecumenici*. The need for information, at least among those most directly involved in the work of the Consilium, especially concerning the progress being made by the individual study groups, had been keenly felt from the very beginning. Information on the Consilium's work, before the publication of the journal, gradually emerged in two phases.

During the first phase the information was reserved only to Consilium members and consultors. These reports were called *Relationes*. The first two issues of *Relationes* came out in March 1964 and gave summaries of the Consilium's first and second plenary sessions. The third issue of *Relationes* was dated July 5 and contained news of the third and fourth plenary sessions as well as other information. The last issue of *Relationes* was dated December 4, 1964, and dealt primarily with news from the various study groups.

The change to the second phase of reporting from the Consilium came about after the meeting with the editors of liturgical publications at the end of the year. On that occasion it was requested that the liturgical publishers be periodically informed about the progress of the work of reform.

The initiative was readily welcomed, so much so that the presidents of episcopal commissions and of national liturgical commissions, as well as many other people interested in liturgy, immediately asked to receive the journal. The publication became particularly interesting as it broadened its scope to include some clarification of the more complicated points of the instruction and the Constitution, as well as solutions to questions sent to the Consilium. In this manner it was possible to achieve a certain uniformity of interpretation of the liturgical documents.

In order to proceed with the publication of this journal, Bugnini sent a report on the project for publication to the Secretariat of State on March 8, 1965. Cardinal Lercaro then followed with an official request for permission to publish the journal during an audience on March 16. Soon afterward the Vatican press, La Tipografia Vaticana, published the first edition of the journal *Notitiae*, nos. 1–4, January–April 1965.

The publication of this journal after just a year of the Consilium's existence had a significance all of its own that made it more than just a publication. It was yet another confirmation of the Consilium's vocation to be an international Office open to the needs of the whole church. The publication then became the expression of a more collegial reforming spirit, which the Consilium was anxious to carry forward in the relationship between the Holy See and the particular churches and within the Roman Curia. Moreover, the journal demonstrated that the Consilium had come of age.

The Publications That Followed the Instruction

By the end of 1964, with the numerous publications that appeared immediately after the instruction *Inter oecumenici,* it was evident that there had been a change for the better for the Consilium. In just three months a total of five publications were issued. Three of these dealt with the practical implementation of the instruction, which was to take effect on March 7, 1965. The other two were about concelebration and Communion under both species. Those regarding the instruction were the following: *Kyriale Simplex* (Dec. 14, 1964);[20] *Chants for the Roman Missal* (Dec. 14, 1964);[21] the *New Order of Mass and Rites of Celebration* (Jan. 27, 1965).[22] Regarding concelebration and Communion under both species, the publications were *Rite of Concelebration and the Rite of Communion Under Both Kinds* (Mar. 7, 1965);[23] *On Changes in Holy Week* (Mar. 7, 1965).[24]

Evidence that the Consilium has succeeded in freeing itself from the Congregation for Rites' tutelage was the ease with which these new rites were published in such a short time. After a year of experience it had become a dynamic, efficient entity in the Curia.

The first two publications for the practical implementation of the instruction were both short collections of plainchants: one was the *Kyriale Simplex,* the other, *Chants for the Roman Missal.* Both of them were dated December 14, 1964. They were the first to be published because in both cases it was simply a matter of a collection of Gregorian chants, and therefore putting them together was relatively easy. Although the *Kyriale* bore the same date as the *Cantus,* work on it began several months earlier, and it had its own special story. Only the change in relationship between the Consilium and the Congregation for Rites assured a happy ending to the story.

On May 9, 1964, Father Cardine, secretary of Study Group XXV, which was working on the books of liturgical chant, presented a memo to the Consilium in which he stated that *SC* 54 and 117 expressed a need for a more

---

[20] See *EDIL* 376; *DOL* 530. In the first group of publications, the *Kyriale Simplex* was the one least connected with the application of the instruction. In fact, the *Kyriale Simplex* had been drawn up and scheduled for publication before the instruction but could only actually be published in that more favorable atmosphere that followed publication of the instruction. However, some chants included in it, such as the *Pater noster* and the *Libera nos,* were actually implementations of the directives given in the instruction.

[21] See *EDIL* 378; *DOL* 531.

[22] See *EDIL* 393; *DOL* 454.

[23] See *EDIL* 387–392; *DOL* 222.

[24] See *EDIL* 393; *DOL* 454.

simple collection of Gregorian chants. The Benedictine Abbey of Solesmes had decided to publish a *Kyriale Simplex,* the first proofs of which were already available. Study Group XXV had examined the draft, amended it, and decided to suggest that the Apostolic See make it an official edition, to be published by the Belgian publisher Desclée. The proposal was favorably accepted by the Consilium, and on May 21 the Consilium itself presented a report on the matter to the Secretariat of State. At that time the Congregation for Rites still had considerable influence, and therefore the Consilium's report found its way to that Congregation, which on June 6 asked the Consilium for a copy of the *Kyriale* project in order to form its own opinion on the subject.

The project was sent to the Congregation for Rites on June 10. Two months passed and the situation remained unchanged, that is, until July 13, when Solesmes Abbey sent a reminder to the Consilium requesting a decision on the matter. Bugnini, who in the meantime had sought more than once to speed up the process by demanding information from the officials in the Congregation, reported the situation to the Secretariat of State. In his letter to the Secretariat, dated July 23, he noted that thirty minutes would have been enough for the Congregation for Rites to examine the manuscript, since the Mass formularies were simply taken from manuscripts of the eleventh and fourteenth centuries. Up to that point he had received nothing but promises.

Bugnini's intervention was extremely effective. The very same day the Congregation for Rites' answer was drafted and enclosed. With it were the answers of three consultors who had been appointed by the Congregation. On July 27 the reply reached the Consilium. On August 19 Solesmes composed an answer to the "Observations" of the Congregation for Rites and sent it to the secretariat of the Consilium. The text, reworked by the same secretariat, was called "Remarks on the observations made by the Congregation for Rites concerning the 'Kyriale Simplex.'" The final draft bore the date of October 27, 1964. By the end of October the Consilium had overcome its inferiority complex and reached full stature in relationship to the Congregation for Rites.

This document, promulgated under the norms established by the instruction, went through several steps before it was printed. On December 22 the Congregation for Rites approved the decree of promulgation. Between mid-December and mid-January, various printer's proofs were prepared. The edition was announced and presented in an article called "Il Kyriale simplex" by L. Agustoni, which was published in *L'Osservatore Romano* on January 30, 1965.[25]

The way in which the document on chants for concelebration *(Cantus)* was approved was far less complicated than was the case with the *Kyriale*. This document was compiled during the last months of 1964, when the Consilium was finally able to issue liturgical publications. On October 27 the Consilium presented the Congregation for Rites with a report entitled "Melodies required for compliance with the *Instruction* and for the Rite of Concelebration." The purpose of the report was explained in the preamble:

> The recently published instruction *Inter oecumenici* envisages that certain parts of the Mass, hitherto called "secret," may be sung by the celebrant; other formulas, hitherto sung by the celebrant, may now be sung also by the people. The rite of concelebration also provides that some formulas may be sung. Hence there was a need to prepare suitable melodies.

No sooner had the report been delivered than the drafting of the document began. Between mid-December 1964 and the end of January 1965, various drafts were worked and reworked.[26] The *Cantus,* like the *Kyriale Simplex,* was presented and commented on by Luigi Agustoni in an article published in *L'Osservatore Romano,* February 1–2, 1965.

The instruction *Inter oecumenici* was to take effect on March 7, 1965. This was an important date in the history of the liturgy of the Roman Catholic Church because it marked the beginning of the implementation of the liturgy of Vatican II. The basic principle of the reform was that the formation of the faithful and the pastoral activity of the clergy would have their summit and source in the liturgy (*Inter oecumenici,* art. 5). The application of this principle could not be separated from changes in the rites and texts. Indeed, the whole second chapter of the instruction was devoted to the changes to be carried out in the Mass beginning on March 7, 1965. These changes concerned not only rites. After March 7 it would be possible to have a bilingual

---

[25] For the record, it is perhaps worth mentioning the slight controversy that followed the publication of the *Kyriale Simplex*. The *Kyriale* was criticized in an article published in the magazine *Psalterium*, 2 (1965) 63–64 and 81–83, written by Raffaele Baratta, one of the three experts who had been consulted by the Congregation for Rites. Luigi Agustoni replied with an article called "A response to criticism of the *Kyriale simplex*," published in the magazine *Musica Sacra*, 4–5 (1965) 128–33.

[26] The booklet was printed by the Vatican Polyglot Press (see *EDIL* 378; *DOL* 196) and also by Benziger Brothers, New York.

Missal in Latin and the vernacular. Many bishops' conferences had already approved and obtained official confirmation of vernacular translations. A new version of the Missal in various countries was therefore a necessity. However, to apply the new directives, a revised Latin *editio typica* of the Order of Mass would also be necessary.[27]

A liturgical publisher had made a request for an updated edition of the *Ordo Missae*. In a letter dated November 6, 1964, the Belgian publishing house Desclée presented a draft that included corrections for the *Ordo Missae* of 1962, based on instructions given to Bugnini by Professor Pierre Jounel, one of the Consilium's consultors. It was a very simple project: a list of the changes and a copy of the 1962 *Ordo Missae* with the corrections written in by hand. Because the edition the publisher had in mind was to be for France, the project included, besides the *Ordo Missae* and the prefaces, several Latin-French prayers, sample prayers of the faithful, etc.

The question had been raised, and the secretariat of the Consilium realized that a response had to be provided as soon as possible if the implementation on March 7 was to be orderly. It would not suffice to add a few variations in the text of the *Ordo Missae* in order to carry out the directives of the instruction. The *Ritus servandus* of the 1962 Missal (the rubrics that regulated the celebration of the Mass) would need to be revised. Work was begun simultaneously on both the revision of the *Ordo Missae* and the *Ritus servandus*.

By November 28 a first draft (Schema I) was ready. It had been drawn up by the secretariat and was much more detailed than the "Desclée project." This *schema variationum* (changes) to be inserted into the *Ordo Missae* was sent out for examination to several consultors that same day, November 28.[28] The motivation for the redrafting of the schema was explained in the accompanying letter: the intention was to facilitate the preparation of bilingual editions of the Roman Missal commissioned by bishops' conferences, as well as to provide priests with a rite of Mass in harmony with the dispositions in the instruction in time for March 7. The deadline for replies was set for

---

[27] The most recent edition of the Roman Missal of Pope Pius V was that of 1962. Although the *Ritus servandus* of that Missal contained a few minor corrections of earlier editions, it essentially reproduced the rites codified on July 15, 1570. See P. Jounel, *Les rites de la Messe* (Rome: Desclée, 1967) 5–19.

[28] The schema was sent to the following consultors: Dirks, Famoso, Franquesa, Gy, Hänggi, Jounel, Lisi, Martimort, Schnitzler, Trimeloni, Wagner.

December 8. By December 20 the secretariat had a new draft ready (Schema II), which was sent out to the consultors the same day.

In an accompanying letter Bugnini emphasized the following points. Only those changes that were necessary for the implementation of the instruction had been added to the text. Other amendments, for example a reduction in the number of signs of the cross and some bows, would be discussed during later phases of the reform. The first part of the Mass had been arranged so that the rites of introduction would end with the collect at the altar. For the Liturgy of the Word, the celebrant would move to the chair. Norms were given both for High Mass and for Low Mass. For the other parts of the Mass, only changes judged to be really necessary had been made. The new parts were the introduction in the Order of Mass; the conclusions of the "orations," which until then had been constricted by the *Codex rubricarum;*[29] and the description of the rite of Communion for the faithful, until then contained in the Ritual. At the end of the schema there was a paper with a few particular matters. The deadline for a response was January 5.

Between January 8 and 9 a new draft of the *Ordo Missae* was prepared (Schema III: January 9, 1965). The changes introduced were as follows. The opening psalm was to be omitted, and the antiphon *Introibo ad altare Dei* was indicated as an antiphon with a response. At the *Adiutorium nostrum* the sign of the cross was to be omitted to avoid having two consecutive signs of the cross. For the individual parts of the Ordinary of the Mass, the celebrant would not recite the parts privately, but rather would say them with the faithful. The whole first part of the Mass, from after the kissing of the altar and the opening prayer, could be celebrated from the chair or from the altar, as convenient. In reciting the *Gloria* and the Creed, the bows and the concluding sign of the cross were to be omitted. For the readings fairly detailed indications were given, according to the various forms of celebration. This was the newest part of the ritual order. During the Creed, at the words *Et incarnatus est,* only a bow was to be made, not a genuflection. The place and mode for the prayers of the faithful was indicated. Only a few slight changes in terminology were inserted into the offertory. The prayer over the gifts was to be proclaimed aloud. There were also changes in the

---

[29] The *Codex rubricarum* was actually the revision of the rubrics of the Breviary and of the Roman Missal by the Congregation for Rites on July 26, 1960: *Rubricae Breviarii et Missalis Romani*" (Typis Polyglottis Vaticanis, 1960). On the basis of these rubrics, the new edition of the Roman Missal and the *Ritus servandus* had been produced in 1962.

rubrics for the beginning of the preface and the *Sanctus-Benedictus*. The rubric for the doxology of the Canon had been reworked. At the end of the Our Father the *Amen* was removed. The embolism ("Deliver us") was to be said out loud. The formulas for Communion of the faithful were added. The rubrics after the *Placeat* were slightly altered to adapt them to the omission of the last gospel.

The draft of the Order of Mass was sent to the printer along with the revised text of the Canon. The first proofs were ready January 23, the corrected proofs on January 27. The work was at last completed. The decree for the *Ordo Missae et Ritus servandus in celebratione Missae et De defectibus in celebratione Missae occurrentibus*" (The Order to be observed in the Celebration of Mass) was dated January 27, 1965.

For the revision of the *Ritus servandus,* the same procedure was followed as with the *Ordo Missae.* The work of revision was done by the secretariat, with the collaboration of the same consultors who had been engaged in the revision of the Order of Mass. The first draft was sent to the consultors on December 4, 1964, a week after the first draft of the *Ordo Missae.* The rubrical section of the text that was new in comparison with the 1962 *Ritus servandus* was the section dealing with the Liturgy of the Word. A new chapter about celebrating Mass with a deacon had to be included. Apart from these differences, this text represented slight changes and simplification in the rubrics. Finally, from the section of the 1962 Missal that dealt with "defects" in the celebration of Mass, only one page remained, with a few minor changes.

In the enclosed letter to the experts, Bugnini pointed out that in the revision of the *Ritus servandus* the revision of the *Ordo Missae* needed to be kept in mind. But time was the greatest problem. The consultors were given only eight days to comment on and return the text. The situation was further complicated by the fact that many lived outside of Rome and had to rely on the mail service. Most responses arrived after December 12. Nevertheless, a new draft was ready by December 23 and was sent immediately to the consultors—only three days after the *Ordo Missae.* The new draft was essentially a simplified version of the previous one. The deadline for a response was January 5, the same as the deadline for the draft of the *Ordo Missae.* There was then a third revision, on January 11, 1965. This was basically the definitive text. The final draft was dated January 20, 1965, and was sent to the printer. It included the complete text of the "defects," only one page of which had been given in the previous drafts. The first proofs were ready by January 23, and several days later the second proofs were delivered.

Appended to the text of the *Ordo Missae* and of the *Ritus servandus* were norms for liturgical publishers established by the Congregation for Rites, entitled *Ad librorum liturgicorum editores* and dated February 15, 1965. This document stated that since the *Ritus servandus* and the *Ordo Missae* were only part of the Missal, the rest of the liturgical book needed to be harmonized with the new directives.[30] A list of forty-seven changes to be included in the Missal was contained in an accompanying booklet entitled *Rubricae in Missali Romano emendandae.*

Even though the revision only took the form of changes in the 1962 Missal, nonetheless the publication of this new Order of Mass constituted an event of fundamental importance in the history of the Roman Catholic liturgy. For the first time the principles of liturgy established by Vatican II were applied to the worship of the church, even though in a marginal and transitory manner.

The 1965 rite contained John Burchard's text (1485), which had been the basis upon which the liturgical commission instituted by Pope Pius V had drawn up the *Ritus servandus* in the Tridentine Missal of 1570. But the spirit of the *Ritus servandus* could no longer be found in the text of 1965. For example, a variety of choices were now open to the celebrant in several parts of the Mass; a similar possibility would have been unthinkable in the 1570 *Ritus*. Furthermore, the model for celebration up until 1965 was that of the "private" Mass, or Mass celebrated by the priest with a server, whereas the 1965 *Ritus* was based on a sung Mass or Mass celebrated with a congregation *(concurrente populo)*. The *Ritus servandus* of 1965 was essentially a rite of transition: "Heir of the liturgy of yesterday, introducing today essential elements of the liturgy of tomorrow, the *Ritus servandus* of 1965 is a ritual of transition."[31]

Apart from considerations of content, the publication of the *Ordo Missae* and of the *Ritus servandus* constituted yet another proof of the capacity of the Consilium to implement the reform in a dynamic way. In just over two months, the Consilium had succeeded in completing a task that had not been anticipated. No one had imagined that it would be necessary to rework the *Ordo Missae* before March 7 when the instruction *Inter oecumenici* was published. Even though Study Group X, which dealt with that topic, had

---

[30] *DOL* 1341.

[31] P. Jounel, *Les rites de la Messe* (Rome: Desclée, 1967) 19. See A. Bugnini, "Il nuovo Ordo Missae," *L'Osservatore Romano* (January 29, 1965).

already begun its work, it was believed that the reform of the Mass would move much more slowly.

As for the topic of concelebration and Communion under both species, a new period of experimentation began. In June 1964 the plenary meeting had examined a draft on concelebration and another on Communion under both species. On that occasion the members of the Consilium decided that the drafts would have to be used *ad experimentum* for a set period of time. The drafts were presented to the Pope on June 26, 1964. During that audience the Pope gave permission for experimentation to a limited number of monasteries chosen by the Consilium.[32] The local ordinary was to be informed. The number of concelebrants was not to exceed twenty. For each monastery one of the Consilium's members or consultors, chosen by the president himself, would be responsible for the concelebration and would report to the Consilium every two months, explaining the difficulties encountered in the rite and proposing suggestions for its improvement.

The first two requests for concelebration did not come from monasteries. The first arrived on June 17 from Cardinal Vincenzo Scherer, archbishop of Porto Alegre. It was a request for two concelebrations: on July 19 and 26, on the occasion of a meeting for theologians and pastoral experts of Latin America. The second request was made by Cardinal Giuseppe Ferretto on June 24, 1964, to accommodate a pilgrimage of priests to Lourdes.[33] It was because of these two requests addressed to the Holy Father that the Secretariat of State asked the Consilium to propose guidelines for these concelebrations. On July 3 the guidelines proposed (for not more than twenty concelebrants) were approved, and the two permissions were granted. At the same time permission was given to Cardinal Lercaro, as president of the Consilium, to grant permission for concelebration *ad experimentum* for individual cases within that current year.

Inevitably, experimentation was destined to become more and more widespread. Other monasteries besides those that had been granted permission soon began to ask for the possibility of concelebration "ad experimentum." The first group of monasteries was joined by the Benedictine Monastery of Chevetogne, Belgium (end of July), the Cistercian Monastery of Hauterive,

---

[32] See as above, p. 64, n. 36.

[33] Cardinal Ferretto referred in his application to the news, published in *L'Osservatore Romano* on June 21, of the concelebration carried out at Sant' Anselmo in Rome on the occasion of the third plenary session.

Switzerland (mid-September), and the Oratorians of Leipzig, East Germany (end of September).

The two drafts on concelebration and Communion under both species were submitted to the Pope with the draft on the instruction and with the problems involved with the instruction. On July 23 the Congregation for Rites presented its observations on the three drafts that it had received for examination from the Pope on July 1. The Congregation was most concerned about the instruction. The observations on the other two schemas were only intended to confirm their serious critique of the instruction on the reform being carried out by the Consilium, which they believed went beyond the intentions of the council.

On July 23 the Congregation for Rites issued its "Observations on the Schemas on Concelebration and Communion Under Both Species." This document referred to matters of a general character as well as some particular elements of the actual rites. In its general observations on concelebration, the Congregation for Rites intended to safeguard "a true celebration, proper respect for the dignity of the Sacrament, and the edification of the Christian people." So once again the Congregation for Rites was affirming its exclusive right to defend the truth and the dignity of the liturgy. Its observations, though, dealt with the concelebrants' position around the altar, limiting their number according to the size of the altar, the recitation of the whole of the Canon in Latin, and the vestments to be used. These comments demonstrated that the Congregation for Rites' ideas were really not very different from those laid down by the Consilium.

There was a contrast, however, between the Congregation's general observations and their conclusion. In commenting on the Consilium's proposal, it stated: "If such principles are to be accepted, then all the directives proposed by the Consilium in the *Ritus servandus in concelebratione* must be revised." The Congregation for Rites, in beginning its comments with minor rubrical observations, seemed to want to create an atmosphere of apprehension and alarm and then call for the complete revision of what the Consilium had proposed.

The particular observations on various parts of the rite of concelebration were consistent with this same strategy. First, at ordinations only the newly ordained were to be allowed to concelebrate; anyone else was considered superfluous. Second, the possibility of permission for a priest to celebrate two Masses on the same day was to be removed from the draft, since it was within the competence of other Congregations, not the Congregation for Rites.

Third, the use of a paten for each concelebrant was to be made compulsory. Fourth, drinking directly from the chalice was excluded; only the use of the *calamus,* or metal straw, was to be allowed.

The overall impression given by the Congregation for Rites' critique was that these comments were based, not on a deep knowledge of the history, theology, and the pastoral practice of concelebration, but rather from a desire to find errors at any cost.

The Consilium's answer to the Congregation for Rites, entitled "A Response to the Observations Made by the Sacred Congregation for Rites Concerning the Rite of Concelebration" and "A Response to the Observations Made by the Sacred Congregation of Rites on the Rite of Communion Under Both Species,"[34] was prepared August 31 and sent to the Pope on September 2. These documents were considerably lengthier than the Congregation's critique, since its "Observations" were easy to challenge historically and pastorally, given the approach championed by the council. For example, the Consilium, in its "Response," was able to offer documentation of the traditions and practices of the Latin church to demonstrate that the Congregation for Rites' contention regarding the necessity to limit the number of concelebrants and the need for them to be physically close to the altar could not be historically supported. Similarly, it was not difficult to show the complete lack of foundation for the Congregation's request that "all the concelebrants recite the whole of the Canon in Latin, from the *Te igitur* up to and including Communion." This blatant error—especially not understanding what constituted the text of the Canon—only served to diminish the credibility of the Congregation's observations.

Moreover, the odd insistence on limiting the number of concelebrants; on the possibility of priests celebrating two Masses on the same day; on Communion of the precious Blood by a metal straw only; on reserving the permission for Communion under both species to the Holy See, all of these positions only confirmed the absence of balance in the Congregation for Rites and its lack of willingness to consider the problems of the renewal from a pastoral point of view, in contrast to the spirit of the council. These were just some of the negative aspects that the Consilium highlighted and that explain why the "Observations" made by the Congregation for Rites were rejected.

However, it should not be forgotten that the fate of the two drafts on concelebration and on Communion under both species was tied to that of the

---

[34] See Appendix I, Document N.VII, B.

instruction *Inter oecumenici*. The difficulties with this document, which were ironed out in mid-September, also marked the beginning of the final phase for the drafts on concelebration and Communion under both species.

Difficulties with the Congregation for Rites did not impede experimentation, nor did they delay the final preparation of the rite. As a matter of fact, during the heated debates of August and September, the faculty for allowing concelebration was not suspended. On the contrary, experimentation became more and more widespread. According to a report by Bugnini:

> . . . from July 3, 1964, to March 21, 1965, as many as seven hundred and twenty permissions were given to bishops and priests. Furthermore, for some nations—three in Europe, five in Africa, eight in the Americas—collective permissions were given to bishops' conferences for concelebration. In exceptional cases and under the usual conditions each president of the conference in question was to communicate the faculty to individual bishops. Moreover, in addition to the abbeys that already had permission to concelebrate, over two hundred other religious communities requested the same concession. Eight of these communities received a positive response, allowing the superior general, who could then delegate the faculty to individual provinces of the order or institute. To put it briefly, there were more than fifteen hundred concelebrations *ad experimentum* in various parts of the world in a variety of circumstances. The Consilium archives have dossiers on these concelebrations: reports, suggestions, photographs, in some thirty files.[35]

In the meantime, conditions for permission to experiment had been made more rigorous, taking also into account the Congregation for Rites' "Observations." The conditions laid down in the decree of concession were the following:[36] first, the rite provided by the Consilium had to be used; second, the number of concelebrants could not exceed twenty, except in the case of ordinations, and they should stand near the altar; third, the priest who received delegation was deputed to do what the rite demanded and was responsible for its worthy execution; fourth, after the concelebration a report should be given to the secretary of the Consilium, indicating any

---

[35] *Res Secretariae*, 17 (April 1965) 4; report to the fifth plenary session of the Consilium.

[36] The conditions given here are those laid down for concessions made to bishops. Priests had to be in contact with the local ordinary.

major difficulties. If possible duplicate photographs should be sent along for the use of the Consilium archives.

Experimentation was further broadened by the numerous permissions granted to bishops attending the third session of the council who concelebrated in churches near their residences in Rome. Moreover, that session of the council began and ended with a solemn concelebration in St. Peter's presided over by the Pope.[37]

The final phase in the preparation of the schema on concelebration was defined by a meeting on November 11 between the Consilium and the Congregation for Rites. At this meeting a definitive text to be presented to the Pope was to be decided upon. During the month of October the secretariat of the Consilium had been asked to put an end to the experimentation. This meant that the work of revising the text had to be completed. And so the above-mentioned meeting was arranged.

The meeting of November 11 took place at the Congregation for Rites. Representing the Congregation were Archbishop Dante, secretary of the Congregation for Rites; Father Antonelli, promoter of the faith; and Monsignor Frutaz, a historical expert from the Congregation. Participating for the Consilium were Father Bugnini, Father Braga, and members of the Consilium study group charged with working on the rite and who were then present in Rome: Monsignor Wagner, Canon Martimort, Father Vagaggini, Father Franquesa, and Father Dirks.

It is interesting to read the minutes of the meeting. Issues on the agenda were the following: (1) Should all the concelebrants be near enough to the altar so as to be able to touch it? (2) Must all the concelebrants say all the prayers from the offertory onward, so that what the president says out loud must be recited by each of them in a low voice? (3) Is it appropriate for all the concelebrants to extend their hands toward the offerings at the words of consecration? (4) Should each concelebrant have his own paten when receiving the Host at communion?

---

[37] Lercaro, *Lettere dal Concilio,* 254. At the liturgy that concluded the third session of the council, the Vatican Press printed a special booklet entitled *Ordo Concelebrationis clausurae tertiae sessionis Concilii œcumenici Vaticani II, die 21 novembris 1964.* At that time, too, Benziger and Einsiedeln published two booklets commissioned by the German bishops' conference, one of which was for concelebration. It included the rubrical revisions of the Order of Mass and the Roman Canon, with the rubrics for concelebration and the other directives for distribution of Communion under both species. It also included the decree granting the permission for these two rites.

In regard to the first question, it was said that the recurrent formula *iuxta altare* used in the liturgical books does not mean that all concelebrants must be near enough to be able to touch the altar; it does mean that they should be relatively close to the altar. Moreover, according to the Roman Pontifical, in the rite of the ordination of priests, the concelebrants could possibly be some distance from the altar. The Eastern church also interprets the rule by stipulating that concelebrants must be "near the altar." History also helped interpret the rule inasmuch as altars were small in the past—about the size of a boundary stone—and therefore not all the concelebrants could stand near enough to touch the altar. It was then pointed out that this question was connected with the problem concerning the number of concelebrants. A long discussion followed. In the end unanimous agreement was reached on the solution expressed in the following text:

> The number of concelebrants must be regulated in such a way that from the offertory, up to a maximum of fifty concelebrants, may stand comfortably around the altar. Where special reasons to go beyond that number exist, a request must be made to the Holy See.

The main reason supporting this resolution was respect for the intention of the council based on the *Acta*. The council seemed to want to carefully avoid concelebrations with an unlimited number of concelebrants, becoming oversized rites that could not be carried out with due reverence and the necessary dignity. At the same time, the council purposely refrained from directly limiting the number of concelebrants out of consideration for some of the larger communities, in which abuses of this nature were to be less feared. Therefore, there was an agreement to establish a general rule that the number of concelebrants should not go beyond fifty, in such a way as to make it clear that the Holy See would take into consideration those cases where there would be a good reason for exceeding this number. Furthermore, the rite would indicate that it was the duty of an ordinary or a major superior to limit the number of concelebrants if, in his opinion, the dignity of the rite so required.

With regard to the second question, all agreed that each concelebrant should recite only the parts of the Canon from the *Hanc igitur* to the *Supplices* inclusive. The main reasons supporting this decision were practical and theological. The recitation of a number of texts by a group of persons would necessarily be slow and would therefore render the concelebration too long and heavy. Experience had shown that this often occurred in the rite of priestly ordinations. From a theoretical point of view, the orations now said at the offertory (of recent origin, and according to the unanimous opinion of the experts, to be abolished or changed in the subsequent reform of the *Ordo Missae*) were texts that were to be accompanied by a gesture. Therefore these prayers should naturally be recited only by the one who makes the gesture.

Moreover, while the first phrase of the *Te igitur* is merely a formula of transition after the preface, the *In primis quae tibi offerimus,* the *Memento,* the *Communicantes,* the *Memento etiam,* and the *Nobis quoque peccatoribus* are formulas introduced later into the Canon and related to the diptychs, which were recited by the deacon; therefore it would be appropriate that these different texts be recited by different concelebrants, following the example of the Eastern church. Such an arrangement would also give a greater variety to the proclamation of the prayer.

Furthermore, in the part of the Canon that goes from the *Hanc igitur* to the *Supplices,* all the essential and traditional concepts of the Roman Canon are expressed: the request that the offerings be accepted, the institution narrative with the words of consecration, the *anamnesis,* the offering, and the prayer for a fruitful Communion. It is worth noting that this part of the medieval text of the Canon (from the *Hanc igitur* to the *Supplices*) is essentially the same as is found in the fourth-century catechetical work of St. Ambrose called *De sacramentis.*

Regarding the hand gesture at the moment of the consecration, the group decided unanimously that this rite should be preserved as described in the *Ordo* for the following reasons. The ancient tradition is confirmed by the *Apostolic Tradition,* which, according to the common opinion of scholars, represents a possible early Roman practice.[38] The same gesture is prescribed in a number of other early texts. There is a parallel practice in other sacramental rites in which some sort of concelebration occurs. All the concelebrants extend a hand at the central point of the rite. A good example of this would be the rite of priestly ordination, when all the priests present, after laying hands on the ordinand, keep a hand extended during the consecratory prayer that follows. In some Byzantine Catholic traditions, for example, the celebrant extends his hand toward the host, which remains on the paten, and toward the chalice.

---

[38] Bernard Botte, *La Tradition apostolique de saint Hippolyte. Essai de Reconstitution* = Liturgiewissenschafliche Quellen un Forschungen 39 (Munster: Aschendorffsche Verlagsbuchhandlung 1963) 10.

All the concelebrants extend a hand toward the host and the chalice as they pronounce the words of consecration. Something similar occurs also among the Orthodox, at least at the moment of the epiclesis. This common gesture by the concelebrants demonstrates a participation in the same act. If there is any fitting time in the celebration for this common gesture of the concelebrants, it would be during the words of institution. Both the experience of concelebration as well as reports received by the Consilium indicated that this gesture was appropriate and heightened the sacral meaning of the prayer.

Other responses followed. With regard to the use of individual patens, all agreed that it should be permitted as an option among the other possible ways of receiving Communion. Other than the issue of the hand gesture, the problems posed were exactly those raised by the Congregation for Rites in its "Observations" of July 23. During the meeting, however, they were considered with greater scholarly depth. As a result of the November meeting, therefore, a new draft on concelebration was produced and was distributed on December 20, 1964. The draft was sent to a large group of consultors[39] together with the draft on Communion under both species for final observations prior to publication. These comments were to be sent to the secretariat by January 5, 1965. This new draft was then sent to the Congregation for Rites on January 31.

The Consilium and the Congregation for Rites then resumed their work together, meeting on February 10, 23, and 27, 1965. During the last two meetings special attention was given to five points that presented some difficulty. They were the same problems discussed during the joint meeting in November 1964: the number of the concelebrants; their proximity to the altar; recitation of the Canon; hand gestures; use of multiple patens.

Only two points were slightly altered: the number of concelebrants and the hand gesture. The paragraph referring to the number of concelebrants was shortened by removing reference to limiting their number to fifty and the ordinary's faculty to permit a higher number. Regarding the concelebrants' hand gesture at the moment of consecration, in order to avoid the appearance of a "hand raising" similar to the Mussolini Roman salute, the expression was mitigated with the addition of *si opportunum videtur.*

---

[39] Consultors to whom the schema was sent: Wagner, Hänggi, Righetti, Schnitzler, Jounel, Vagaggini, Franquesa, Gy, Jungmann, Martimort, Fischer, Botte, Neunheuser, Falsini, Dirks, Trimeloni, Diekmann, Pinell, Marsili, Schmidt, Famoso, Buijs, Lanne, Matéos, Van Doren, Rousseau, Feder, Borella.

These and other explanations were sent to the Secretariat of State by Bugnini on February 27, 1965. Interestingly, these five points had been previously submitted to the Holy Father for an authoritative decision; he in turn was asked his opinion on the matter. This was the latest sign of the esteem that Bugnini had earned in the eyes of the Pope.

Finally, all was ready for the final approval of the concelebration text, to which had been added the text of Communion under both species. Approval was given by the Pope during an audience with Cardinal Larraona on March 4, 1965. The approved draft was practically the same as that of January 20, 1965, except for some correction of style and rubrics. The same could be said for the draft of Communion under both species of February 10, 1965. Both rites were promulgated and published together on March 7, 1965. Also included were most of the musical texts published earlier in a small book called *Cantus qui in Missali Romano desiderantur iuxta Instructionem ad exsecutionem Constitutionis de Sacra Liturgia recte ordinandam et iuxta ritum concelebrationis,* dated December 14, 1964.

As Bugnini himself wrote in an article that appeared in *L'Osservatore Romano* on March 26, 1965, concelebration was the first rite to be restored by the Vatican II liturgy and constituted the first fruit of the Consilium's efforts. Not only had the rite of concelebration been restored after having fallen into disuse in the Western church since the twelfth century,[40] but it also represented the Holy See's new way of understanding the liturgy. No longer was it purely an imposition of norms laid down by Rome, but the result of consultation and experimentation that lasted eight months and involved practically the whole church. In this the Consilium was most gratified to see some progress in its efforts.

Next on the agenda was Holy Week. It is not quite known how the initiative originated for a revision of the texts for the Chrism Mass with its blessing of oils and other Holy Week texts. The call for such a revision was first found in a report on this work carried out by the Consilium that was sent to the Congregation for Rites on February 10, 1965. It spoke of this revision being requested by "the competent authorities." Like other publications derived from the instruction, it was directed by the secretariat of the Consilium. The work had been started in October 1964 and was divided into three parts: the Chrism Mass, the blessing of oils, and the solemn prayers of Good Friday.

---

[40] See P. Jounel, *La concelebrazione* (Rome: Desclée, 1967) 24.

The first draft of the revised Chrism Mass had been sent out to a group of consultors on December 1 and was reworked several times before becoming the definite text sent to the Congregation for Rites on February 10, 1965. Regarding the blessing of oils, the first draft was prepared and ready by November 6; a second draft followed on November 28. Father Braga prepared a report on the simplification of the consecration of the oils based on conversation at a meeting held on January 5. A new draft was ready on January 7; except for a few minor amendments, it was the one presented to the Congregation for Rites on February 10, 1965.

The first draft of the solemn prayers of Good Friday was issued on October 27. This text was reexamined by the study group at the Consilium on December 23, 1964. Another revision (the third) was done on January 1, 1965. At a meeting on January 5 at the Consilium, all three drafts were examined together; after further study and emendation, they were presented to the Congregation for Rites on February 10. In addition to a general presentation, each draft also had its own detailed introduction.

The general presentation referred to all three documents. Regarding the Chrism Mass, the readings had been changed to accommodate the *Graduale Simplex* for the whole year, and a collection of "simpler melodies" was presented. The draft on the blessing of oils contained only minor emendations intended to simplify the rite. One exception to this simplification was the inclusion of concelebration. It should be noted, however, that these emendations were not meant to compromise an in-depth revision of the rite, which would necessarily include a reexamination of the texts. The major change in the Good Friday texts was the elimination of some prayers that were considered inappropriate, given the council's new emphasis on ecumenism and interreligious dialogue.

The manuscript was then sent to the printer, and on February 26 the first proofs were ready. The changes in the Holy Week liturgy, like the rite of concelebration, were published with a decree dated March 7, 1965.[41] Compared with the speed of the earlier efforts at reform, the Consilium was now working more expeditiously. The goal pursued by Bugnini and Lercaro from the very beginning of the Consilium had been reached: an agency that was international, dynamic, and independent from the Roman Curia. Unlike the first ten months of 1964, now it was the Consilium which, after having

---

[41] Bugnini wrote a commentary on the publication in an article printed in *L'Osservatore Romano* (March 19, 1965).

carried the work, asked for the Congregation for Rites' opinion; the Congregation appeared to have become merely a consultative body.

In the letter of February 10 presenting the drafts of the changes in the Holy Week liturgies to the Congregation for Rites, Bugnini wrote:

> This draft has already been submitted to the Holy Father for general approval. On January 23, 1965, he asked the Cardinal Secretary of State to write: "I fulfill the venerable charge of communicating to Your Eminence that all appears to be in order. Will you therefore be so good as to arrange for the opportune revision, approval, and promulgation, so that these innovations may be enjoyed by the church for the coming Easter celebrations?"

All that remained for the Congregation for Rites was to give its consent for publication. This consent was to be given without delay in order to facilitate the translation and publication of these texts by the end of February.

It could be said that March 7, the date when the instruction *Inter oecumenici* went into effect, marked the end of the first period of the reform, which had begun with the publication of the instruction. This document had opened the door for the liturgical reform. For its part, the Consilium had gradually gained the Pope's highest esteem and confidence, thereby diminishing the role of the Congregation for Rites. Once it was free to act, the Consilium was able to exercise competent leadership in the implementation of the reform. In just over three months, five publications of reformed liturgical rites were already in print, constituting the first implementation of the Vatican II liturgy according to the procedures given in the instruction. In retrospect, the instruction proved to be even more important than originally anticipated. It could be said that it constituted the *culmen et fons,* the "summit and source," of the Consilium's first year of existence.

Conclusion

This chapter has treated the activity of the Consilium from the publication of the instruction *Inter oecumenici* to its promulgation. This was certainly the most positive period since the Consilium's establishment, characterized by enthusiasm for the new instruction. More specifically, the activity focused on the implementation of the document. This would be accomplished through the preparation of a series of publications that would offer the church a first look at the liturgy desired by the Second Vatican Council.

In order to fully appreciate the significance of the fourth plenary meeting of the Consilium, it is necessary to consider its context. It took place roughly between the end of September and the beginning of October. The last meeting of the assembly was held in mid-November, when the final preparations for the publication of the instruction were taking place. At that time it was obvious that the Consilium's approach to reform would prevail. On opening the meeting, Bugnini, the secretary, announced that the instruction would soon be circulated. It is evident that the decisions made by the fourth plenary session concerning the future reform of the Missal and the Divine Office, approved by a large majority, expressed confidence in the Consilium's work. This confidence was officially expressed in the imminent publication of the instruction.

The session on November 16 was especially significant. Just prior to that meeting there had been several positive developments in favor of the Consilium, such as the papal audience at the end of October and the meetings with the liturgical commission presidents and with the editors of liturgical periodicals. Moreover, at that point there was widespread satisfaction with the publication of the instruction. In this particularly favorable atmosphere, the secretary decided to raise the question of the preface of the Eucharistic Prayer in the vernacular. This move may have seemed rather risky considering that the newly published instruction, which was to take effect on March 7, did not allow this as a possibility. The positive response of the plenary members to this proposal was a sign that enthusiasm for the reform was beginning to pervade the whole Consilium.

While on the one hand it was clear that the newly published instruction was but one further step along the road to liturgical renewal, Bugnini wisely recognized that it would be important to move forward cautiously in developing the Consilium's relationship with the Congregation for Rites in order to accomplish the desired goals. This growth in their relationship was evidenced in a meeting between the Congregation for Rites and the Consilium that took place several days prior to the fourth plenary meeting. It was during this meeting that certain problematic issues, such as concelebration, were jointly resolved.

The fourth plenary meeting, then, took place in an atmosphere of restrained enthusiasm for the publication of the instruction. However, in addition to its study of various drafts of new rites, the plenary meeting, by approving the use of the vernacular in the preface, opened the Eucharistic Prayer itself to the vernacular. Once again the Consilium was acting as a spokesman for the bishops' conferences, many of which were already pressing for decisions in that direction.

From the second half of October 1964 to March 1965, the life of the Consilium was characterized by a series of positive events that were indicative of the favorable climate surrounding the Office: the papal letter dated January 7, in which the prerogatives of the Consilium vis-à-vis the Congregation were confirmed; Bugnini's appointment as undersecretary of the Congregation's section *De sacra Liturgia;* the founding of the Congregation's liturgical review *Notitiae.* All this demonstrated that the Consilium was indeed gaining favor, especially within the Roman Curia but also internationally.

The meeting of directors of national liturgical commissions marked a reorientation of the liturgical life of the church by reaching out to diverse corners of the globe, held for too long at a distance from the church's liturgical decisions. It created a healthy climate of collaboration and exchange of ideas between the Roman Curia and the world church. This was one of those important elements that made the Consilium an advocate for local churches and helped to lead the renewed liturgy mandated by Vatican II away from being the expression of a local church or interest group to become the liturgy of the universal church.

A concrete expression of this collaboration was the founding of the review *Notitiae.* The proposal was made by the editors of liturgical periodicals, who were anxious to be regularly informed about the reform's progress. The review, first published at the beginning of 1965, soon became the main source of information on the activity of the Consilium, but it also contained information on the activities of the national liturgical commissions. It became an important point of reference on the progress of the conciliar liturgical reform throughout the church.

These positive events—especially the support of the Pope and the collaboration of those forces that had long awaited the liturgical renewal—made it possible for the Consilium to begin producing the new revised rites. All this was made possible by two further crucial factors: the efficient functioning of the Consilium and the marginalization of the Congregation for Rites. By this time the Consilium had completed almost a year of activity, during which it had gradually improved the working of its individual sections. Under the secretary Bugnini's leadership, the secretariat, following the activity of the bishops' conferences and the liturgical commissions and challenged by the Congregation for Rites' observations and maneuvers, had become a most efficient center of activity and organization. By the end of 1964 it was able to face with confidence the complex work of the immediate implementation of the instruction: the direct preparation of the different schemas in collaboration with the *periti* and the consultors, and contact with the other Congregations and with the Secretariat of State. The publications edited in only a few months were the most evident sign of the efficiency of the Consilium's secretariat. The favorable climate and the confidence that had grown up around the Consilium made all this possible.

The second factor that facilitated this progress was the marginalization of the Congregation for Rites from the implementation of the reform. Until then the Congregation's opposition to the Consilium's approach to reform had succeeded at least in blocking and deferring the publication of several draft texts. The "Observations" made by the Congregation on the draft of the instruction *Inter oecumenici* had held up the document for three months (July 1–October 1). Other drafts were also delayed, such as the *Kyriale Simplex* and the rite of concelebration. Miraculously, from the end of October 1964 onward, all the difficulties were solved. The Consilium's projects were able to proceed speedily and to be published without difficulty. Evidently the balance of power between the two Offices had altered, even though the leading figures of the Consilium and of the Congregation for Rites were the same. Now it was the Consilium that had the upper hand. The Congregation for Rites, which only months earlier had been able to attack the Consilium and its approach, holding up the draft of the instruction for three months, now had to submit to the authority of the Consilium and accept its line of reform unconditionally. The only prerogative left to the Congregation was that of signing documents prepared by the Consilium, beginning with the publication of the instruction *Inter oecumenici*.

This reversal of power was further illustrated during the approval phase of *Variationes in ordinem Hebdomadae Sanctae inducendae*. On that occasion the Consilium presented the Congregation for Rites with a draft for which it had already obtained approval in principle from the Pope. Moreover, the Consilium set the deadline for the publication of the document. The Congregation's input on the reform was no longer necessary, and its role had been reduced to a mere bureaucratic formality. The Congregation for Rites had been marginalized in the implementation of the reform. It is plausible that this drastic turn of events would not have happened had the

Congregation softened its hostility and intransigence both with regard to the reform and the Consilium.

Just twelve months after its establishment, the Consilium was fully functional—a modern and efficient Office, independent of the Curia, fully supported by the Pope, appreciated and respected internationally. The reform's greatest difficulties seemed by now to have been overcome.

Chapter Six

✠ Activity of the Study Groups

The study groups began their work in 1964, holding their meetings in Rome and various other places, as can be seen from some of the reports presented to the members at the plenary meetings. The story of these groups is necessarily connected to the various drafts that were prepared step by step as the work was completed. Apart from the documents on concelebration, Communion under both species, and the revised Holy Week ceremonies, none of the groups was able to complete its work in the time allotted, although almost all of them did get started. To have a more complete picture of the Consilium's activities in the period just before the instruction took effect, it will be helpful to review the activities of the study groups that met from March 1964 to March 1965.

Groups I–IX: The Calendar and the Divine Office

Study Group I dealt with the reform of the calendar mandated by the Constitution on the Sacred Liturgy, which was the starting point for both the Breviary and the Missal. Consequently, the work of the other groups was subordinate to that of Group I. During 1964 this study group held only two sessions—one at Louvain in May and a second in Rome during June, at which time it mainly concentrated on problems regarding the church year. The group planned to present its work at a meeting of the plenary group in October. They were unable to achieve their goal, however, because the group's reporter, Father Bugnini, was busy with other matters. The first report was dated February 12, 1965, and sent to the consultors for comment. Taking into account the replies received from the consultors, a second draft was drawn up on March 15.

Group II had the task of implementing article 91 of the Constitution: "The work of revising the Psalter, already happily begun, is to be finished as soon as possible, and is to take into account the style of Christian Latin, the liturgical use of the psalms, also when sung, and the entire tradition of the Latin church." This group was one of the first to begin its work. On February 14, 1964, the group held a first meeting at Cardinal Lercaro's residence at the Benedictine convent of Santa Priscilla. However, the group members and the Consilium's secretary had met previously at Bugnini's residence at San Silvestro al Quirinale on February 6. The study group actually began meeting twice a week on March 5. Working at this pace, they were able to revise more than fifty psalms, which were then sent to scholars of various nations. These scholars were trained in various fields: orientalists, liturgists, musical experts. They were not associated with the Consilium team in order to assure accurate and objective evaluations.[1] They held meetings in Rome as well as in other places. The work of revision progressed as follows: the first five psalms were ready on March 23, 1964; the following five on May 10; Psalms 11 to 25 on July 5; Psalms 26 to 52 on December 19. By February 19, 1965, they had completed Psalm 75.

Group III focused on the distribution of the psalms in light of article 91 of the Constitution: "So that it may be really possible in practice to observe the course of the hours proposed in Article 89, the psalms are no longer to be distributed throughout one week, but through some longer period of time." This study group began work in April 1964. The members of the group first dealt with the weekly Psalter. The group's reporter and secretary prepared various drafts, which they sent to the consultors for examination.

On June 20 and 21 the group met in Rome under Canon Martimort's direction and agreed on a number of guidelines to submit to the Consilium in September. The reporter and secretary produced a draft "On the Breviary," dated July 19, 1964, from the consultors' observations and the guidelines. The draft also included two proposals for the distribution of the psalms over a period of four weeks.

---

[1] From "Relazione sull'attività del 'Consilium' dal 21 aprile al 21 giugno" (prepared for the audience of June 26, 1964) and from *Notitiae* 2 (1965) 4.

The next draft prepared by this study group was dated September 28, 1964. It consisted of two questions to be put to the members of the Consilium during the fourth plenary meeting: maintaining the entire Psalter in the weekly cycle and the number of psalms for Vespers. The text had been prepared by the group's reporter and the secretary on September 24 and 25, 1964. The schema was presented to the Consilium on October 1, 1964.

Before leaving Rome on October 11, Father Joseph Pascher, a Consilium member, sent the group a letter containing a draft concerning the beginning lines of the psalms and "The Psalter Distributed over Two Weeks." In a letter addressed to Bugnini on the same day, Pascher proposed a meeting of the group in Milan for January 15, 1965. Another report by Pascher, "On the Distribution of the Psalms," was dated March 1, 1965. But the group's third draft was completed only in April 1965 in view of the fifth plenary session.

Group IV was to implement article 92a of the Constitution: "Readings from sacred Scripture are to be arranged so that the riches of God's word may be easily accessible in more abundant measure." Martimort chaired this group at its inception. The first draft, dated October 27, 1964, included an extract from a report that Martimort had delivered to the bishops of the Consilium on October 1. The group held its first meeting at Neuilly-sur-Seine, just outside of Paris. On that occasion basically two questions were raised: Should the traditional method of continuous or semicontinuous readings be followed, or should pericopes be chosen according to biblical themes to correspond to the different seasons of the liturgical year? Second, would it be necessary to wait for the decisions of the group studying the calendar and the Scripture readings of the Mass to select the pericopes? In the meantime, five advisors were asked to make a selection of pericopes from the Old Testament suitable for the readings of the Divine Office. The second meeting was held on February 20, 1965, and dealt in particular with the choice of books from the Old Testament. A report dated April 26, 1965, described the results of these meetings.

Group V was assigned the task of choosing patristic readings for the Divine Office based on article 92b of the Constitution: "Readings excerpted from the works of the Fathers, Doctors and other ecclesiastical writers ought to be better selected." The group developed several drafts over the next few months, but its work was impeded because it awaited decisions on the setting of the calendar, the determination of the Scripture readings of the Office, and lastly on the structure of the Office of Readings, which had not yet been established. Its third draft on the patristic readings was a reworking of the

September 3 draft done for the Consilium plenary meeting of October 1, 1964. A subsequent draft was presented on January 25, 1965, and offered an abbreviated collection of patristic passages for the season of Advent. The final draft was sent out by the secretariat of the Consilium with a letter from the secretary on February 8, 1965.

Group VI was entrusted with the responsibility of dealing with the Breviary's historical readings, dealt with in article 92c of the Constitution: "The accounts of martyrdom, of the lives of the saints, are to be in accord with the facts of history." A first draft on historical readings was prepared by the Société des Bollendistes (Bollandists) on September 10, 1964. It was a scholarly presentation of the problems the Consilium would have to face and solve regarding this topic. The same questions presented on September 10 were immediately reworked in view of the fourth plenary gathering. The Consilium members limited themselves to merely accepting the possibility of having hagiographic readings in the Divine Office.

Group VII worked on hymns in the Breviary, guided by article 93 of the Constitution: "To whatever extent may seem advisable, the hymns are to be restored to their original form, and any allusion to mythology, or anything that conflicts with Christian piety, is to be dropped or changed. Also as occasion arises, let other selections from the treasury of hymns be incorporated." The first handwritten report was prepared on May 12, 1964, providing a general idea of the work to be accomplished. However, the first formal report was issued on June 27, 1964, and dealt with the specific problems concerning hymns. The third report on hymns was sent to the members of the group on August 29 and treated the various hymns of the Ordinary of the Psalter and of the Sanctoral. The first list of hymns for the new Breviary was contained in a draft of February 15, 1965. This was the first concrete result after the various meetings of Group IX (charged with the general structure of the Breviary) and of the fourth plenary meeting. Following the meeting of March 1–2, 1965, the final draft, dated March 30, 1965, was issued.

Group VIII was to revise the musical responses, antiphons, verses, absolutions, and blessings in the Divine Office. While these were not mentioned in the Constitution itself, there were particular elements, nonetheless, that needed revision. The first draft was prepared on February 15, 1965, and introduced the problems to be solved. Some of these problems were dealt with at the already-mentioned meeting of Group IX on March 2 in Rome. Following that meeting and the observations on the first draft, a second draft was prepared on April 26, 1965, in view of the plenary meeting of the same month.

Group IX was particularly important, since its task was to synthesize and coordinate all the groups working on the reform of the Divine Office. Canon Martimort, the reporter for this group, acted as an overall coordinator for all the work concerning the reform of the Breviary. Present at this group's meetings were the reporters and secretaries of the different groups working on Breviary reform. In the beginning the group's activity centered on problems concerning the Breviary in general in order to launch the work of the various study groups.

The first report on the reform of the Breviary was presented by Martimort to the consultors on April 16. The report was the result of a synthesis of information given by the reporters and secretaries of the groups working on the Breviary, under Martimort's direction. It consisted of a systematic presentation of the questions to be tackled. The same report was presented, after some correction, to the plenary group on April 18. On June 20 and 21 the study group met again. On July 3 Martimort sent a number of questions on the Divine Office to the members of Group IX. A preliminary proposal was ready on July 20. It was a draft of a report that Martimort was scheduled to give to the fourth plenary meeting of the Consilium in September.

After the April and June meetings, Group IX met again four times between the end of September and the beginning of October 1964. The meetings on September 26 and 27 and October 2 centered on reports on the work of Groups III, V, VI, VII, and VIII and on decisions determined during the Consilium meetings. The report from Group IV on the Scripture readings was not among those presented because it was awaiting decisions from the group studying the readings for Mass. A synthesis of these meetings was dated December 1, 1964. Subsequent meetings were held at the Consilium offices in Santa Marta on February 20, March 1 and 2, 1965. Thus, at the beginning of 1965, while Breviary reform was under way, there was still much that remained to be done.

Groups X–XVIII: The Reform of the Mass

Group X worked on the Order of Mass. The first list of problems regarding the reform was presented to the consultors on April 15, 1964. The paper dealt with disputed questions concerning the Roman Missal. This list, revised and reworked in a more systematic manner, was presented to the members of the Consilium on April 18. The first meeting for this study group was held in Trier May 8–10 at the Liturgical Institute, of which Johannes Wagner was director. The results of the first meeting were discussed on May 19 at the Benedictine abbey at Einsiedeln, Switzerland, and on May 24 at All Saints Church in Basel. The report drafted at these meetings served as the basis for the next gathering at Einsiedeln, scheduled for June 5–7, 1964.

Rather than work on a schema for the new *Ordo Missae* to present to the Consilium, the group preferred to look at the question as a whole and discuss principles and methods to be followed in solving difficulties. In particular, it was decided, on Bugnini's advice, that it would be necessary to contact the reporters of the other study groups involved in the reform of the Missal and to submit certain questions for study by a number of experts in order to have their opinion on the matter. Monsignor Wagner reported on the results of the first two meetings to the Consilium during the third plenary meeting in June 1964.

Group X's next meeting was held in Fribourg, Switzerland, August 24–28, with the secretary of the Consilium present. On August 26, the reporters and the secretaries of the other groups involved in the reform of the Missal arrived. In Fribourg, Father Franquesa and Monsignor Schnitzler prepared a first provisional draft of the *Ordo Missae,* which proved to be unsuccessful. The greater part of the meeting was taken up with the examination of a number of proposals *(voti)* on particular matters sent in by the experts. The first set of proposals dealt with the *Memento* and the acclamation of the Canon; the names of the saints in the Canon; the *commixtio* (commingling); and the blessing at the end of the Mass. A second group of proposals from the group members themselves dealt with the Canon of the Mass and the rite after Communion; the acclamation after the readings, offertory prayers, the rite of the breaking of the bread, and the question of the greeting of peace; the offertory and Communion. Finally, there were also proposals from other consultors; they also examined a particular proposal on the signs of the cross in the Canon.

The group met a fourth time in Rome on September 21–23 and reconsidered the results of the previous meetings. A report was prepared for the Consilium and distributed to its members the following month during the fourth plenary meeting. This draft was not really a detailed revision, but rather a further attempt to present general questions regarding the reform of the Order of Mass. A first provisional draft of a new *Ordo Missae* was finished on October 22, following observations received on previous documents. The second provisional Order of Mass was to have been drafted during a meeting planned for February 14–23 at Le Saulchoir, near Paris. The meeting, however, had to be postponed until June because the reporter was ill. During 1964, then, Group X devoted its activity above all to considering the complex problem of the reform of the *Ordo Missae* and avoided working on particular problematic issues.

Only a few basic questions were resolved; for the more controverted issues it was thought better to postpone any decision. This was certainly a wise move. In fact, some questions regarding the *Ordo Missae* as well as a number of uncertainties about the Constitution were resolved with the publication of the *Ritus servandus* on January 27, 1965. The publication of the new rite of concelebration on March 7 marked yet another step forward in the reform of the *Ordo Missae*. Moreover, this initial reform put into practice throughout the church gave episcopal conferences, individual bishops, and liturgical experts an opportunity to put forward concrete proposals on the basis of their experience with the new rite. All this was particularly helpful for the experiments that the study group began to carry out regularly during its meetings, beginning with the meeting at Le Saulchoir.

Group XI, charged with the Mass readings, was to suggest implementation of article 51 of the liturgy Constitution: "The treasures of the Bible are to be opened up more lavishly, so that richer fare may be provided for the faithful at the table of God's word. In this way a more representative portion of the Holy Scriptures will be read to the people over a set cycle of years." Work began for the group in April 1964. On April 28 the group's secretary sent the consultors a set of questions regarding the direction the work should take and some important issues to be considered. The replies were somewhat complicated. From May 17 to May 20, the group's secretary, G. Fontaine, and its reporter, Godfrey Diekmann, O.S.B., worked together at St. John's Abbey, Collegeville, Minnesota, on a synthesis of the replies. The result was a report sent to both the group members and the reporters of the other groups involved in the reform of the Mass. After this the group's secretary met in Fribourg, Switzerland, August 26–28, with all the reporters and secretaries of those groups engaged in the reform of the Mass.

Group XI held its first real meeting in Brescia, Italy, from September 9 to September 12, 1964. Five group members took part in the meeting: H. Schurmann, E. Kahlefeld, P. Massi, E. Lanne, and the group's secretary, G. Fontaine. Present for the secretariat of the Consilium was Carlo Braga. The topic for the discussion was the text prepared in May by the reporter and the secretary. When the three-day meeting ended, a report was drafted and sent to the secretariat of the Consilium. Subsequently, the draft was reworked at least twice. This document was the basis for the draft on the Lectionary for Mass dated October 1 and presented to the Consilium on October 6. Like the reports that preceded it, the draft was divided into two parts: (1) the principles on the Lectionary from the liturgy Constitution; (2) proposals for implementation. The members of the Consilium approved this text on October 6.

The second meeting was held in Rome on October 12 and 13, 1964. Present were G. Diekmann, H. Schurmann, P. Massi, G. Fontaine, C. Braga for the secretariat of the Consilium, and J. Wagner, general reporter for the Roman Missal. During that meeting discussion was centered on a three- or four-year cycle for the Sunday Lectionary and planning for weekday Mass readings. At the end of the meeting the work was distributed and organized. This was the group's last meeting in the period with which we are dealing. It was also the last meeting to be directed by Father Diekmann, who, due to his many engagements in his own country, asked to be relieved of the presidency of the group. As of June 1965 the new reporter was to be Father Cipriano Vagaggini.

Group XII was entrusted with suggesting how to implement article 53 of the liturgy Constitution: "Especially on Sundays and holydays of obligation, there is to be restored, after the Gospel and the homily, 'the universal prayer' or 'the prayer of the faithful.' By this prayer in which the people are to take part, intercession shall be made for holy church, for the civil authorities, for those oppressed by various needs, for all people, and for the salvation of the entire world."

It was a question of restoring to the Mass an element that formerly existed but was to be given a new form. On April 24, A.-M. Roguet, the reporter, sent the group members a questionnaire in order to draw up a first draft of "the prayer of the faithful." Following the replies received, Roguet and J.-B. Molin, the group's secretary, went to Trier on May 15–16 for two reasons. First, they wanted to visit the library of the Liturgical Institute and examine examples of intercessory prayers. Second, they wished to talk over some fundamental points with Wagner and Fischer. The results of the first phase of work were collected in a fifty-six-page draft, divided into eight chapters. The project was sent to the group members on July 17, 1964.

A new, more mature draft was proposed on October 8. This draft was revised again and reworked for presentation to the Consilium in November 1964. This was the basis for the final document, which comprised a historical part, a part containing practical guidelines, and a third part containing drafts of prayers of the faithful proposed as examples for the bishops' conferences. The Consilium decided to approve this document, which, after having been corrected, was published as a booklet called *De oratione communi seu fidelium*. It was presented by Bugnini on behalf of the Consilium on January 13, 1965. The booklet had two parts: a practical directory, with some examples of prayers of the faithful, and an appendix, which included the history of the prayers of the faithful and some examples set to music.

While the book proved to be initially helpful, it soon became obvious that it was inadequate to meet the demand for a greater variety of texts, especially for the various seasons of the liturgical year. This was expressed in a letter written by Bugnini to Roguet and Molin on February 8, 1965, thanking them for their work. Work on a second edition, however, began immediately.

Group XIII was charged with the task of revising the existing collection of votive Masses in the Missal and to compose new formularies to better suit the situations of the modern world. The group's reporter, H. Schmidt, thought that it would be better to wait until some general guidelines were produced by the other study groups working on the reform of the Missal before outlining principles for the reform of the votive Masses. Those principles were discussed at a meeting held in Fribourg, Switzerland, in early September and reworked to produce a draft on votive Masses, dated September 10, 1964. The draft described several fundamental problems with six questions on the future work of revision. Sent to the group members on September 12, the draft was then revised on September 29 and became the final document presented to the Consilium on October 6. At the close of 1964, this study group's initial activity ended. It would resume some years later when the group was recomposed.

The work of the following three groups (Group XIV: songs in the Mass; Group XV: overall structure of the Mass; Group XVI: concelebration and Communion under both species) was substantially treated by the Consilium itself.

Group XVII was to revise some particular rites of the liturgical year not included in the revision of the Office and the Mass. In addition, it was to revise the special rites of Holy Week. The reporter, M. Righetti, and the secretary, F. Vandenbroucke, met in Genoa on June 3, 1964, to organize the work. They identified a series of problems, which were presented to the consultors. During the summer the secretary sent the group members a report on the opinions expressed by the consultors. The group's first formal meeting was held in Milan on September 8–9, 1964. In addition to the reporter and the secretary, Borella, Pascher, Kolbe, Nocent, Falsini, and Miller were present. During the month of September, a report on the problems debated at that meeting was prepared. Subsequently, various observations on the part of consultors and other people were sent to the reporter and the secretary.

Related to Group XVII, the meeting for editors of liturgical publications held in Rome on November 13 and 14, 1964, gave the secretary and almost all the members of the group an opportunity to meet for further discussion on the subject. On that occasion it was decided that the basic outline of the work should be submitted to the Consilium. So the group prepared its third draft with the title *Quaestiones "Consilio" proponendae*. But Bugnini felt that before the "Questions" were presented to the Consilium, the work of the liturgical year group should be harmonized with the work of the calendar group. To this end, three consultors from Group XVII took part in a meeting with Group I, held in Rome on April 1–2, 1965. After that meeting Group XVII's work was ready to be submitted.

Group XVIII was to carry out the revision of the Common of the Missal and the Divine Office. Work had already begun in April 1964. The first report, drafted by the group reporter, B. Neunheuser, was dated April 30. In addition to the conversations with various consultors and their observations, a group member, R. J. Hesbert, wrote a document entitled "Preliminary Report on the Competence of This Commission and Its Working Method," which first appeared in French, dated August 13, 1964. Two weeks later Neunheuser, as reporter, drafted a supplementary document to add to his report of April 30. It was obvious that in the initial phase of work the group could not proceed until other fundamental problems were solved by other study groups. However, for the plenary meeting at the end of the year, the reporter did prepare a two-page report containing four questions on the principles to be followed and some explanations. Because the project was still at an early stage, it could not be put to the Consilium.

Almost a year later, having taken into account the corrections and recommendations suggested by other study groups and by the consultors, Neunheuser, as reporter, was finally in a position to draw up a definitive draft on March 4, 1965. It was this draft that was distributed to the consultors by Bugnini on April 6 as material for revision before presentation to the Consilium.

Group XVIII*bis* had not been included in the original division of work for the general liturgical reform that had been approved on March 15, 1964. It was added in early September 1964. It was only during the fourth plenary session that a few members of the group had a chance to meet for the first time. On that occasion Bugnini gave some general orientations to the group. It was at that time that Bugnini asked the group to prepare a revision of the solemn prayers of Good Friday and the prayers of the Chrism Mass as soon as possible. Plans were already under way for a document entitled "Changes to be introduced into the Rites of Holy Week," eventually published on March 7, 1965.

The group's first draft was drawn up on October 27, 1964. It contained the first proposals for the revision of the prayers of Holy Thursday and Good Friday. Subsequently, the draft was incorporated into the work being directed by the secretariat for the changes in the Holy Week liturgy. A subsequent meeting was held at Faenza, south of Bologna, on January 10–12. Present were the reporter and the secretary of the group. During that meeting the group revised all the prayers for the different seasons of the liturgical year in use at the time. The group's work was limited to examining and revising some of the prayers of the Roman Missal without delving into more general problems, such as the nature and duration of the various liturgical seasons. The first draft was prepared for February 1, 1965, and then further modified during a group meeting at Louvain, April 5–10, 1965.

Groups XX and XXI: The Reform of the Pontifical

Group XX worked on the Roman Pontifical. Study on the reform of the first book of the Pontifical was begun by B. Botte in mid-1964 in a draft presentation that dealt with questions concerning the ordination rite of a bishop, of priests, and of deacons. It also included the "blessing" of subdeacons and the minor orders. As Bugnini wrote in *Relationes,* dated December 4, 1964, the reform of holy orders was also in the competence of other Congregations, and therefore to avoid pointless work on the part of the Consilium, it would be necessary to first settle some open questions. This delay went on until the month of July 1965, when Bishop Guano hosted an ad hoc meeting in Livorno on the reform of the ordination rites. The first formal meeting of the group took place at the Liturgical Institute in Trier, August 3–5.

Group XXI dealt with books II and III of the Roman Pontifical (Consecration of Churches and Special Celebrations). This group had made some contribution to the draft for the reform of the rite of the blessing of oils on Holy Thursday, contained in the booklet introducing the changes in the Holy

Week rites. Because of the complexity of the subject matter, the real work was yet to be started. In February, J. Nabuco, a Brazilian bishop who had been a member of the preparatory subcommission on sacred art, prepared an introduction on the subject, which was sent out to the group members.

Groups XXII and XXIII: The Reform of the Ritual

The reform of the Ritual was assigned to Groups XXII and XXIII. Their work was to include both the sacraments and the sacramentals and constituted a large amount of material related to several articles in the Constitution on the Sacred Liturgy (63b, 65, 75, 77, 79, 80). That is why the work was assigned to two study groups: one for the sacraments and the other for the sacramentals. It was presumed that there would be ample exchange between the members of the two groups, given the complementary nature of the material in question. At the beginning these two groups met together.

Group XXIII had already prepared "A Synthesis of Responses to the Questionnaire Regarding Funerals" for July 25, 1964. In the period immediately following, Groups XXII and XXIII had several meetings, during which they drafted "A Report Regarding the Approval of the Roman Ritual," dated September 10, 1964. The report discussed general problems regarding the Ritual and examined questions concerning the individual rites: baptism, anointing of the sick, funerals, matrimony, and sacramentals. The report, corrected and reworked, became a formal draft presented to the Consilium on October 9, 1964. After the approval of the questions put to the Consilium at this meeting, the two groups met in Cologne on December 28–30, 1964. Present were Fischer, Gy, Lengeling, Mazzarello, Cellier, Rabau, and Stenzel. Bugnini was present for the first two days.

The chairs of the two groups presided and moderated discussion on the following topics: in the morning of December 28, anointing of the sick; in the afternoon of the same day, various questions on mixed marriages as well as the brief rite of infant baptism, presented by Bugnini; on December 29, adult baptism; and on December 30, the rite of viaticum and the commendation of the soul at death, along with a few special matters concerning the funeral rite. During this meeting they also set the calendar for future meetings: a meeting for the reporters in mid-January; a meeting of the subcommission on baptism on January 15–18 in Trier. Other meetings were planned at Le Saulchoir at the end of March, and the reporters and secretaries of the two groups were scheduled to meet in Rome in April.

Specific Reforms

G roup XXIV was charged with beginning work on the revision of the Martyrology, a task that would take over two decades. Study Group XXV dealt with the revision of the chant books and met for the first time at the Abbey of Solesmes under the direction of E. Cardine from April 27–May 3, 1964. Among those present were L. Agustoni, secretary; M. Altisent, S.P.; J. Harmel, O. Praem.; L. Kunz, O.S.B.; J. Houlier, O.S.B.; J. Claire, O.S.B. The group was to plan for the implementation of article 117 of the Constitution on the Sacred Liturgy, which read: "The *editio typica* of the books of Gregorian chant is to be completed; and a more critical edition is to be prepared of those books already published since the reform of St. Pius X. It is desirable also that an edition be prepared containing simpler melodies, for use in small churches." Article 53, dealing with the prayers of the faithful, and article 54, which referred to the use of the vernacular, were also to be taken into consideration.

The discussion on this topic served as the basis for the formal draft of the first book of chant, dated May 3, 1964. It was during this meeting, too, that the study group examined the *Kyriale Simplex* and proposed its publication to the secretariat of the Consilium. The group's second meeting was again held at Solesmes, September 11–21. Attending were all the group members who had taken part in the first meeting. The results of the meeting were reflected in a draft of the second book of chant, which the reporter presented to the Consilium on October 6. It dealt with problems concerning singing at Mass envisaged in the instruction *Inter oecumenici* and in the rite of concelebration. It also presented the *Kyriale Simplex,* which had been revised after the first meeting. Lastly, there was a list of other questions connected with the reform of the Mass and with the critical edition of the books of Gregorian chant. This was the group's final report for 1964. After the publication of the *Kyriale Simplex* at the end of the year, work began on the *Graduale Simplex* and on a report to present to the Consilium at the plenary meeting in April 1965.

The revision of the Ceremonial of Bishops was entrusted to Group XXVI. One of the guiding principles for their work was found in article 34 of the Constitution on the Sacred Liturgy: "The rites should be marked by a noble simplicity; they should be short, clear, and unencumbered by useless repetitions; they should be within the people's powers of comprehension, and as a rule should not require much explanation." An initial draft of the work was drawn up by Martimort on October 18, 1964, and sent to the group members. The group's first meeting was held in Vatican City on November 7, 1964. During that meeting the participants debated preliminary matters, such as episcopal vesture and emblems in liturgical celebrations—choral robes, the throne or cathedra, etc. The draft was then revised and presented on December 15, 1964. Another meeting of the group was held in the Consilium offices on February 28, 1965, under the direction of Martimort. This group still had much to do.

Group XXVII was to deal with incorporating elements from other liturgical rites into the Roman Rite, while Group XXVIII was to study a code of law for the liturgy. Group XXIX, on the papal chapel, was established in the office of the Consilium on February 22, 1965, and held its first meeting on March 9, 1965, in the presence of Cardinal Lercaro, president of the Consilium.

There was also a special study group established to deal with the important topic of sacred music. In a letter addressed to the Secretariat of State, dated January 15, 1965, Bugnini presented the subject of music and singing in the liturgy and proposed that study should start with the preparation of an instruction or some similar document on sacred music. On January 23 a reply came from the Secretariat that the proposal was opportune; therefore study and careful preparation of the proposed document should begin. A draft was ready on February 12. It was the first draft of what would become the Instruction on Sacred Music in the Liturgy.

Below is a list of the drafts elaborated by the various study groups before March 7, 1965; there were sixty-four drafts, subdivided as follows:

Coetus peculiaris[2] (2):	*De concelebratione:* 6 drafts (1, 11, 14, 18, 53, 58)
Coetus peculiaris	*De Communione sub utraque specie:* 5 drafts (2, 12, 15, 19, 60)
Coetus peculiaris	*De instructione:* 6 drafts (3, 4, 10, 13, 17, 27)
Coetus I	*De calendario:* 1 draft (61)
Coetus II	*De Psalterio recognoscendo:* 4 drafts (8, 9, 22, 54)
Coetus III	*De psalmis distribuendis:* 2 drafts (23, 37)
Coetus IV	*De lectionibus biblicis Officii:* 1 draft (45)
Coetus V	*De lectionibus patristicis in Officio Divino:* 4 drafts (20, 26, 35, 59)

[2] *Coetus peculiaris* indicates a group of consultors or *periti* chosen and directed by the secretariat for a specific task.

Coetus VI   *De lectionibus historicis deque textibus historicis:* 2 drafts (28, 36)

Coetus VII   *De hymnis:* 3 drafts (21, 25, 69)

Coetus VIII   *De cantibus Officii Divini:* 1 draft (63)

Coetus IX   *De generali structura Officii Divini:* 5 drafts (5, 6, 24, 31, 50)

Coetus X   *De Ordine Missae:* 5 drafts (7, 16, 39, 44)

Coetus XI   *De lectionibus in Missa:* 1 draft (40)

Coetus XII   *De oratione fidelium:* 4 drafts (41, 42, 47)

Coetus XIII   *De Missis votivis:* 2 drafts (29, 38)

Coetus XVII   *De ritibus peculiaribus in anno liturgico:* 2 drafts (51, 55)

Coetus XVIII   *De communibus Breviarii et Missalis:* 1 draft (86)

Coetus XVIIIb   *De orationibus et praefationibus recognoscendis:* 2 drafts (46, 57)

Coetus XXI   *De libris I et III Pontificalis (De benedictione oleorum):* 3 drafts (48, 49, 56)

Coetus XXII-XXIII   *De sacramentis et sacramentalibus:* 2 drafts (30, 32)

Coetus XXV   *De libris cantus revisendis:* 2 drafts (33, 34)

Coetus XXVI   *De Caeremoniali Episcoporum:* 2 drafts (43, 52)

Coetus pecularis   *De musica sacra:* draft (62)

Conclusion

A s far as the work of the study groups was concerned, 1964 was basically a time of preparation. It was during this time that the members met, exchanged ideas, and planned the work involved. On the whole, the draft documents sought to offer a global vision of the work to be accomplished and of the difficulties involved, but they did not propose concrete solutions. There were two main reasons for this. The first and most obvious reason was the challenge of launching the groups—determining the path to be followed and establishing a general plan for their work. That is why several study groups, especially those working on the same liturgical book, met together rather than separately, as they would do later when the lines of the reform became clearer. This was the case for the study groups working on the Missal and on the Breviary, whose reporters and secretaries often met under the respective direction of Wagner or Martimort. The same was true for the study groups entrusted with the reform of the Roman Ritual.

The second reason for the tentative nature of the documents produced by the study groups arose from the status and activity of the Consilium during this particular period. Initially the Office's activity had to go through a period of adjustment. Only after the first months of experience did the role of the plenary group, the *Consulta,* and the secretariat (which had in practice replaced the ordinary meeting) become clear. Until the beginning of 1965, moreover, almost all the activity of the Office, and therefore also a good part of that of the consultors who were part of it, was devoted to the preparation of *Inter oecumenici* and various publications concerning its implementation. This was in addition to the Consilium's persistent difficulties with the Congregation for Rites in regard to the publication of the documents of reform. This makes it understandable why the study groups moved slowly and self-consciously during this time and did not realize all of their potential.

Looking back, the motives that had limited the study groups' activity during 1964 can be seen in a positive light. In the final analysis, conditions permitted a more profound meditation on the principles and the appropriate way of proceeding. Nevertheless, at the end of 1964 a good deal of the initial work of the future liturgical reform had been done. The decisions made by the fourth plenary session on the general structure of the Divine Office and on the *Ordo Missae* constituted a green light for the various study groups.

Chapter Seven

✠ The Aftermath of the Initial Reform
(1965–1980)

While the purpose of this study was to examine the initial liturgical re-form, it seems appropriate to explore the reform's subsequent developments, offering some basic reflections in order to help ground the further develop-ment of the liturgical renewal. There are few historical studies available on the liturgical reform for the period 1965 to 1980. While Enrico Cattaneo has offered the best overall historic synthesis of this period[1] and the facts are more easily identified, thanks to *Notitiae,* which has reported the more significant events that accompanied the implementation of the reform since it began publication in 1965, there is still more of the story to be told.

The Consilium (1965–1968)

O nce the Consilium had gone beyond its initial difficulties in 1965, it swung into full action. The first two months of that year, as we have already seen, were completely taken up with preparing publications for implementing the instruction *Inter oecumenici.* After the beginning of the implementation of this instruction on March 7, the Consilium resumed its work on the reform with renewed enthusiasm.

---

[1] *Il culto cristiano in occidente, note storiche* (Rome: Edizioni Liturgiche, 1978).

The year 1965 was marked by two plenary sessions and by a conference on translations of liturgical books. The fifth plenary meeting was held April 26–30.[2] It examined several reports from study groups regarding the calendar, different aspects of the Liturgy of the Hours—the distribution of the psalms, the patristic readings, the hymns and antiphons—the *Ordo Missae,* the anointing of the sick, funerals, a catechumenate for adults, the Ceremonial of Bishops, the Instruction on Sacred Music in the Liturgy. The fifth plenary session also approved the *Graduale Simplex.* Furthermore, because new appointments needed to be made to replace members who had died, at the suggestion of the Consilium's secretariat a vote was taken for names of bishops from places not represented in the Office (England, Spain, Ireland, Hungary, Central America, South Africa) to serve on the Consilium. Due to this change in personnel, the Consilium became even more international.

One of the first issues that needed to be dealt with was that of the preface of the Eucharistic Prayer in the vernacular. At the end of April, after a lively exchange of letters with the Secretariat of State, the goal of the preface in the vernacular was reached.[3] The Consilium, of course, had already approved this innovation on November 16, 1964, during its fourth plenary meeting. This was another step forward in the direction of the full, active, and conscious participation so desired by the council.

An international conference for translators of liturgical books was held November 9–13, 1965, taking its impetus from the letter of June 30 on liturgical renewal written by Cardinal Lercaro to the presidents of the conferences of bishops.[4] The secretariat of the Consilium organized this symposium for the translators of liturgical books. This initiative had been approved by the sixth plenary session, which also named an organizing committee for the meeting. Seventeen papers were given, workshops were held, and a display of new liturgical books in various languages was set up, along with an exhibition of ancient liturgical codices from the Vatican Library. The event was another success for the Consilium.[5]

---

[2] See *Not* 1 (1965) 99–104.

[3] See *EDIL* 395; *DOL* 766.

[4] *EDIL* 406–417; *DOL* 407–8.

[5] The proceedings of the conference were published by the Libreria Editrice Vaticana in a volume called *Le traduzioni dei libri liturgici* (Vatican City, 1966).

From mid-September to early October there was a meeting for the reporters and secretaries of the study groups in order to prepare for the sixth plenary meeting, which was held from October to December,[6] dealing mainly with the draft on the Order of Mass, the rite of a catechumenate for adults, funeral rites, the Ceremonial of Bishops, and approval of the instruction on sacred music. What distinguished the sixth plenary meeting were various "experiments" of what was called the *Missa normativa,* celebrated in the chapel of the Sisters of Maria Bambina. These experiments were the basis for the first votes of the members of the Consilium on the reformed structure of the Mass. In these experiments the revised Roman Canon was used. Some people who were not part of the Consilium were invited to assist at the experiments. This may well have contributed to the spread of rumors that the Consilium was busy preparing quite unimaginable heresies. This opened the door to a new phase of opposition to the implementation of the reform.

The first part of 1966 was devoted chiefly to the preparation of drafts for the Consilium's approval. The reporters and the secretaries of the study groups met twice: May 5–14 and again September 19–October 1.

The seventh plenary session was held October 6–14, 1966.[7] It was one of the most important plenaries due to the large number of participants (forty-one in attendance) and for the amount of work achieved. Moreover, for the first time there were guest "observers"— five members of other ecclesial communions. The drafts presented were on both minor and major holy orders, on the calendar, the readings, the prayers and prefaces of the Mass, on the rites of infant baptism and marriage, on the Breviary, on the instruction on the eucharistic mystery, on the consecration of the oils, and on the Ceremonial of Bishops.

On October 13 Pope Paul VI received the participants of the seventh plenary meeting in audience. Referring in his speech to the *Ordo Missae,* he said, "The issue is of such a serious and universal import that we cannot do otherwise than consult with the bishops on any proposals before approving them by our own authority." [8] A meeting of the Synod of Bishops was already planned for the following year to consider liturgical reform.

[6] *Not* 2 (1965) 3–5.
[7] See *Not* 2 (1966) 312–13.
[8] *DOL* 636.

Besides those already mentioned, only three other initiatives on the part of the Consilium in 1966 merit attention here: a letter dated January 25, addressed to presidents of the bishops' conferences, on certain problems in the liturgical reform;[9] a decree, on January 27, regarding editions of the liturgical books;[10] a pamphlet published on April 17 concerning the prayer of the faithful.[11] In retrospect, 1966 was a relatively quiet year for the Consilium, devoted mainly to preparing draft documents for the renewal and fine-tuning of its organizational structure.

1967, on the other hand, was one of the most traumatic and difficult years in the life of the Consilium. The eighth plenary session was held that year April 10–19 and was concluded in the presence of the Pope. In particular, it dealt with the new Eucharistic Prayers and with the drafts presented to the Synod of Bishops. It had been preceded by a meeting of reporters and secretaries of the study groups, held April 3–8.[12]

Of particular interest was a private meeting held in the afternoon of October 8. Present were seventeen members of the Consilium, without the consultors. The purpose of the meeting was to improve the internal organization of the Consilium in order to make its organization more efficient. It was decided that rules would be drawn up in order to better regulate the meetings of the study groups as well as the plenary meetings. Moreover, the Consilium's "statutes" were to define the competencies of the various internal organizations of the Consilium.

It was decided to establish a Consilium *Praesidentiae*[13] to solve more urgent questions that might arise between plenary meetings. It would also maintain communication between the plenary group and the *Consulta*. The main purpose of the Consilium *Praesidentiae,* however, was to give greater weight to decisions made by the presidency and the secretariat and, in the absence of the plenary group, to render the Consilium less vulnerable to attacks from conservative circles, particularly from within the Curia. On October 11 seven members were elected to form the Consilium *Praesidentiae.* The bishops chosen were among the most open-minded

---

[9] *EDIL* 569–579; *DOL* 419–29.
[10] *EDIL* 580–591; *DOL* 918–29.
[11] *EDIL* 646–668; *DOL* 1891–1928.
[12] See *Not* 3 (1967) 138–46.
[13] See *Not* 3 (1967) 47.

and supportive of the Consilium's role. None of them belonged to the Roman Curia.[14]

The chief purpose of the ninth plenary session, held November 21–28, 1967, and preceded by the meeting of the reporters (November 14–20), was to examine the *modi* (observations) formulated by the Synod of Bishops on the drafts of the Mass and of the Divine Office.[15]

While the eighth plenary was meeting a book was published entitled *La tunica stracciata: Lettera di un cattolico sulla 'Riforma liturgica'* ("The Shredded Tunic: A Letter from a Catholic on the Liturgical Reform"). The volume, written by Tito Casino, was a harsh attack on the work of the Consilium and especially on Cardinal Lercaro, to whom the book was addressed in the form of a letter.[16] The publication caused considerable reaction, particularly because the preface was written by a member of the Roman Curia, Cardinal Bacci. He started the preface with an admission that the book was disrespectful of those involved in the reform, but then went on to support and finally approve it.

Lercaro, seeing the publicity given to the book in the press and aware that the Holy See had not challenged the book's characterizations, sent a written protest to Cardinal Eugène Tisserant, dean of the Sacred College of Cardinals. He then returned to Bologna, leaving the following telegram for Bugnini, making reference to an article about the incident in a Rome newspaper, *Il Messaggero:* "I am leaving for Bologna on a one-way ticket." Later there were official challenges to the claims of this book, and the situation became less tense. Nevertheless, this episode stands as yet another sign of the fierce hostility in certain circles toward the implementation of the reform.

The Synod of Bishops, meeting October 21–25, 1967, turned its attention to the liturgy. The Consilium had prepared a detailed report to the Synod on the situation of the liturgical reform, the progress of the various study groups, and the status of the two drafts—the general structure of the *Ordo Missae* and the other on the Divine Office. Addressing the assembly, Cardinal Lercaro delivered a second report, along with a supplementary document supported by the Pope, in which he put before the Synod four particular questions on

---

[14] The result of the vote was as follows: René Boudon, 31; Michele Pellegrino, 30; Otto Spülbeck, 29; Vicente Enrique y Tarancón, 28; William Conway, 27; Clemente Isnard, 25; Jan Bluyssen, 24.

[15] *Not* 3 (1967) 410–17.

[16] Cattaneo, *Il culto cristiano,* 658.

the celebration of the Eucharist: the new Eucharistic Prayers, the formula of consecration, the Creed, and the chants of the Mass. Following the bishops' examination, another paper, called *Responsiones,* gave the Consilium's opinion on what had been said.

In addition to this paper, the bishops were given an "example" that presented the new one-week structure of the Divine Office. Gift copies of the *Ordo Lectionum* and the *Graduale Simplex* were also distributed. The bishops were also able to attend a celebration of Mass in the Sistine Chapel according to the new *Ordo Missae.* The Synod of Bishops approved the work of reform being carried out by the Consilium by a wide majority, in spite of a few difficulties.[17]

Despite these difficulties, 1967 also saw the publication of several documents of fundamental importance for the future of the reform. Particularly worth mentioning are the Instruction on Sacred Music in the Liturgy (*Musicam sacram,* March 5, 1967);[18] a second instruction on the orderly carrying out of the Constitution on the Sacred Liturgy (*Tres abhinc annos,* May 4, 1967), which also opened the Canon of the Mass to the use of the vernacular;[19] an instruction on the worship of the eucharistic mystery (*Eucharisticum mysterium,* May 25, 1967), which constituted a constant point of reference for the reform;[20] and the *Graduale Simplex* (September 3, 1967).[21]

On June 15, 1967, a survey on the application of the liturgical reform was drawn up to ascertain the difficulties encountered, the degree of consensus reached, and other requests.[22] On June 21 the president of the Consilium sent another letter to the bishops' conferences on experimentation, liturgical adaptation, mixed commissions, the significance of the church universal and local, translations of the Roman Canon, and the rite of holy orders.[23] Therefore, 1967 was a year of lights and shadows. On the one hand, there were attacks against the reform; on the other hand, however, this year saw the first concrete fruits of the renewal and the support for the Consilium's work voiced by the Synod of Bishops.

---

[17] *Not* 3 (1967) 353–70.
[18] *EDIL* 733–801; *DOL* 4122–90.
[19] *EDIL* 808–37; *DOL* 445–74.
[20] *EDIL* 889–956; *DOL* 1230–96.
[21] *EDIL* 1008–1026; *DOL* 4257–74.
[22] Part of the report was published in *Not* 4 (1968).
[23] *EDIL* 974–982; *DOL* 477–88.

Between 1966 and 1967 an attempt was made by the Pontifical Council for the Reform of the Roman Curia to reorganize the offices of the Curia. This was an ad hoc commission established for this purpose. As had been the case in other areas, the Congregation for Rites and the Consilium had two different approaches regarding this reorganization. The officials of the Congregation for Rites envisaged an internal rearrangement of the Congregation and saw this as an opportunity to gain control of the Consilium. On the other hand, the secretariat of the Consilium believed that the Congregation for Rites should be divided into two Congregations—one for Worship and the other for the Causes of Saints. At the very least, they maintained that there should be a distinct separation between these two sections of the Congregation, each with its own secretary, members, and consultors.

At first, the Consilium's position was not taken into consideration. The Congregation for Rites had presented the Commission with a memorandum dated September 30, 1966, suggesting that the Congregation take over the Consilium. Later the plan of reorganization and the memorandum put forward by the Congregation for Rites were made known to the Consilium. On July 15 a reaction to this plan by the Consilium, entitled "Observations on the Plan for Reform by the Congregation of Rites" was presented. The basic request made by the Consilium to divide the Congregation for Rites into two separate sections or into two Congregations was not accepted. However, the revision of the liturgical books and carrying out the reform of the liturgy were recognized as the responsibility of the Consilium, even though its final decisions were to be submitted to a plenary of the Congregation for Rites' department for worship.[24] The reorganization of the Roman Curia, at least as far as the liturgy was concerned, left things just as they were. However, it did give the Consilium secretariat an opportunity to resume talks with the Secretariat of State and the Pope on the subject that had been interrupted at the end of 1963, the organization of a Congregation for Divine Worship.

The year 1968 began with some significant events that would affect the future of the liturgical reform and the Consilium. This year marked the beginning of frequent contact between Pope Paul and the Consilium regarding the structure of the Mass. After the conclusion of the Synod of Bishops on December 11, 1967, a report had been presented to the Pope on the votes taken at the Synod and the observations from the Consilium's ninth plenary meeting. After reading the report, the Pope asked to examine personally

---

[24] *EDIL* 998 §4; *DOL* 657 §4.

the structure of the new *Ordo Missae*. On January 11, 12, and 13, in the Matilde Chapel of the Apostolic Palace, parts of the "normative" Mass were celebrated in the presence of the Holy Father and about thirty others. After these celebrations the Pope communicated his opinion to the Consilium. This was the beginning of the not always unanimous dialogue between the Pope and the Consilium that would eventually lead to the promulgation of the new *Ordo Missae* in 1969.

At the beginning of 1968, two leading figures left the scene—Cardinals Lercaro and Larraona. They were succeeded by the Benedictine Cardinal Benno Gut, who came to find himself not only president of the Consilium but also prefect of the Congregation for Rites.[25] This dual role was part of the plan to reorganize the Congregation for Rites and the Consilium. Cardinal Gut was unaccustomed to the subtle maneuvers of life in the Curia. As a consequence of this appointment, it would be easier to bring about the rearrangement of the two Offices responsible for the liturgy.

The tenth plenary session was held April 23–30 and dealt with several questions regarding the *Ordo Missae*. They were actually the questions raised by the Pope following the experiments in the Matilde Chapel in early January. The plenary group also examined the completed schemas of marriage, confirmation, Holy Week, the consecration of virgins, and the *Institutio generalis* of the Mass.[26] As usual, the plenary gathering had been preceded by a meeting of reporters and secretaries of study groups held April 14–22.

The eleventh plenary meeting took place October 8–17.[27] It completed the examination of the drafts for baptism, funerals, religious profession, Holy Week, the rite of blessing an abbot, and the *Praenotanda* of the Breviary. The meeting of the consultors had been held October 1–7. Also on the agenda was the new *Ordo Missae,* which, by order of the Holy Father, had been previously sent to all the Congregations of the Roman Curia for examination in May 1968. On July 24 the replies of the various Congregations were communicated to the Pope. The *Ordo Missae* was definitively approved by the Pope on November 6, 1968.

Two important documents were published in 1968: the new Eucharistic Prayers and the Rite of Holy Orders. The fact that four Eucharistic Prayers

[25] See *Not* 4 (1968) 3–4.
[26] See *Not* 4 (1968) 180–84.
[27] *Not* 4 (1968) 348–55.

were approved was consistent with the early Roman liturgy, which actually had used several anaphoras. The second publication was also significant in that it was the first completed reformed liturgical book mandated by Vatican II. So 1968 was on the whole positive for the reform with the publication of the *Ordo Missae,* the new anaphoras, and the rites of ordination. Moreover, the departure of both Cardinals Larraona and Lercaro promised a more secure and permanent juridical position for the Consilium within the Curia.

Curial Reorganization (1969–1974)

The year 1969 marked a turning point in the history of the implementation of the Vatican II liturgical reforms. In a consistory on April 28, 1969, Pope Paul VI announced the division of the Congregation for Rites into two Congregations: one for Divine Worship and the other for the Causes of Saints. On May 8 came the publication of the apostolic constitution *Sacra Rituum Congregatio,* establishing the two new Congregations. The very same day the members of the two new Congregations were announced. Prefect of the Congregation for Divine Worship was Cardinal Benno Gut, and the secretary was Father Annibale Bugnini. It was a memorable event. Just as Pope Sixtus V in 1588 had instituted the Congregation for Rites to safeguard and promote the liturgy of the Council of Trent, so now in 1969 Pope Paul VI was instituting the Congregation for Divine Worship to safeguard and promote the liturgy of the Second Vatican Council.

Bugnini's proposal, first presented on the eve of the institution of the Consilium and again presented in 1967, when a reorganization of the Curia was attempted, was being carried out at last, even down to the smallest details. The fourth floor of Piazza Pio XII, Number 10, would house the new Congregation for Divine Worship, as had already been proposed in December 1963. Although Pope Paul VI founded the Congregation for Divine Worship, the idea was conceived and carried out by Bugnini. He was undoubtedly responsible for the appointment of the gentle, collaborative Cardinal Benno Gut.

The new institution was to be organized according to the structures and regulations of the other curial departments. The number of members and consultors of the Consilium had to be considerably reduced.[28] As it

---

[28] Only seven bishops of the Consilium, chosen by vote during the plenary session of November 1969, passed to the new Congregation. The consultors, nominated in April 1970, numbered only nineteen.

happened, the Consilium was not dismantled immediately. It was given the name *Peculiaris Commissio ad instaurationem liturgicam perficiendam* (Special Commission for Implementing the Liturgical Reform.) This was a way to ensure that for a time the work in the new Congregation would continue in the same dynamic, international style already experienced for more than five years. Consequently, work on the reform went ahead without any major changes.

The second aspect that marked 1969 was the significant number of new liturgical books published in that year. The work of the previous years was beginning to bear fruit. The main publications were the following: the Rite of Marriage on March 19;[29] the General Roman Calendar on March 21;[30] the document promulgating the new Roman Missal, the new *Ordo Missae*, on April 3 and 6;[31] the Rite of Infant Baptism on May 15;[32] and the funeral rite on August 15.[33] Moreover, a number of instructions were also published, including *Actio pastoralis,* on celebrations for special groups (May 15)[34] and *Memoriale Domini,* on the manner of giving Communion (May 29).[35]

The twelfth plenary meeting was finally held at the end of 1969, November 10–14.[36] All the activity in the previous months was spent in publishing the completed drafts. Furthermore, the study groups had no new drafts ready for the plenary meeting that should have been held during the month of April. So the meeting was held at the end of the year and dealt with various matters, including penance, the Divine Office, adult baptism, and the anointing of the sick. This meeting had been preceded by a meeting of reporters held November 4–8.

While 1969 was an extraordinary year for the publication of the reformed liturgical books, it also marked the beginning of organized opposition against the reform and against the new Congregation. The first target was the new *Ordo Missae*, published in April of that year. On June 5 two "theologians" of the Curia published a twenty-five-page booklet entitled "A Brief Critical

---

[29] *EDIL* 1249–67; *DOL* 2969–86.
[30] *EDIL* 1268–1332; *DOL* 3767–3827.
[31] *EDIL* 1326–1736; *DOL* 1357–70.
[32] *EDIL* 1774–1842; *DOL* 2248–84.
[33] *EDIL* 1921–47; *DOL* 3373–97.
[34] *EDIL* 1843–57; *DOL* 2120–33.
[35] *EDIL* 1892–1907; *DOL* 2054–69.
[36] *Not* 4 (1969) 436–41.

Examination of the *Novus Ordo Missae*." Among other things, it contended that "today, no longer from without, but from within the very heart of Catholicism, the existence of division and schism is officially recognized."

The attack reached its climax in October when the press came to know of a letter sent to the Pope by Cardinals Ottaviani and Bacci on September 25.[37] In the letter the two cardinals said in summary that "the *Novus Ordo Missae . . .* represents *. . .* an alarming divergence from the Catholic theology of the Holy Mass." The attack had its effect. The Congregation for the Doctrine of the Faith was invited to make a thorough examination of the General Instruction of the new Roman Missal (GIRM). The CDF argued for modifying no. 7 of the GIRM, even though during the November plenary meeting members of the Consilium had specifically rejected any changes. Nonetheless, at the end of 1969, after several sessions with the Congregation for the Doctrine of the Faith, the new Missal was at last practically definitive, but the controversy over the *Ordo Missae* had labeled the new Congregation as being too progressive. Like the Consilium, the new Congregation was born amidst great difficulties.

Not to be overlooked among the events of the implementation of the conciliar reform was Bugnini's work in reforming papal ceremonies. In 1968, together with Monsignor Virgilio Noè and Abbot Gabriel Brasó, Bugnini was appointed Commissioner for Papal Ceremonies. In practice, though, Bugnini was the sole commissioner. In 1970 his term as commissioner came to an end when Monsignor Noè was appointed Master of Pontifical Ceremonies. Noè was highly esteemed by the Secretariat of State and had just been appointed Undersecretary of the Congregation for Divine Worship the previous year.

The two years under Bugnini's direction were decisive ones for pontifical ceremonies because the liturgical reform was applied to papal ceremonies both in St. Peter's and during visits made by Pope Paul VI to other countries. During the meeting of the Latin American Bishops' Conference held at Medellín, Colombia, in 1968, some of the Pope's celebrations were carried out for the first time according to the new liturgy. But critics of the reform spoke of a radical departure from previous forms in the new pontifical

---

[37] See, for example, articles in *Il Messaggero:* "Per i Cardinali Ottaviani e Bacci la nuova Messa 'eretica' è 'profanatoria'" (October 30, 1969); "I Cardinali Ottaviani e Bacci contro la nuova Messa" (October 28, 1969). For further information about the controversy's repercussions, see E. Cattaneo, *Il culto cristiano in occidente,* 650, nn. 61, 62.

ceremonies. Considering the critics' well-known resistance to any change, papal liturgical celebrations would probably never have attained the liturgical goal of noble simplicity desired by the council.

The year 1970 registered less debate over the reform. The new Congregation's activity was devoted almost entirely to preparing the editions of the new liturgical books, the Roman Missal in particular.[38] The Congregation completed its internal organization and its staff and finished fitting out its offices.[39] The last meeting of the Consilium, or Special Commission for the Liturgical Reform, took place during the thirteenth plenary session, April 8–10. Members examined the final sections of the reform: blessings, the Martyrology, the anointing of the sick, and the dedication of a church.

The first plenary meeting of the reorganized Congregation for Divine Worship was held November 3–6, 1970. On the agenda were the following: minor orders, anointing of the sick, the dedication of a church, and blessings. The plenary meeting had been preceded by the new Congregation's first meeting of consultors.

The year 1970 closed with the death of Cardinal Gut on December 8. Two months later, on February 20, 1971, Cardinal Arturo Tabera, archbishop of Pamplona, was appointed the new prefect of the Congregation. It is likely that certain requests made by Cardinal Tabera to the Apostolic See when he was still bishop of Albacete and later archbishop of Pamplona were indications to the secretary of the Congregation of a broad-minded vision in the pastoral-liturgical field. As bishop of Albacete, Tabera had requested permission from the Consilium to celebrate the Liturgy of the Word separately with children and then have them join the rest of the congregation for the Liturgy of the Eucharist. Later, as archbishop of Pamplona, he had asked the Congregation for Divine Worship for the faculty to allow specially trained lay people to distribute Holy Commun-

---

[38] *Ordo professionis religiosae* (February 2); *Missale Romanum* (March 26); *Ordo consecrationis virginum* (May 31); *Instructio de calendariis particularibus atque officiorum et Missarum propriis recognoscendis* (June 24); *Instructio de ampliore facultate sacrae Communionis sub utraque specie ministrandi* (June 29); *Instructio tertia ad Constitutionem de sacra Liturgia recte exsequendam* (September 5); *Lectionarium Missalis Romani* (3 vols.; September 30); *Missale parvum* (October 18); *Constitutio apostolica de Officio divino* (November 1); *Ordo benedictionis abbatis et abbatissae* (November 9); *Ordo benedicendi olea et conficiendi chrisma* (December 3).

[39] See *Not* 6 (1970) 230–31; 336–38.

ion or to allow the faithful to take the consecrated Host directly from the ciborium. The Apostolic See's answers to both requests were negative, but this pastorally sensitive approach, together with an increasing "internationalization" of the Roman Curia, may have influenced Tabera's appointment as prefect.[40]

In the offices of the Congregation, a meeting of the secretaries of national liturgical commissions was held on February 25 and 26, 1971. Discussion during the meeting centered on how the work of reforming the liturgy was progressing and how the results were being applied in various countries. There was also consideration of children's Masses and Eucharistic Prayers— subjects that would continue to keep the Congregation busy for several years.[41]

Lastly, it should be said that in 1971 study was begun on two problems vitally important for the life of the Congregation: Masses with children and Eucharistic Prayers. In the course of the year many liturgical commissions were consulted about these two matters.

The year 1972 opened with the episcopal ordination of Bugnini by Pope Paul VI on February 13. Aside from being a customary practice for secretaries of Congregations to be ordained bishop, Bugnini's ordination was an affirmation for all the secretary had achieved.

The second plenary meeting was held March 7–11, 1972. The agenda included a draft dealing with the insertion of the name of the bishop in the Eucharistic Prayers, drafts on the Holy Eucharist, blessings, rites in the Pontifical, the Ceremonial of Bishops, the Eucharistic Prayers.[42] As usual, the plenary meeting had been preceded by a *Consulta,* held January 25–February 1.

The third plenary meeting was held November 21–24. The matters discussed were the following: the rite of candidacy for holy orders, the institution of lectors and acolytes, the promise of clerical celibacy, the Rite of Reconciliation of Penitents, the Directory of Masses with Children, the revision of the Martyrology, and the Ceremonial of Bishops. A General Instruction of the Liturgy of the Hours had already been published in 1971. In 1972 the work on the Breviary was completed with the publication of the

[40] *Not* 7 (1971) 81.

[41] R. Kaczynski, "Directorium und hochgebetstexte für Messfeirern mit Kindern," *Liturgisches Jahrbuch* 3 (1979) 157–75.

[42] *Not* 8 (1972) 118–34.

fourth volume. Lastly, the third and final volume of the Lectionary for Mass was published that same year.[43]

On September 14, 1973, Cardinal Tabera, prefect of the Congregation of Worship, was transferred to the Congregation for Religious. This move gave Bugnini, the secretary, complete autonomy in leading the reform. Tabera was a kind, intelligent man of uncommon pastoral balance. In the thirty-two months he served as prefect of the Congregation for Divine Worship, his stature gave prestige to the Congregation, even within the Curia itself. But the resistance he encountered as prefect continued after he left office and contributed in no small way to undermine the dominant position of the Congregation's secretary within the higher circles of the Curia.

The year 1974 marked ten years since the establishment of the Consilium and the beginning of the implementation of the liturgical reforms of Vatican II. During this time nearly all the liturgical books had been published, and the work that remained was already well advanced. The reform had entered its third phase, which focused on the adaptation of the texts of the reform to meet the needs of the local churches.[44]

On January 25, 1974, Cardinal James Robert Knox, archbishop of Melbourne, was named prefect of the Congregation for Divine Worship. In wel-

---

[43] The following liturgical books were approved during 1972: *Ordo initiationis christianae adultorum* (January 6), *Not 9* (1973) 44–46; *Ordo cantus Missae* (June 24), *EDIL* 2639–2800, *DOL* 2328–2488; *Notificatio de Liturgia Horarum pro quibusdam communitatibus religiosis* (August 6), *EDIL* 2832–59, *DOL* 4275–4302; *Declaratio de concelebratione* (August 7), *EDIL* 2865–72, *DOL* 3728–35; *De nomine episcopi in Prece eucharistica proferendo* (October 9), *EDIL* 2873–76, *DOL* 1813–16; the apostolic constitution and the *Ordo unctionis infirmorum* (November 30; December 7), *EDIL* 2913–17, *DOL* 1970–74; *De institutione lectorum et acolythorum, de admissione inter candidatos ad diaconatum et presbyteratum, de sacro coelibatu amplectendo* (December 3), *EDIL* 2924, *DOL* 2939. In 1973, although there were no plenary meetings, the following books were published: *Normae circa Patronos constituendos* (March 19), *EDIL* 3015–29, *DOL* 3971–85; *Normae circa imagines B.V.M. coronandas* (March 25), *EDIL* 3031–36, *DOL* 3890–95; *Litterae circulares ad Conferentiarum episcopalium Praesides de Precibus eucharisticis* (April 27), *EDIL* 3037–55, *DOL* 1975–93; *Editio typica altera Ordinis Baptismi parvulorum* (August 29); *De sacra Communione et de Cultu mysterii eucharistici extra Missam* (June 21), *EDIL* 3060–3108, *DOL* 2089–2103, 2193–2226; *De interpretatione textuum liturgicorum* (October 25), *EDIL* 3110–14, *DOL* 904–8; *Directorium de Missis cum pueris* (November 1), *EDIL* 3115–69, *DOL* 2134–88; *Ordo paenitentiae* (December 2), *EDIL* 3170–3216, *DOL* 3063–3109.

[44] A. Bugnini. "Dieci anni," *Not 9* (1973) 397–99.

coming the new prefect, Bugnini recalled his activity in 1973, when the Fortieth International Eucharistic Congress was held in Melbourne. On that occasion the cardinal had expressed an active interest in the liturgy and had requested a special Eucharistic Prayer for the aborigines. It is possible that this interest and openness positively influenced Bugnini, who supported Knox's appointment, as had happened earlier in regard to Cardinal Tabera.

The year 1974 saw the publication of the following liturgical documents: the apostolic exhortation *Marialis cultus* (February 2);[45] circular letters concerning Particular Calendars, Masses and Offices (February);[46] *Jubilate Deo* (April 14);[47] *Notificatio de obligatorietate novi Missalis* (October 28);[48] Eucharistic Prayers for Masses with Children and for Reconciliation (November 1);[49] *De editione typica altera Gradualis Simplicis* (November 22).[50] Of this list, the Eucharistic Prayers for Children's Masses and for Reconciliation and also the *Notificatio* on obligatory use of the (new) Roman Missal deserve some attention.

A specially formed study group had drafted three Eucharistic Prayers for Masses with Children and two for Reconciliation; the latter were to be used during the 1975 Holy Year. Bugnini did his utmost to obtain approval for the five texts, putting pressure both on the Secretariat of State and on the Congregation for the Doctrine of the Faith. The situation became tense when *Notitiae* published a confidential note from the Secretariat of State on the use of Eucharistic Prayers for Masses with Children, meant only for the attention of the heads of the Congregation.[51] The *Notificatio* on the obligatory use of the new Missal was in response to some opposition against the "new" Mass beginning to appear in certain quarters with a continuing nostalgia for the old rites. This opposition was seen in some European countries and in England. In France, Archbishop Marcel Lefebvre took the leadership of the neo-Tridentine movement.[52]

---

[45] *Not* 10 (1974) 153–96. The text of the exhortation was prepared by the Congregation.

[46] *Not* 10 (1974) 87–88.

[47] *Not* 10 (1974) 122–26.

[48] *Not* 10 (1974) 353.

[49] *Not* 11 (1975) 4–12.

[50] *Not* 11 (1975) 292–96.

[51] See *Not* 11 (1975) 5, note 3.

[52] For further information on opposition led by the French bishop, see Cattaneo, *Il culto cristiano in occidente,* 664. See also *Not* 12 (1976) 377, 417–27.

{ A) ',

Bugnini Leaves the Scene (1975)

The early months of the year 1975 were uneventful except for the publication of the *Editio typica altera Missalis Romani* on March 27.[53] The most notable events took place during the summer. Bugnini, secretary of the Congregation, continuing the policy of internationalization followed by the Consilium, sought to solve problems according to suggestions from experts in various countries, often not taking into account the point of view of the Curia and the limits set by legislation in force. He was especially concerned with the question of the Eucharistic Prayer, by then of great interest to a number of national conferences of bishops that supported a solution that went beyond the compromise reached in the circular letters of 1973.

It was in this context that Bugnini tried to settle the question of new Eucharistic Prayers for Belgium. The Belgian bishops had already dealt with a problem of the proliferation of new, unauthorized Eucharistic Prayers composed by individuals. Belgium was feeling the influence of the more serious situation in the Netherlands, where even more unauthorized experimentation was taking place. In 1969 the Belgian bishops had approved five of the eleven Eucharistic Prayers that had already been authorized by the Dutch bishops. These were the years during which the Congregation for Divine Worship was working on guidelines for the composition of new Eucharistic Prayers; these guidelines were completed on April 27, 1973, and entitled *Litterae circulares*.

Thus the solution of the problem, postponed in 1969, was eventually faced in 1975. Bugnini was in favor of allowing a limited number of new prayers for Belgium and the Netherlands. But by this time the secretary's action with regard to this issue was regarded with suspicion. For this reason Pope Paul VI decided that the solution proposed in 1975 should be debated by a meeting of the two Congregations—Divine Worship and the Discipline of the Sacraments. This was the first time that such a measure had been taken. The meeting was held on June 19, 1975. In addition to the cardinal prefect, eight other curial cardinals were present, and all of them voted unanimously against granting approval of the use of the prayers. Moreover, they affirmed that according to legislation in force, not even one new

---

[53] See *Not* 11 (1975) 297–337.

Eucharistic Prayer could be allowed.[54] The gap between the point of view of the secretary of the Congregation for Divine Worship and that of other members of the Curia was now quite evident.

At the beginning of July following that mixed meeting, while Bugnini was away from Rome on vacation, several private meetings led to the decision that he should no longer have a leadership role in the liturgical renewal and that the Congregation for Divine Worship that he had established ought to be disbanded. For his part, Bugnini suspected that something was happening. Among other things, his contact with the Secretariat of State had become strained and more infrequent during the preceding few years. Also, early in 1975 he had discovered the existence of a special commission set up within the Congregation without his knowledge. Its scope was to prepare a plan for rearranging how liturgical matters were to be treated within the Roman Curia. Part of the plan was the institution of a Congregation *pro vita liturgica,* which would bring together the different responsibilities in the liturgical field, at that time divided among various curial Congregations.

It is highly probable, however, that the Congregation's future had already been decided. With the promulgation of the apostolic constitution *Constans nobis stadium,* published in *L'Osservatore Romano* on July 17, the Congregations for Divine Worship and the Discipline of the Sacraments were fused in order to form the new Congregation for Divine Worship and the Discipline of the Sacraments.[55] While this change was described as a renewed commitment to maintain the conciliar vision of reform,[56] it really entailed the end of the Congregation for Divine Worship. The Congregation was forced to move from its headquarters on the fourth floor and relocate in a corner of the first floor, where the Congregation for the Sacraments had its offices. Moreover, the ten persons who made up the permanent staff of the Congregation for Divine Worship were, in a matter of months, reduced to five. Bugnini was sent to Iran as apostolic pro-nuncio. Thus the Congregation for Divine Worship was reduced to a minor section of the Congregation for the Sacraments.[57]

---

[54] See *Litterae circulares* 6 (April 27, 1973).

[55] *Not* 11 (1975) 209–12.

[56] See *OR* (July 20, 1975).

[57] Among various comments published about the event, two articles merit attention, one in the newspaper *Paese Sera* (August 8, 1975), entitled *"Lo sfratto alla Liturgia"*

July 1975 marked the end of the reform's most interesting period. Subsequent events contradicted the protestations that the council's vision of renewal would continue. In the five years from 1975 to 1980 only two meetings were convoked: one plenary meeting of the new Congregation for Divine Worship and the Discipline of the Sacraments, held on November 22–23, 1976, and a *Consulta* of the section for Divine Worship, held on February 21–22, 1978. The two meetings need be remembered simply for the record. They were unproductive.

Several liturgical documents begun by the Congregation for Divine Worship were completed after it had been merged with the Congregation for the Sacraments in July 1975: "Letter to the Presidents of Bishops' Conferences concerning the introducing of the vernacular in the Sacred Liturgy" (June 5, 1976);[58] "The Rite of Dedication of a Church and Altar" (May 29, 1977);[59] "Instruction on Norms Concerning the Worship of the Eucharistic Mystery," (April 3, 1980).[60] It should be said that the first two documents lacked only the finishing touches for their publication in July 1975. At the end of 1980, none of the other projects begun by the Congregation for Divine Worship had been continued or completed.

The only outstanding event in the period 1975 to 1980 consisted in several new appointments made in the Divine Worship section of the new Congregation in 1977.[61] The new appointments, though, did nothing to improve the situation. They stand merely as proof of Pope Paul VI's desire to restructure the Congregation that he had founded and then agreed to suppress. In spite of his advanced age, he was perfectly aware that the suppression of the Congregation for Divine Worship in 1975 had been, at the very least, a hasty decision. But this Pope, under whose leadership the greatest liturgical reform in the church of the West had taken place, was exhausted. He died on August 6, 1978.

("The Dismantling of the Liturgy"), signed Lillo Spadini. The contents of the article, as well as the style in which it was written, made it clear that it was written by someone using a pseudonym—probably inside the Curia itself. The supposed author simply would not have had access to the "insider" information referred to in the article. The other article was entitled *"Rivolta di 19 cardinali in Vaticano contro un potente monsignore,"* by Luciano Capovilla, in *Il Tempo* (September 12, 1975).

[58] *Not* 12 (1978) 300–302.
[59] *Not* 13 (1977) 364–90.
[60] *Not* 14 (1980) 287–96.
[61] See *Not* 13 (1977) 476.

Reflections on the Contribution of the Consilium

After briefly looking at the most significant events in the implementation of the liturgical reform initiated by Vatican II, it would be helpful to suggest some possible interpretations. These cannot give a complete picture of the role played by the Consilium and the Congregation for Divine Worship.

The Consilium that existed for a little more than five years—from 1964 to 1969— was different from the other organizations in the Roman Curia. This made it possible for the Consilium to promote liturgical renewal from the perspective of the local churches rather than succumb to the tendency of the traditional curial organizations to move very cautiously. Therefore the Consilium was able to achieve a reform that was an answer to the widespread needs of the whole church rather than simply the expression of its central bureaucracy.

The Consilium was shaped by its own activity and in turn even influenced the Congregation for Divine Worship. The principal characteristics of the Consilium could be summed up by the adjectives "competent, international, collegial, efficient, and unconstrained by precedent." It was competent in that bishops, consultors, and experts were chosen on the basis of their specific knowledge of liturgy. The Consilium was international in that its members were selected in light of representing not only each continent but also, when possible, each larger Catholic nation (see *SC* 25). It was collegial, since, unlike other consultants to Congregations of the Roman Curia, practically every appointed expert was called to collaborate in the work of the Consilium. It was efficient thanks to the secretary's remarkable capacity for work. The organization of the secretariat was notable for its coordination of the work of the forty study groups, its promotion of a team spirit, and the pastoral openness of the members of the secretariat, which served as the basis for the work of reform. Finally, the Consilium, unlike the Congregations of the Roman Curia, was not bound by any procedural practices or particular regulations. Although the lack of juridical definition of its area of competence and activity at times strained its relations with the Curia, it also gave the Consilium the freedom of initiative necessary to tackle the reform in depth as well as to deal with daily problems as they arose. In this, the Consilium was greatly aided by the direct access of the president and the secretary to the Pope.

These very characteristics led to opposition from the Roman Curia, which considered the Consilium a kind of foreign interloper. The Consilium's international membership threatened the members of the Curia, who were largely Italian. The absence of a precise juridical status for the Consilium within the Curia, as well as its direct contact with the Pope, naturally led to difficulties in an organization used to respecting lines of authority and customary procedure.

The Consilium, though, was supported by local churches. This was due to its international membership and its innovative approach to reform, which was closer to reality and more suitable for implementing a liturgical renewal able to fulfill the desire of Vatican II by meeting the needs of the modern world. Interestingly, when the council was in session, this support of the local churches was evident and aided in developing the most satisfactory liturgical reforms. The presence of the world's bishops in Rome naturally minimized the influence of the curial Congregations. It was mainly thanks to these favorable circumstances that the Consilium was able to overcome the many difficulties encountered along the way.

However, none of this would have been possible if the Pope had not played his part. It was Pope Paul VI who put the administration of the Consilium into the hands of two men who were certainly more popular outside of Rome than in the Curia. These appointments were made at the beginning of his pontificate, when he most felt the need for renewal within the church and for dialogue on the problems of the contemporary world. It is no coincidence that at the same time, in the autumn of 1963, it was this same Pope who worked to improve the relationship of the Holy See with the Italian state.[62] It can be said, therefore, that the establishment of the Consilium as a new Office not modeled on existing Offices in the Curia, and the discreet but ongoing support of the Pope for the Office's work of reform, made those first years of the pontificate of Paul VI the most open and fruitful of his reign.

The convergence of the various factors mentioned above led to extraordinary results. In five short years of life, the Consilium planned and set in motion the implementation of the entire reform. When the Congregation for Divine Worship was instituted in May 1969, almost all the drafts for the new liturgical books, as well as the documents on the reform, were very near completion. All that remained for the new Congregation was to complete the work. By the end of March 1969, the Consilium had already completed work on 324 out of 400 drafts proposed in 1965.

[62] See S. Magister, *La politica vaticana e l'Italia 1943–1978* (Rome: Riuniti, 1979) 311ff.

But more important than the quantity was the outstanding quality of the work achieved by the Consilium. The new liturgy, thanks to the extremely qualified and scholarly work of the Consilium's experts, became a model that not only expresses the genuine liturgical tradition of the Roman Rite, but that can be used as a basis for liturgical adaptation in different nations and cultures. For the first time in the history of the church, we have a liturgy today which, rather than being an expression of a particular church, responds to the concept of the church universal. "What is essential for liturgy is that it not be the product of one epoch or one nation, but rather that it be Christian—that is, an expression of the timeless faith of the church."[63] This, it would seem, is the fundamental characteristic of the liturgy of Vatican II implemented by the Consilium.

In 1969 the Congregation for Divine Worship was created, putting an end to the Consilium and effectively taking over the reform. This event certainly had a number of positive repercussions, but it also marked the beginning of a process of "curialization" of the work of reform.

After Cardinal Lercaro's resignation in 1968 as president of the Consilium, Bugnini remained as the reform's sole leader. He enjoyed the greatest influence during the years that immediately followed. The reform of the papal liturgy, in Bugnini's hands during that period (1968–1970), was one of the most visible signs of his uncontested leadership in every area of the reform. In this context the good and gentle figure of the new Congregation's first prefect, Cardinal Benno Gut, had little or no influence on the progress of the reform, due to his untimely death on December 8, 1969.

The establishment of the Congregation was the realization of Bugnini's dream. This accomplishment was confirmed by his episcopal ordination in 1972, which came as a result of the dedication and dynamic ability with which he led the reform. Furthermore, the Consilium maintained its juridical independence in directing the liturgical renewal. By 1965 the Consilium had become independent of the Congregation for Rites' tutelage through a series of events. This new status was guaranteed by the support of the Pope. But before it could publish any document, the Consilium still had to obtain the Congregation for Rites' formal authorization. In 1969, however, the

---

[63] «L'essentiel d'une liturgie, ce n'est pas d'être d'un siècle ou d'une nation, c'est d'être chrétienne, c'est-à-dire d'être l'expression de la foi de l'Église qui est de tous les temps.» B. Botte. *Le mouvement liturgique. Témoignage et souvenir* (Tournai: Desclée, 1973) 38.

establishment of the Congregation for Divine Worship gave formal juridical authority to its decisions, which obviated the need for additional approval.

The establishment of the Congregation also gave it greater prestige and authority within the Roman Curia. The Consilium had certainly not enjoyed the same consideration and respect in the Curia as a formally established "Congregation." But once the approach of the Consilium became the approach of the Congregation for Divine Worship, it acquired greater influence within the Curia. The earlier secondary status had been replaced by an official recognition of the equality of the organization in charge of the liturgical reform and the other curial Offices.

The 1967 "reform" of the Curia did not get very far. In fact, hopes that the curial Congregations would be reformed to meet the new needs of the church were dashed. Therefore, once the young, dynamic Consilium had become a Congregation, it was forced into the mold of a Curia that had yet to be renewed. The first casualty was its international and representative characteristics. Only seven of the Consilium's bishops were able to belong to the new Congregation. It is true that they were chosen purposely from among those who had been the most active members of the Consilium, but from a numerical point of view, they found themselves in an Office in which the curial members had far greater weight than they ever had in the Consilium. The consultors, too, had to be reduced from more than two hundred to just eighteen. The necessary adaptation to norms regulating the functioning of the Vatican Congregations was modifying the fundamental characteristics of the Consilium.

In addition to the Consilium's special way of functioning, two factors concerning its outside relationships made it possible to achieve, in only five years, the planning and realization of the greater part of the work of reform: its independence from the Curia and its direct contact with the Pope. Once the Consilium became a Congregation, not only was it forced to rearrange its internal composition, thus losing most of its international flavor and representation, but it also had to modify its relations with the other curial Congregations, which could no longer be simply "consulted." Ever more frequently it had to consider and accept the opinions of other Congregations that were not always open to the solutions proposed by the Congregation for Divine Worship.[64] That is why direct contact with the Pope also began to be less effective.

---

[64] For example, in a controversy over the amendment of no. 7 of the *Institutio Generalis Missalis Romani,* the Consilium's text had to be altered according to indications

The creation of the Congregation for Divine Worship was in practice official confirmation of the validity of Bugnini's action in five years of directing the Consilium. In the new Congregation he continued that "international" style already successfully employed in the previous organization. Here, too, questions were tackled and solved mainly on the basis of requests from national liturgical commissions.[65] The Congregation's eighteen consultors were not always appointed following the regulations of the Roman Curia but were chosen because they were experts in the liturgy or secretaries of liturgical commissions from all over the world. Although this offered a wider vision of the problems, it possibly alienated some consultors. Some who had previously been supporters began to sow doubts about the policies of the Congregation in the soil of the Curia. Also, the way the Congregation for Worship related to other Congregations, particularly the Congregation for the Doctrine of Faith, illustrated such a different mentality that real collaboration was very difficult, and only rarely were these relations tension-free.

Finally, Bugnini's style of working began to create difficulties even with the prefect of the Congregation. Beginning in 1964, Bugnini had been the *de facto* uncontested executor of the liturgical reform. This was due to the confidence placed in him by Pope Paul VI. He had become the point of reference for the Consilium and the Congregation for Divine Worship. Lercaro, the Consilium's first president, lived in Bologna and gave free rein to Bugnini as secretary. Cardinal Benno Gut, second president of the Consilium and first prefect of the new Congregation, lived as an ordinary monk at Sant'Anselmo on the Aventine Hill of Rome. Like his predecessor, he had such confidence in Bugnini that he appeared only once a week in the Congregation. Cardinal Tabera, the Congregation's second prefect, attempted to take a more activist approach in leading the Office but was transferred shortly afterward to another Congregation. It is quite probable that Bugnini's difficult relations with Tabera constituted one of the most decisive elements leading up to the suppression of the Congregation for Divine Worship in 1975.

---

given by the Congregation for the Doctrine of the Faith in the 1970 *Missale Romanum* published by the Congregation for Divine Worship. See *EDIL* 1402; *DOL* 1397.

[65] Most solutions advanced on such crucial problems as the new Eucharistic Prayers, the Directory and Eucharistic Prayers for Masses with Children were dealt with on the basis of consultation with liturgical commissions and liturgical centers on various continents. Considerable pressing for an open-minded solution to these matters came from the meeting of liturgical commission secretaries held on February 25–26, 1971, in the Congregation's offices.

The problematic and complex situation in which the Congregation for Divine Worship found itself was illustrated by some particular aspects of the liturgical reform: the new Eucharistic Prayers; the Directory and Eucharistic Prayers for Masses with Children; the Eucharistic Prayers for Reconciliation; and the Rite of Penance. Work on the new Eucharistic Prayers, begun in 1971, was concluded in 1973 with the publication of *Litterae circulares de precibus eucharisticis*. After a debate that had lasted three years, the matter was solved with a compromise. Bugnini would have preferred a solution more responsive to requests made by the liturgical commissions and bishops' conferences. He was probably wrong to have held his position too adamantly. There was disagreement even within the Congregation on this matter, so much so that one consultor wrote a pamphlet on the dangers of the proposed solution. The paper, distributed among the Congregation's members, caused considerable alarm also in the highest offices of the Curia.

The rite of penance was another disputed area. The most debated topics were the various versions of the words of absolution, the rite of general absolution, and the different penitential celebrations proposed by the document. In this case as well, years of discussion and argument had embittered some members of the Curia against the Congregation.

No less heated was the controversy over the Directory for Masses with Children and the related Eucharistic Prayers. The publication in *Notitiae* of a note on the use of these Eucharistic Prayers that should have remained confidential resulted in diminishing confidence in the Congregation's work.

These three major questions gradually eroded the confidence of members of other curial Congregations and of the Secretariat of State in the reform being carried out under the direction of the Congregation for Worship.

In the light of these events, the decision reached in 1975 would seem to have been the logical conclusion to a long process that had really started when the Congregation was established. Unfortunately, only later, after the decision reached in mid-July 1975, did it become apparent, once peace had been restored, that not only the person of the secretary of the Congregation had been eliminated, but the institution charged with promoting and safeguarding the liturgy of the Second Vatican Council had also been suppressed.

The decision reached in 1975 can only be seen as a negative event in the history of the church's liturgy. The Congregation for Rites, instituted in 1588 to safeguard the Tridentine liturgy, existed for almost four centuries. However, the Congregation for Divine Worship, instituted to implement the liturgy of the Second Vatican Council, lasted for a mere six years. Even the most optimistic historian would be forced to suspect that the institutional suppression was hardly wise and that in the heat of that month of July, personal resentment seems to have prevailed.

The Consilium, through its original distinctiveness and its effectiveness, was made possible due to a convergence of a variety of factors: the winds of change unleashed by the Second Vatican Council; the readiness to dialogue on the problems of the contemporary world that characterized the early years of the pontificate of Pope Paul VI; and the energy and expertise of a few charismatic individuals, Lercaro and Bugnini in particular.

At a later phase, the need for a permanent Office in harmony with the liturgy of Vatican II and having more authority to regulate its implementation led to the change from a free and independent Office like the Consilium to the more formal structure of a Congregation within the Roman Curia. But it was precisely the fact that the new Congregation acted more like the suppressed Consilium than like a traditional Roman Congregation, coupled with the single-mindedness, even stubbornness, of the secretary, that led to an overreaction among the other Congregations of the Roman Curia. Consequently, with the reorganization of the Congregation, more traditional personnel who were more representative of the Roman Curia came to be part of the new Congregation.

Conclusion

With the change of the Consilium into a Congregation in 1969 and the transformation of the Congregation for Divine Worship to a subsection of another Congregation in 1975 (Congregation for Divine Worship and the Discipline of the Sacraments), the distinctive style of the Consilium was gradually absorbed into the more traditional style proper to the Roman Curia. This was probably one of the first signs of a tendency to return to a preconciliar mindset that has for years now characterized the Curia's approach. As more and more time passes since the Second Vatican Council, an event charged with such hope and desire for renewal, its distinctive contributions seem to be increasingly questioned. Nevertheless, the Consilium and the Congregation for Divine Worship remain in the history of the church as institutions connected with the liturgical reform of Vatican II. Instituted and then suppressed by Pope Paul VI, they stand as witnesses to the prophetic vision as well as the limitations of his pontificate.

✠ Editors' Epilogue

Archbishop Marini's account of the beginning of the Consilium demonstrates how that body, born of the council, based its *modus operandi* firmly on the decisions of the Constitution on the Sacred Liturgy. For the first time since the Council of Trent, authority was restored to bishops of local churches, in collaboration with the Holy See, to promote the liturgical life in their dioceses. While the language is careful, article 22 §2 of the Constitution on the Sacred Liturgy is the first indication that the Second Vatican Council would give new authority and recognition to the local episcopates, referred to in the document as "the competent territorial bodies of bishops legitimately established." A constant in Marini's account is the pastoral intent of the bishops in authorizing and carrying out the liturgical reform. This pastoral goal is nowhere more strikingly evidenced than in the bishops' overwhelming decision in favor of opening the church's worship to the living languages. This decision simply makes no sense divorced from the bishops' preeminent pastoral concern.

A related characteristic of the process followed by the Consilium was the willingness of the bishop members to seek the opinion of international liturgical experts and to work closely with them in carrying out the mandate of the council. These experts were not limited solely to academic authorities in the field but also included pastors who had long experience in promoting the prayer of the people. Attention to the important cultural dimension of worship was a key concern for both bishops and experts working within the Consilium and left the door open for further development. It was this balance between the scholarly and pastoral that allowed the Consilium to achieve its goals.

Would the bishops of the Second Vatican Council recognize the faithful implementation of their decisions in the present contentious liturgical climate? Would they see verified in the life of the church today all that they had hoped for and envisioned?

> In this restoration, both texts and rites should be drawn up so that they express more clearly the holy things which they signify; the Christian people, so far as possible, should be enabled to understand them with ease and to take part in them fully, actively, and as befits a community (*SC* 21).

 **Appendix**

DOCUMENT I

MOTU PROPRIO *PRIMITIAE* ET ADNEXA *INSTRUCTIO*

Introduction

The text of the motu proprio *Primitiae* and the appended Instruction, given here, is the final draft of several projects prepared in October and November 1963.

The texts of the two drafts of documents do not carry the same date.

The text of the motu proprio bears a note in Father Bugnini's handwriting: "With correction by Fr Dirks—November 2nd 1963."

The text of the Instruction bears two notes by Bugnini:

a) "This text in 5 copies to Cardinal Lercaro, November 21st. Same text written especially for the Holy Father."
b) "2nd draft after the additions (in red) agreed upon with Cardinal Lercaro."[1]

---

[1] The additions were most probably approved by Cardinal Lercaro on Sunday, November 24, according to a statement in a letter written by Lercaro himself on November 24, 1963: ". . . then some work with Fr. Bugnini to prepare for presentation to the Holy Father the liturgical innovations that may be carried out immediately." G. Lercaro, *Lettere dal Concilio 1962–1965,* ed. Giuseppe Battelli (Bologna: Dehoniane, 1980) 234.

Text

APOSTOLIC LETTER MOTU PROPRIO
CONTAINING SOME NORMS AND PRESCRIPTIONS OF
THE CONCILIAR CONSTITUTION ON THE SACRED LITURGY
TO BE PUT INTO EFFECT IMMEDIATELY

The **First Fruits** (*Primitiae*) of the Second Vatican Ecumenical Council have already been seen in the Constitution on the Sacred Liturgy, approved by the same Sacred Council, and solemnly sanctioned and happily promulgated by Us at the end of the Second Session.

Truly the completion of the work initiated, the general liturgical renewal, for which a special Pontifical Commission must be by Us instituted as soon as possible and which will suitably renew the public worship of the Church, can only be brought by degrees and gradually to the desired result, and given the nature of the matter, it will also require no little time. For this reason numerous Council Fathers have addressed to Us continuous requests that those norms of the Constitution applicable now may be carried out immediately. After careful examination of the matter, for the greater good of the faithful and more efficacious ministry of the holy pastors, We have decided to approve this noble and opportune proposal.

In fact, as we watch over the apostolic work, we wish above all that the Liturgy, in order to meet the present needs of Christ's flock, may be the summit towards which the activity of the Church is directed and at the same time the fount from which all the Church's power flows (cf. *Const.* article 10).

Therefore, with Motu proprio, in full consciousness and with our full Apostolic authority, we establish as follows:

I. That the Bishops and all ministers zealously strive with suitable and congruous means to instruct the faithful in those biblical, theological and pastoral principles, by which the foundations of the whole Constitution are supported and confirmed, and which must inspire all pastoral activity.

II. From the whole Constitution have been extracted those elements of general renewal applicable immediately. We therefore attribute the value of law, to this Letter, the Appended Document, containing these things.

III. The typical editions of the liturgical books maintain their validity, until they have been duly revised; nevertheless the additions or variations mentioned here must henceforth be considered as authentic.

IV. Primarily Article 22 § 1 of the Constitution must be observed: "Regulation of the liturgy depends solely on the Authority of the Church, that is, on the Apostolic See and, accordingly as the law determines, on the bishop." So, "Therefore, no other person, not even if he is a priest, may on his own add, remove, or change anything in the liturgy" (*Const.* article 22 §3).

V. The competent territorial bodies, mentioned in Article 22 §2 of the Constitution, may *in the meantime* be understood as follows:

- a) Bishops' Conferences, provincial or regional, constituted in conformity with Canon 292 of the Code of Canon Law.
- b) Other Bishops' Conferences, whose members are individual territorial Bishops in charge according to the legitimate knowledge of the Apostolic See.

VI. The things established in this Apostolic Letter will come into effect on the next Feast Day of the Nativity of Our Lord.

May the local Ordinaries, the heads of institutes of perfection for both sexes, and the pastors who care for souls, make every effort to see that the clergy, the religious, and all the faithful are clearly informed about the above-mentioned liturgical and pastoral significance of the Constitution on the Sacred Liturgy. With immediate and constant catechesis may they be instructed in the new forms of liturgy to be introduced, so that they may not only be attracted by the novelty of the things, but may consciously and fruitfully become, in mind and in spirit, participants in the liturgical action.

INSTRUCTION ON ELEMENTS OF THE LITURGICAL REFORM IMMEDIATELY APPLICABLE

In relation to the norms of the above given *Motu Proprio,* the elements of liturgical reform to take effect from the 25th of the month of December 1963 are as follows:

THE MYSTERY OF THE HOLY EUCHARIST

I. re: *article 50*

- a) If the chants of the *Proper* and the *Ordinary* of the Mass are sung, they are not to be read by the celebrant on his own; except for the "Sanctus," which is either to be sung by the celebrant together with those assisting or it is recited without being sung.

b) In the prayers at the foot of the altar, at the beginning of the Mass, psalm 42 is to be omitted, and be placed in the Masses in Passion Time.

c) The Secret, or "Super oblata" (prayer over the offerings) must be audible, whether sung or recited.

d) In the Canon of the Mass the words from *Qui pridie* up to *Calicem salutis perpetuae* must be said out loud.

Furthermore, at the end of the Canon, after the words *benedicis et praestas nobis,* the rubrics must be changed as follows: "He uncovers the Chalice, he genuflects, and raising the Chalice and the Host, omitting the signs of the cross, says out loud: *Per ipsum* up to *per omnia saecula saeculorum.* When the people have said *Amen,* he replaces the Host, covers the Chalice with the pall, genuflects, rises, and with joined hands, says in an audible voice, or sings: *Oremus. Praeceptis.*"

e) In distributing Holy Communion, the sign of the cross with the Host is omitted, and the following formula is used: *"Corpus Christi,"* to which the communicants reply: *Amen.*

f) Mass ends with the blessing of the celebrant, followed by the admonition *Ite, Missa est.* The last Gospel is omitted; the Leonine prayers are suppressed.

II. re: *article 53*

Before the offertory, having said *Oremus,* there may be the "Oratio communis" or "of the faithful." Pending the creation of proper formulas, it is lawful to use either the old existing formulas in use in individual nations, or formulas approved, or about to be approved, by the Bishop, or the final part of the Litanies of the Saints. In this latter case, beginning from *Kyrie eleison.* R. *Kyrie eleison; Christe eleison.* R. *Christe eleison; Kyrie eleison.* R. *Kyrie eleison,* followed by: *Ut Ecclesia, tuam* up to *Filii Dei* included, and after repeating as above the *Kyrie eleison* three times, the following prayer is added: "Lord, we ask you to accept the prayer of your Church so that free from all adversities and errors, she may freely serve you. Through Our Lord Jesus Christ. R. Amen."

Whatever the form adopted, be it maintained that the celebrant or the deacon express the intention and the people respond.

III. re: *article 54*

The readings, Epistle and Gospel, are to be read in the vernacular, facing the people, and, when possible, from the lectern. For the text, meanwhile the version approved by the Bishop may be used.

In the same manner the *"oratio communis"* (common prayer) is to be said in the vernacular; but only in Masses which are not sung may the Lord's Prayer be in the vernacular.

IV. re: *article 57*

Concelebration, in the cases foreseen by the Constitution, may be carried out only after the rite of concelebration has been approved and published.

THE SACRAMENTS

V. re: *article 63b*

In places where no bilingual Ritual exists, *in the meantime the Bishop may use bilingual Rituals already approved,* if available in a language known to the faithful.

VI. re: *article 66*

To be preferred for the Baptism of adults is the "Order of Baptism for adults divided in stages"; however when celebrated all at one time, it is permitted to omit the renunciations, see the Rituale Romanum tit. II, cap. 4, nn. 6 and 7, and the second series of exorcisms, see numbers 18–21, for men and numbers 24–27 for women.

VII. re: *article 69*

   a) In the "Rite of supplying ceremonies omitted in infant baptism" Rituale Romanum, tit. II, cap. 5, the exorcisms in no. 6, 8, 10 (*Exorcizo te, immunde spiritus,* and also *Ergo maledicte*), and in no. 15 *(Exorcizo te, omnis spiritus)* are to be omitted.
   b) In the "Rite of supplying ceremonies omitted in adult baptism," found in Rituale Romanum tit. II, cap. 6 the exorcisms in no. 5, 14–25, 31–35 are to be omitted.

VIII. re: *article 71*

    a) Confirmation, if opportune, may be conferred during Mass, immediately after the reading of the Gospel and the homily.

    b) It is good for the rite of Confirmation, when possible, to be preceded by the renewal of baptismal promises according to the Easter Vigil rite except for the preparatory instruction which concerns the conclusion of the Lenten period, or according to the rite in legitimate use in individual places.

    c) At the words "In the name of the Father and of the Son and of the Holy Spirit" which follow the formula "I sign you with the sign of the cross and I confirm you with the anointing of salvation" only one sign of the cross is to be made.

IX. re: *article 74*

When the Anointing of the sick and the Viaticum are administered at the same time, after confession if necessary, first to be administered is the holy Anointing, then the Viaticum, omitting the formulas and prayers, which must be repeated differently, such as, for example, the priest's blessing upon entering, the *Confiteor* etc., which can be recited together.

X. re: *article 76*

In the Consecration of Bishops it is lawful for all bishops present to perform the laying on of hands.

XI. re: *article 78*

Matrimony, according to custom, should be celebrated during Mass, immediately after the reading of the Gospel and the homily. If it is celebrated without Mass, the Epistle and the Gospel should be read for the spouses at the beginning of the rite.

The prayers over the spouses, after the "Our Father" and before the final blessing, may be recited in the vernacular, in a version approved by the Bishop.

XII. re: *article 79*

Blessings hitherto reserved, contained in the Rituale Romanum tit. IX capp. 9, 10, and 11, may be imparted by every priest, except for the blessing of a bell for use of a blessed church or oratory (cap. 9, no. 11), of a corner stone of a church (ibid., no. 16), of a new church or public oratory (ibid., no. 17), of a new cemetery (ibid., no. 22), except for papal blessings (cap. 10, nos. 1–3).

THE DIVINE OFFICE

XIII. re: *article 89*

An appropriate adaptation of the Divine Office to suit the pastoral needs of the clergy requires a reform of the entire Roman Breviary, in which a new arrangement of texts and a more abundant and suitable selection of the readings from Holy Scriptures and the Father will permit a more efficacious celebration of the Divine Office. Meanwhile:

a) Prime may be omitted. Nevertheless, pending a different arrangement of the Office, it should be recited so that an important part of the psalms and selected prayers will not be totally neglected;

b) outside of choir, from the three minor Hours, Terce, Sext, None, one can be chosen to suit the time of day.

DOCUMENT II

THE "MEMORANDUM" OF THE FRENCH LITURGICAL COMMISSION

Introduction

The "Memorandum" from the French Liturgical Commission was sent to Cardinal Paolo Giobbe by Archbishop Joseph-Marie Martin of Rouen, president of the commission, with a letter on February 7, 1964. The letter also carried the note of the date of arrival: "February 15, 1964."

Probably the text was also sent to other offices of the Roman Curia.

The French "Memorandum" is one of the most significant proofs of the reaction aroused by the publication of the motu proprio *Sacram Liturgiam* (and by number IX in particular) in L'Osservatore Romano of January 30, 1964.

Archbishop Martin's letter and the text of the "Memorandum" follow.

Text

Paris, February 7, 1964

Your Eminence,

As President of the National Liturgical Commission of the French Episcopate, I believe I must make known to you the emotion aroused in France by the final disposition of the "Motu Proprio" on the subject of translations into living language.

For your information, I allow myself to communicate to Your Eminence the Memorandum, enclosed herewith, which summarizes the reflections made by the Bishops of the Commission gathered in Paris since yesterday morning.

Please accept, Your Eminence, the homage of my sentiments of profound, religious respect.

Joseph-Marie MARTIN
Archbishop of Rouen
President of the Episcopal Commission for Liturgy

His Eminence, Cardinal GIOBBE

Memorandum of the Liturgical Commission of the French Episcopate

The French Bishops, having requested the consent of the Secretariat of State, held a plenary assembly in Rome on November 30 and December 2, 1963, during which, with a two-thirds majority by secret ballot, they reached a certain number of decisions in view of the application of the *"De Sacra Liturgia"* Constitution, to be promulgated two days later. It was in fact impossible to envisage assembling the bishops again in France for a Plenary, after the closing of the Council Session, when the bishops would be returning to their dioceses after such a long absence; this is why their decisions were to be made public only after the publication of the Motu Proprio by means of which the Pope would give the assemblies the temporary statutes necessary for the exercise of their responsibilities according to articles 22 and above all 36–40 of the Constitution "De Sacra Liturgia." The results of the votes of the Plenary Assembly were communicated immediately to the Secretariat of State.

As soon as the Motu proprio of January 25 was published, the French Episcopate issued its first "Regulation," concerning mainly the readings of the Mass, in agreement with article 54 of the Constitution. Both clergy and faithful in fact were awaiting with great impatience some progress in this field that the conciliar decisions and the text itself of the Constitution were welcomed with joy and seen as an important pastoral event.

But now, press communications have spread a rumor that the Apostolic See disapproves this Regulation. These statements by irresponsible newspapers have begun to cause incredible concern among public opinion and among the clergy in particular, and now we come to know of an article, signed S.M., published in the January 30 issue of the *L'Osservatore Romano,* most displeasing to the bishops' conferences and which proposes, for article number 36 of the Constitution, an interpretation absolutely contrary to what was said and voted by the Council Assembly on this subject, to which the Holy Father himself gave his approval before promulgating the Constitution.

The council did not decide that the Assemblies would propose this or that concession for the vernacular for approval by the Apostolic See: it purposely discarded a similar disposition and decreed that the bishops' assemblies would make the decisions and that their decisions would be *probata seu confirmata* by the Apostolic See (cf. report by Mgr. Calewaert). Neither did the council state that the bishops' conferences would submit translations for approval by the Apostolic See; it agreed that the translations would be approved by the bishops' conferences, that is all. Any other disposition would contradict the council's decisions, as it would also contradict the trust in the episcopal conferences already shown earlier by the Apostolic See when it gave them the task of arranging translations of the *Ordo Baptismi adultorum*, a task which for its part the French Episcopate did not fail to carry out. This is true also for article 101 on the Divine Office, which refers in particular to the translations carried out according to article 36, and not through the intervention of a Vatican Congregation which cannot consider itself more competent than the Episcopates in matters concerning exact translations into a national language.

Already public opinion is alarmed by the interpretation in the Motu Proprio proposed, in a manner it would appear little authorized, in *L'Osservatore Romano*. People are saying that just two months after its promulgation, the Constitution is beaten in the breach, that the decisions made by the episcopal assemblies may be effectively neutralized by the Roman Curia, that the role of the bishops' assemblies is being undermined at the very moment of their establishment by the council, that the decisions of the council are being contested even before the council has finished.

If the interpretation put forward in *L'Osservatore Romano* were exact, it would in fact justify, on the part of the bishops and of the whole Catholic world, grave concern and the strongest of protests, because it would in no way be possible to recognize therein true application of the Constitution or of the encouragement given in many ways by the Sovereign Pontiff Paul VI.

Before the gravity of the ministerial problems and all manner of difficulties which priests encounter daily in their ministry, real distress threatens to take hold of them should they see deceived their legitimate hope for the renewal which the liturgical Constitution, in particular with regard to the language, had given them. This distress could cause some to fall into disobedience and perhaps even, we dare to say, into despair.

But no doubt, opportune clarification will reassure the bishops and will confirm them in the right which is theirs in the terms of the Conciliar Constitution.

DOCUMENT III

PROMEMORIA ON THE INTERPRETATION OF THE LITURGICAL CONSTITUTION

Introduction

The "Promemoria" was prepared by Father Bugnini in mid-February, when the situation concerning the office responsible for the implementation of the liturgical reform had reached the height of confusion.

The Sacred Congregation for Rites had already commenced its maneuvers to take by force the direction of the reform and relegate the Consilium to the simple role of a consultative office of the Sacred Congregation for Rites.

The "Promemoria" was intended to press for a decision of clarification in favor of the Consilium.

Nevertheless, given the delicacy of the situation, Bugnini thought it wiser not to dispatch the "Promemoria" intended for the Holy Father.

Text

CONSILIUM AD EXSEQUENDAM CONSTITUTIONEM DE SACRA LITURGIA

Prot.n. 76/64   February 15, 1964

Promemoria
on the interpretation of the Liturgical Constitution

1. It is urgently necessary that the interpretation of the Constitution on the Sacred Liturgy be entrusted to one, clearly defined Office, in order to avoid resolutions which could be in contrast to the spirit of the Document and also to each other.

2. The competent Office may seem today to be the Sacred Congregation for Rites, as it is the Holy See's administrative office in matters of liturgy.

But the polemical position taken regarding the Constitution, from the beginning of its preparation, by the majority of persons of whom this Sacred Congregation is today composed would seem to render it less suited to interpret the Constitution. Moreover, this position being well known in international ecclesial circles, were the Sacred Congregation to offer resolutions, these would not enjoy the necessary trust.

There are also precedents which would seem less favorable to entrusting the interpretation of the conciliar document to the Sacred Congregation for Rites.

In 1960, with the Code of Rubrics, and in 1961, with the Instruction for the revision of diocesan Propers, a sound legislative base, both firm and clear, had been reached. Unfortunately, after a few months, the first indults were conceded and then other wider concessions, quite contrary to the whole spirit of the Documents just issued.

3. The most suitable Office, on the other hand, would seem to be the "Consilium ad exsequendam Constitutionem de sacra liturgia," being composed of persons well prepared, in that they followed the progressive development of the Constitution, who are widely trusted in the area concerned, and technically suited for this work. In this manner the interpretation would be also in full harmony with all the work of the implementation of the document.

4. The formation of a commission for the interpretation, once the members of the "Consilium ad exsequendam Constitutionem de sacra liturgia" have been nominated, would not be difficult, seeing that the Eminent Cardinals who belong to the "Consilium"—four of whom are in the Curia and one, Cardinal Lercaro, who has no difficulty in coming to Rome—could at the same time be charged with forming the commission for the interpretation. These eminent Cardinals would then need to be assisted by a good number of experts who, at a study center, would prepare the resolutions.

5. It should, however, be noted that in its present form the "Consilium ad exsequendam Constitutionem de sacra liturgia" has no administrative power; there is need, therefore, of new powers, announced by an official, public Pontifical Act, as in 1917 for the Code of Canon Law, with the institution of a special commission "ad canones Codicis Iuris Canonici authentice interpretandos" (cf. A.A.S. [1917] 483–484).

DOCUMENT IV

PRINCIPLES AND NORMS FOR THE CONFIRMATION OF THE ACTS OF THE EPISCOPAL CONFERENCES

Introduction

During the ordinary meeting of March 20, the secretary reported on the problems deriving from the decisions made by bishops' conferences concerning various parts of the liturgy.

In order to proceed with the confirmation of these decisions, some general principles had to be established. These principles were presentèd in the paper *Quaestiones tractandae,* 1.

The principles reworked were presented in the paper *Quaestiones tractandae,* 3, for examination by the plenary body, which approved them on April 17 and 18, 1964.

After the plenary session the members' decisions were approved by the Pope on April 21 and successively put on three typescript pages: *Res Secretariae,* 3, given below.

At the bottom of the texts presented to the Pope, Cardinal Lercaro added the following handwritten note: "Placet ex audientia diei 21 aprilis 1964, Iacobus Cardinal Lercaro."

Text

PRINCIPLES AND NORMS FOR THE CONFIRMATION OF DECISIONS OF EPISCOPAL CONFERENCES APPROVED BY THE CONSILIUM IN A PLENARY MEETING ON APRIL 17 AND 18, 1964

1. The experiments, of which article 40, 2 of the Constitution speaks, refer, not to existing rites, but to "elements of local tradition and culture that may be introduced into public worship."
   25 in favor, 1 against

2. The principle that the vernacular may be used even in sung Masses is accepted, providing the melodies are approved by the competent territorial authorities.
   25 in favor, 1 in favor iuxta modum

3. The readings may be proclaimed directly in the vernacular in all Masses.

   all voted in favor

4. The readings, in a sung Mass, may be proclaimed, without being sung.

   all voted in favor

5. The readings must be proclaimed facing the people.

   all voted in favor

6. A rite is to be prepared for the proclamation of the readings facing the people.

   all voted in favor

7. Pater noster: the Our Father:
   a) in read Masses it may be recited by the people with the celebrating priest in the vernacular;
   b) in sung Mass it can be sung by the people together with the celebrating priest, either in Latin or in the vernacular, to melodies approved by the competent territorial authorities.

   a) *all in favor*
   b) *25 in favor, 1 against*

8. The formulas *Ecce Agnus Dei* and *Domine, non sum dignus* may be said in the vernacular in Masses either sung or read.

   all voted in favor

9. The present formula for the distribution of the communion of the faithful must be replaced by the formula (the Body of Christ) *Corpus Christi* R. *Amen.* This formula may be said in the vernacular.

   all voted in favor

10. If the competent territorial authorities judge it to be opportune, the acclamations, greetings, and formulas of dialogue, in all the Liturgy, may be said in the vernacular, and also sung, to melodies legally approved.

    all voted in favor

11. The collect, the prayer over the offerings, the postcommunion, the prayer over the people may be said in the vernacular.

    all voted in favor

12. a) The prayer over the offerings and the embolism of the Lord's Prayer may be recited out loud and in the vernacular.
    b) The whole question of the other parts of the Canon of the Mass to be said out loud and in the vernacular is postponed until the general liturgical reform.
       To both: 23 in favor, 3 against

13. a) Psalm 42 in the prayers at the foot of the altar may be omitted.
    b) The remaining prayers at the foot of the altar may be said in the vernacular.
    c) The question of the revision of these prayers is postponed until the general liturgical reform.
       all in favor

14. a) The chants of the Ordinary of the Mass, that is the *Kyrie, Gloria, Credo, Sanctus- Benedictus* and *Agnus Dei* may be either sung or recited in the vernacular, to melodies legitimately approved.
    b) In read Masses, instead of the Nicene-Constantinopolitan Creed, the faithful together with the celebrating priest may say, in the vernacular, the Apostles' Creed.
       to a) *25 in favor, 1 against*
       to b) *22 in favor, 4 against*

15. The chants of the Proper of the Mass, that is the *Introit, Gradual, Offertory, Communion:*
    a) in sung Mass may be chanted in the vernacular, to melodies legitimately approved;
    b) in read Masses they may be recited in the vernacular.
       all in favor

16. a) The Leonine prayers are to be omitted.
    b) The Last Gospel is to be omitted.
    c) The prayers at the foot of the altar may be omitted when preceded by a penitential liturgical action, such as sprinkling with blessed water.
       all in favor

17. a) The vernacular may be used, even for the essential forms, in Baptism, Confirmation, the Eucharist, Penance, the Anointing of the Sick, Matrimony and Funerals.

b) In the conferring of Holy Orders, the vernacular may be used in the initial Allocution both in Ordinations and in Consecrations, in the Admonition, and in the examination in an Episcopal Consecration.

c) The vernacular may be used, in the same parts, in the rite of blessing of an Abbot and an Abbess and in the Consecration of Virgins.

all in favor

18. The vernacular may be used in Sacramentals, those present in the Missal and in the Ritual.

all in favor

19. Until an official version is given for the recitation of the Divine Office in the vernacular, according to the cases foreseen in article 101 of the Constitution, the competent territorial authority may approve an existing version already published.

all in favor

Vatican City, April 20, 1964

DOCUMENT V

FORMULA OF PROMULGATION
OF DELIBERATIONS OF A GENERAL CHARACTER

Introduction

The "Formula for the promulgation of deliberations of a general character" accepted by the SCR and by the Consilium put an end, although only temporarily, to the pointless disagreement which had occupied the entire month of May, 1964.

The text was approved by the Pope, following the agreement of both offices and it was transmitted back to them on May 28, 1964.

Text

SACRED CONGREGATION FOR RITES

The Consilium ad exsequendam Constitutionem de Sacra Liturgia, in an assembly held on _____, discussed certain matters concerning the Constitution, and His Eminence Cardinal Giacomo Lercaro, President of the Consilium, submitted the responses to His Holiness.

The Holy Father, after having examined these responses with due care assisted in this task by the said Consilium as well as this Sacred Congregation for Rites, has decreed that these responses be suitably drafted in their definitive form; and during the Audience conceded on the day _____ to His Eminence Arcadio Maria Larraona, Prefect of the Sacred Congregation for Rites, he confirmed the same and ordered that they be made public and diligently observed, as they are here given.

_____
_____
_____

Given at Rome, on _____year 1964

Arcadius Maria Card. Larraona
Prefect

Henricus Dante
a Secretis

DOCUMENT VI

DIFFICULTIES BETWEEN THE CONSILIUM AND THE SCR ON THE DRAFT OF THE INSTRUCTION

Introduction

The SCR's "Observations on the Instruction" and the Consilium's "Response to the Observations by the Sacred Congregation for Rites," respectively dated August 23 and August 31, 1964, were put in two separate files.

File 1 contained:
– A letter of presentation by Cardinal Larraona.
– Introduction on the three documents prepared by the Consilium: Instructio, Ritus concelebrationis, and Ritus communionis sub utraque specie.
– Observations on the Instructio:
Preface; Chapters I–IV ; The formula for the promulgation for the "Instructio" and of the Consilium's other documents.
– Symbol of the faith (historical treatise on the Symbol of the Apostles and the Nicean Symbol of Constantinople, by Father A. Frutaz).
– Observations on the schemas on Concelebration and Communion under both species.
– Two notes on the Instruction sent to the Pope by Bishop Guano.

File 2 contained:
– A letter of presentation by Cardinal Lercaro.
– I.   Remarks on the Sacred Congregation's observations on the Instruction:
  - Introduction
  - Part I: Some general remarks
  - Part II: Particular questions
  - Formula of approval and promulgation

– II.   Remarks on the observations made by the Sacred Congregation for Rites on the rite for concelebration:
  1. General questions
  2. Particular questions
  Conclusion.

- III. Remarks on the observations made by the S.Congegation of Rites on the rite of Communion "sub utraque specie."

The following documents are included:

A. Schema of Instruction prepared by the Consilium (nos. 55, 56, 57, 59)

In fact numbers 55, 56, 57, and 59 of the Instruction project prepared by the Consilium (schema n. 17, *De Instructione* 5, June 21, 1964) were at the center of the controversy.

B. Observations by the SCR on the Instruction prepared by the Consilium

C. The Consilium's Response to the Observations by the Sacred Congregation for Rites

Selection of the parts of the "Observations" and the "Response" concerning the above-mentioned Instruction project was done as follows:

From the SCR's "Observations" (file 1)

1. Introduction
2. Observations on numbers 55 and 59
3. Formula of promulgation for the Instruction and the other Consilium documents.

From the "Response" by the Consilium (file 2)

1. Some general remarks
2. Answers to numbers 55 and 59
3. Formula of approval and promulgation.

Criteria for the selection are the following:

From number 1 it is possible to have a general idea on the respective positions of the Rites and of the Consilium regarding the implementation of the liturgical reform.

In number 2 these positions are concretely expressed with regard to the most topical problem at that time: the space to be given to the vernacular language in the Liturgy.

From number 3 it is possible to discern the respective role of which each of the two offices felt it was capable.

Text

A. Schema of Instruction prepared by the "Consilium" (nn. 55, 56, 57, 59)

Chapter II: *THE MOST SACRED MYSTERY OF THE EUCHARIST*

V. *Parts of the Mass that may be allotted to the vernacular* (re: article 54)

55. In the Mass, either sung or read, celebrated with the people, the competent territorial authority, their deliberations having been approved or confirmed by the Apostolic See, may introduce the vernacular:
   a) particularly in the proclamation of the readings, the Epistle and the Gospel, and also the common prayer or prayer of the faithful;
   b) then, according to conditions in the various places, also the chants in the Mass, that is the Kyrie, Gloria, Credo, Sanctus-Benedictus and Agnus Dei, and the antiphons to the introit, the offertory and communion;
   c) furthermore, the acclamations, greetings and formulas of dialogue, in the formulas: *Ecce Agnus Dei, Domine, non sum dignus,* and *Corpus Christi,* R. *Amen,* in the communion of the faithful and in the Lord's prayer, including its preface and embolism.

56. It falls only to the Apostolic See, on the other hand, to concede the vernacular in the other parts of the Mass, which are sung or recited by the celebrant alone.

57. The pastors of souls should diligently see that the faithful are able to recite or sing together also in the Latin language those parts of the Mass belonging to them, particularly if more simple melodies have been adopted.

Chapter III: *THE OTHER SACRAMENTS AND SACRAMENTALS*

I. *Parts which can be allotted to the vernacular* (re: article 63)

59. The competent territorial authority, their deliberations having been approved or confirmed by the Apostolic See, may introduce the vernacular:
   a) in the rites of Baptism, Confirmation, Penance, Anointing of the Sick and Matrimony, except for the minimum essential formulas, and also in the distribution of Holy Communion;
   b) in conferring Holy Orders: in the allocution at the beginning of every Ordination or Consecration, and also in the examination of the elect in an Episcopal Consecration, and in the admonitions;

c) in Sacramentals, present either in the Missal or in the Ritual or in the Pontifical;

d) in funerals.

If then in some places a wider use of the vernacular would seem opportune, the prescriptions in article 40 of the Constitution must be followed.

B. Observations by the SCR on the Instruction prepared by the *Consilium* (July 23, 1964)[2]

1. *Introduction*

1. The Holy Father, during the audience on July 1, 1964, gave His Eminence Cardinal Larraona, Prefect of Rites, three Documents recently prepared by the *Consilium,* namely an ample *Instructio* for the execution of the liturgical Constitution, the *Ritus servandus in Concelebratione Missae* and the *Ritus servandus in distribuenda Communione sub utraque specie,* for opportune review and examination.

2. The three Documents have been carefully read and discussed during 14 board Meetings of which the participants were: H. E. Cardinal Larraona, Prefect, formerly President of the Conciliar Commission for S. Liturgy and a member of the Consilium; Msgr. Dante, Secretary of Rites, member of the Conciliar Liturgical Commission; Fr. Antonelli, formerly Secretary of the Conciliar Liturgical Commission and a member of the Consilium; Msgr. Ferraro, Expert of the Conciliar Liturgical Commission; Msgr. Frutaz, Expert of the Conciliar Liturgical Commission and Consultor of the Consilium for historical matters.

3. The examination of the Instruction, the most complex of the three, gave rise first of all to two preliminary questions: one on the *nature and limits of the Instruction,* and the other on *the gradual application of the Constitution.*

Something on both questions should be said immediately.

– *First preliminary question: the nature and limits of the Instruction*

---

[2] The title in the SCR's original text was the following: "Observations on three Documents prepared by the Consilium: Instructio, Ritus Concelebrationis and Ritus Communionis sub utraque specie."

4. In the sound tradition of the Roman Curia there are two types of Instructions: one *autonomous,* that is, having no relation to any previous document, as some Instructions of a legislative character from Propaganda Fide, or others of a doctrinal character from the Holy Office; the other is the type of Instruction which hinges on a previous Document.

There are many Instructions of this kind, such as for example that following the Apostolic Constitution *Deus scientiarum Dominus,* or that of the Rites in 1955, which follows the General Decree *Maxima redemptionis nostrae mysteria* on the liturgical reform of Holy Week.

The present Instruction from the "Consilium" is certainly of this second type and hinges on the Constitution on the Sacred Liturgy and on the Motu Proprio *Sacram Liturgiam,* which establishes the initial and partial application of the former.

From this arises an important consequence, namely, that the dispositions of the *Instructio* can and must illustrate and explain first the various points of the Motu Proprio *Sacram Liturgiam;* they may also, if it be the case, amplify the concessions foreseen by the *Motu Proprio,* given the necessary approval of the Holy Father; but they may never exceed the Constitution.

This must be said, because some points of the Instruction seem in fact to overstep the Constitution, in spirit and perhaps even in letter.

– *Second question: on the gradual application of the Constitution*

5. The Instruction intends to guide the clergy and the faithful to a *gradual and progressive* application of the Constitution. This principle is certainly good; its application, however, given the psychological and real conditions of today, must be carried out with caution and moderation. Many of the faithful and many of the clergy too, are tired of this trickle of small modifications, especially as it has been said more than once that there will be a thorough revision of the Missal and of the Breviary; and in view of this everyone, to a greater and a lesser degree, is intolerant of partial modifications. The opinion, tacit or spoken, of the great majority of the clergy is this: give us, once and for all, the definitive Breviary and the Missal; we will then carry out all the required changes, and the matter will be closed.

In this general state of mind, the principle of a gradual application of the Constitution must be applied with great moderation, keeping in mind two criteria: that it must be, first, a question of things easily applied; and second a question of elements considered to be certainly definitive. Under no circumstances, in fact, must hasty concessions be allowed in any way to compromise the definitive reform which, within the limits of the Constitution, must be actuated with full freedom of movement.

6. After these general observations, we now pass to concrete observations on the text of the Instruction. These will be made step by step, following the progressive numbers.

These observations are dictated by a sincere desire to cooperate, in the best possible manner, for a full, happy and fruitful application of the Constitution.

We wish also to say that the Instruction is undoubtedly the result of much work; this is however a complex subject with many delicate points. Even one incautious word could have unpleasant consequences. Therefore much caution must be taken, because of the matter in itself, and also to avoid a repetition of the case of bitter, unpleasant controversy, which arose over certain points in the Motu Proprio of January 25, 1964.

2. *Observations on numbers 55 and 59*

No. 55   This number deals with the vernacular language in the Mass. Article 54 of the Constitution, to which this number of the Instruction refers, was one of the most debated. Now, while in the said article 54 of the Constitution, together with the possibility of a *congruus locus* for the vernacular in the Mass, there is the manifest desire to limit in it the use of the vernacular, number 55 of the Instruction seems on the contrary to favor a wider use. Therefore the Holy See itself would seem to be in favor of a wider use of the vernacular in the Mass, and this is against the spirit and the letter of §1 of article 36 of the Constitution, which foresees the preservation of Latin as the basis of the Liturgy. Nor should it be forgotten that the great majority of the Fathers approved the various dispositions concerning a wider use of the vernacular, precisely because of the existence of that first paragraph which ensured substantial preservation of the Latin, apart from a few particular cases *(salvo iure particulari),* such as the concessions made to China.

Consequently, to approve number 55 such as it is, would be to directly violate the above-mentioned §1 of article 36 which is fundamental, and create this paradox: Latin imposed as a basis would become an exception, and the vernacular, which must be given a secondary place, would occupy the main position.

This having been affirmed, here is what we think in concrete terms of this number 55:

55a) It is acceptable, because the Constitution also foresees the *Epistle,* the *Gospel* and the *Oratio communis* in the vernacular.

55b) It is not opportune, at least for the moment, to allow the *Kyrie, Gloria, Credo, Sanctus-Benedictus, Agnus Dei* to be *sung in the vernacular.* This is a matter of many consequences and certainly premature. It must not be forgotten that whereas article 36 §2 foresees the possibility of a vernacular version of the acclamations, in article 54, which regulates the vernacular in the Mass, the acclamations have not been inserted.

It should also be added that certain acclamations, which come from the Jewish liturgy, are said by everyone and cannot be translated, should be retained just as they are. Take for example: *Hosanna, Alleluia, Amen.* Furthermore the proposal to change the *Amen* is illogical, because those who wish to translate the Amen into the vernacular, wish to maintain intact the word *Alleluia.*

No. 59 This number deals with the use of the vernacular in the Sacraments (except for the Eucharist) and in Sacramentals. The Constitution speaks of this point in article 63, in which it says that the use of the vernacular in the Sacraments and Sacramentals may often be most useful and therefore *"amplior locus huic tribuatur";* and the procedure to be followed to obtain this wider use is laid down, namely, the procedure foreseen by article 36 familiar to us all.

The Constitution is wise. It foresees a more restricted use of the vernacular in the Mass (*congruus locus,* article 54), and a wider use (*amplior locus,* article 63) for the Sacraments, because although the liturgy of the Sacraments has also a communal character, like every liturgical action, it is directed however toward the individual.

Now, number 59 of the Instruction goes much further than article 63 of the Constitution. According to the Instruction the competent territorial authority, "actis ab Apostolica Sede probatis seu confirmatis," may extend the vernacular to the rites of all the Sacraments (Baptism, Confirmation, Penance, Anointing of the Sick, Matrimony), without limit, also including therefore the sacramental formula; an exception is made for the Eucharist, because it is part of the Canon, and for Holy Orders, for which however the vernacular may be proposed— and rightly so—for the allocution at the beginning, the examination of the elect and the final admonition.

As far as sacramentals are concerned, all of them, including those contained in the Missal, such as the Blessing of Ashes or Palms, and the Blessing of Candles on February 2, or contained in the Pontifical, such as the Blessing of an Abbot, the consecration of a church, an altar, of the chalice and paten, in other words for all sacramentals, the territorial authority may decide on the use of the vernacular, "actis ab Apostolorum Sede probatis seu confirmatis."

Naturally if the Holy See itself declares that the vernacular may be proposed for all these rites, in examining the Decisions it will be unable to go back on its word unless for exceptional motives.

In conclusion, according to this number 59, in the liturgy of all the Sacraments and Sacramentals Latin remains in the Eucharist and in part of the Sacrament of Holy Orders. But even for this it is advised that "sicubi autem amplior usus linguae vernaculae opportunus videatur, servetur praescriptum art. 40 Constitutionis," invoked here analogically, because article 40 does not deal directly with the vernacular, but rather profound structural adaptations of a rite.

This being the case, it must be said that this number 59 oversteps the spirit and the letter of the Constitution, which in the mentioned article 63 foresees, in the Sacraments and Sacramentals, not a total change to the vernacular, but rather "amplior locus" given to the vernacular.

In the final analysis, after what has been proposed for the vernacular in the Mass, as we have seen, to approve this number 59 on the generalization of the vernacular in the Sacraments and Sacramentals, would be to give the impression that the Holy See wishes to promote the total elimination of Latin from the Liturgy.

For all these reasons we are of the opinion that it is not convenient to approve number 59 of the Instruction.

Also because almost every country has for some time been in possession of the so-called bilingual Ritual, ritually approved, which foresees ample use of the vernacular, in the Sacraments, and even more so in Sacramentals and Funerals.

Any nation lacking a bilingual Ritual may request one and it will be granted.

3. *The formula for the promulgation of the Instruction and other documents of the Consilium.*

At the end of the *Instructio* the Consilium proposes a formula for its promulgation.

Keeping in mind the generic formulary already agreed upon, and given also the *path* actually followed for the preparation, discussion and revision of the Instruction, it would seem that the formula proposed by the Consilium could be considerably modified.

We therefore take the liberty of proposing the following formula:

The present Instruction, diligently prepared and carefully discussed by the Consilium instituted to execute the Constitution on the Sacred Liturgy, was submitted by the Cardinal President of the said Consilium to the Holy Father Pope Paul VI for his supreme approval.

The Holy Father, however, before giving his approval transmitted the Instruction for examination to the Sacred Congregation for Rites, which exercises in the Church on behalf of the Holy Father ordinary powers in liturgical matters, in order that it might have the opportunity to formulate its own eventual observations: which, the said Congregation has dutifully accomplished.

Successively the Holy Father, all things diligently weighed after having heard the Cardinal President of the Consilium and the Cardinal Prefect of the Congregation for Rites, has deigned to approve this Instruction and has ordered the said Prefect of the Congregation for Rites to make it public so that it may be diligently observed by all to whom it applies, from the day _____.

Notwithstanding any contrary disposition.

Arcadius M. Card. Larraona, S.R.C. Prefect
Henricus Dante, Secretary

Rome, July 23, 1964

C. Response from the Consilium to the Observations made by the Sacred Congregation for Rites (August 31, 1964)

1. *Some general remarks*

In the letter from His Eminence Cardinal Larraona and in the introductory part of the observations on the Instruction, there are certain remarks of a general character which it will be best to examine individually.

1) The call for prudence first of all. This is a concern which appears here and there, and also frequently in the single observations. It is motivated generally by two arguments: the difficulty of the questions, and fear of giving support to those who are called "extremists," "exaggerated," or "fanatics."

The need to proceed with due prudence because of the difficulty of the subject, may we be allowed to say, has never been underestimated by the Consilium either. However we think it is also necessary to avoid the obstacle dictated by over-prudence, which results in undue immobility. Hitherto the response to proposals or requests for reforms has always been a postponement pending a statement from the council. Now that the council has spoken, and spoken clearly, we see no reason to defer further those points of reform, awaited and desired by all. To act otherwise would be to humiliate all those, who with good will and honest intentions, intend to carry out the council's resolutions.

Neither must we take prudence to an extreme, not executing or postponing, for fear of favoring the so called "extremists," "exaggerated," or "fanatics." First, they are a minority and cannot be considered so authoritative as to impede the progress of a balanced majority. And if the center gives the feeling of moving, then the "exaggerated" will have a limited field in which to spend their energy within the sphere of obedience, whereas, in the opposite case, seeing in the central authority an excessive delay in proceeding on the line of decision clearly established by the council, they could find an excuse for arbitrary action to the detriment both of the reform to be carried out and of the authority itself.

Lastly may we make one final consideration, the fruit of experience of the last few years. Many of the liturgical reforms which have taken place and the norms which today regulate the liturgical pastoral activity in the Church were only codified after having been considered for a long time with circumspection as the initiative of those liturgists, who themselves in turn, had been defined as "extremists," "exaggerated," or "fanatics." Whereas it would have been much better and more helpful if the indications to be followed had been spontaneously given by the authorities.

2) Another remark of a general character, which appears at the beginning and in many of the observations, is the fear that some points of reform introduced now may *compromise the future general reform.*

This consideration too has been constantly kept in mind by the Consilium, which in the successive drafts of the Instruction always removed whatever appeared in need of further examination. For example, a more ample disposition of some rites and formulas for the Offertory, the breaking of the bread and the conclusion of Mass, at first inserted into the schema, was suspended precisely because the respective study groups expressed the need for further examination, in spite of the qualified studies already completed.

The points of reform dealt with in the Instruction are those which, from the studies carried out, from the judgment made by the study groups, and from the concrete schemas elaborated since the time of the preparatory Commission, can be considered as accepted by all liturgists and experts in the liturgical-pastoral field, inasmuch as they have doctrinal and historical foundation and are most useful for promoting the active participation of the faithful. Therefore introduced now, they will not be touched again in the definitive reform.

And all this was said during the meetings of the Consilium, each time the single points presented were discussed.

3) The third remark: concerning the *gradual application* of the reform, a principle seen as essentially good, but perhaps inopportune due to the weariness it generates in the clergy and the faithful with an uninterrupted succession of partial reforms.

We can see no reason to question the need for the principle of gradualness. The reform triggered by the conciliar deliberations will, in certain fields, be considerably profound and could cause some disorientation among the clergy and faithful, were it not carried out in stages, at least in the various sectors of the liturgy.

Furthermore, if the clergy (but which part of the clergy?) has said it is tired of the partial reforms actuated so far, it is because it knew that none of those reforms were definitive. This is so for Holy Week, for example, and the Code of Rubrics; precisely because they were defined simply as steps towards the general, permanent reform. Nevertheless, even these gradual reforms have served their purpose.

Now, at long last, a systematic plan of revision is beginning to emerge. It will take time, but already from its first steps it already fits into the context of the entire reform desired by the council, and is therefore definitive. And if there was a complaint when the Motu Proprio *Sacram Liturgiam* was published it arose precisely from the disappointment of seeing further postponed these points of reform proposed by the Instruction, already acquired and therefore expected.

4) It is asked that, at least in introducing these reforms, only those *more easily actuated* be carried out.

But to judge the greater or lesser difficulty of actuation, especially in the liturgical-pastoral field, which requires first an effort of study and personal conviction on the part of the clergy and then long and patient work of formation of the faithful, is not always easy; everything is both difficult and easy at the same time, depending on the angle from which it is considered. As it happens, we are of the opinion that in the reforms proposed, an element of simplicity does exist; namely, to render liturgical actions more simple, more clear, more comprehensible, and therefore more easily open to active, communal participation by the faithful.

5) There is finally the remark of major importance, which criticizes the text of the Instruction for "overstepping the Constitution in its spirit and perhaps even in letter," especially with regard to the use of the vernacular in the Liturgy.

The individual remarks will be answered with the respective articles, appealing less to considerations, impression and sentiments, and more to the authentic documents and the story of the successive formulation of these same articles on their conciliar path.

For the moment, may we be allowed to emphasize that these numbers of the Instruction faithfully reflect and codify the directing principles approved by the Consilium in the plenary meetings of last April, for the confirmation of decisions made by national Bishops' Conferences. At the basis of the discussion were the same arguments amply explained later on.

The articles of the Instruction concerning the vernacular were already presented for the Holy Father's consideration during the Audience on April 21, 1964, and they were approved by him, with authorization to proceed, using them as a basis, with the confirmation of Decisions by the Bishops' Conferences. In fact some of these points have already been applied, to the deep satisfaction of the Episcopates involved, while for others it was said the Instruction must be awaited.

After establishing these considerations of a general character, we will now consider the individual observations made by the SCR. Many of them are clarifications of the text or a completion of it, others are simply expressions of doubt on the disposition's practical convenience; a brief response will be given to each. More space, demanded also by the importance of the subject, will be dedicated to the questions concerning the introduction of the vernacular in the Liturgy.

2. *Response to numbers 55 and 59*

n. 55   The SCR sees in the text of article 55 of the Instruction too great a concession to the vernacular in the Mass, to the point of being a violation of article 36,1 of the Constitution: "Linguae latinae usus, salvo peculari iure, in Ritibus latinis servetur." To approve this article as it is, says the SCR, "would be to reach this paradox: that Latin, imposed as a basis, would become an exception, and the vernacular, which should have a secondary place, would occupy the main place."

Response: 1) Number 36,1 of the Constitution must, in our opinion, be interpreted together with paragraph 2 of the same article: to the vernacular "amplior locus . . . tribui valeat . . . iuxta normas quae de hac re in sequentibus captibus singillatim statuuntur."

Now in the chapter on the Mass, in article 54, there is mention of the parts in which the concession of the vernacular is foreseen: "praesertim in lectionibus et oratione communi, ac, pro condicione locorum, etiam in partibus quae ad populum spectant."

The authentic interpretation of the text is given by the Report read in the Council Assembly before the vote. It is worthwhile to give the corresponding passage:

Pro diversis vero Missae partibus, in quibus lingua vernacula adhiberi potest—et nullam partem expresse excludimus, quamvis consideratione digni sunt illi Patres qui Canonem excludunt—modum
statuimus, quo talis usus obtineri poterit.

a) Pro lectionibus et oratione communi, in quibus specialissimo
   modo apparent rationes, quae usum linguae vernaculae commen-
   dant, competens erit auctoritas illa territorialis, de qua in art. 36
   locuti sumus. Specialis autem condicio harum partium insinuatur
   per verbum "praesertim."

b) Reliquas partes Missae, sive in Proprio sive in Ordinario, in duo
   capita distinguimus. Etenim vel dicuntur aut canuntur a fidelibus,
   vel dicuntur aut canuntur a sacerdote. Pro prioribus competens erit
   auctoritas territorialis ad normam art. 36. Pro aliis autem servetur
   art. 40.

Nemo tamen inquietari velit, si videat art. 54 nihil expresse dicere
de cantibus; quia in cap. VI "De Musica sacra," ad art. 113 dicetur:
"Quoad linguam adhibendam, serventur praecepta art. 36; quoad
Missam, art. 54, etc." Quae ergo in hoc art. 54 statuuntur, intelligun-
tur sive de his quae recitantur sive de iis quae canuntur" (Schema
Constitutionis de sacra Liturgia. Emendationes. VI. P. 18).

Even without being, a priori, a promoter of the vernacular, one cannot
fail to note in the official Report the expression: "et nullam partem
expresse excludimus, quamvis consideratione digni sunt illi Patres
qui Canonem excludunt". Hence, according to the official Reporter,
also the non-exclusion of any part from the possibility of saying it in
the vernacular is not yet against paragraph 1 of article 36.

2) Also to be underlined in the text of article 54 is the expression
"etiam in partibus quae ad populum spectant." What parts belong
to the people is not said. But the expression (the fruit of long and
heated discussion by the Consiliar Commission) is derived from the
"Instructio de Musica Sacra et Sacra Liturgia" number 14b): "In
Missis lectis sacerdos celebrans, eius minister, et fideles qui una
cum sacerdote celebrante actioni liturgicae directe participant, id
est, clara voce illas partes Missae dicunt quae ad ipsos spectant (n.
31), unice linguam latinam adhibere debent."

And number 31 of the same Instruction indicates as parts belonging
to the people: the simpler responses such as Amen, Et cum spiritu

tuo, etc. (lett. a), the parts said by the server (lett. b), the chants of the Ordinary of the Mass (lett. c) and the chants of the Proper of the Mass (lett. d).

Now, precisely in these parts "quae ad populum spectant," and which in 1958 it was prescribed to say in Latin in the case of direct liturgical participation, article 54 of the Constitution foresees the possibility of the vernacular, pro condicione locorum.

Therefore it does not seem to us, on the basis of these considerations, that the Instruction violates either article 36 §1 or article 54 of the Constitution.

3) And we come to the individual parts of the article of the Instruction.

55 a) For the use of the vernacular in the readings and in the "oratio fidelium" the SCR finds no difficulty either; so far so good.

55 b) For the use of the vernacular in the chants of the Ordinary of the Mass, the SCR holds this as premature, and proposes "to wait at least until the Ordo Missae is revised."

Response: On the basis of what has been explained above, there is nothing against the Constitution. So much so that it seems that the SCR itself admits this for Mass which is not sung; it excludes it however for sung Mass. But this distinction is contrary to article 113 of the Constitution, which makes no distinction between sung Mass and Mass without singing.

There remains the postponement of the matter until the Order of Mass has been revised. Not even this seems acceptable, because it would mean prolonging the present precarious situation further, after the general reform, with new trials and new experiments on texts and melodies. Something which would be better done during this transition period instead, so that at the moment of the general reform we may really achieve definitive stabilization.

55 c) The SCR is also against section three of the article.

Let us examine the issues one by one because there must be some misunderstanding. In fact:

— The observations of the SCR mention the *Agnus Dei*. Evidently this is an error of transcription, because the Instructio speaks of the *Ecce Agnus Dei* and the other formulas relative to the communion of the faithful. The Agnus Dei was dealt with in the previous letter, together with the other chants of the Ordinary of the Mass.

— Again, the observations of the SCR speak here of the Introit, the Offertory, the Communion: parts which are included in letter b) instead, because they are more directly part of the formulas which fall to the people, after the chants of the Ordinary.

But let us take a concrete look:

1) The SCR is against the translation of the acclamations, greetings, formulas of dialogue, and observes that "whereas §2 of article 36 foresees the possibility of the translation of the acclamations into the vernacular, in article 54, which regulates the Mass, the acclamations are not inserted."

Response: First, article 36 §2 speaks of "admonitions" not of "acclamations": and between the two there is a great difference! Furthermore, the fact that article 54 makes no explicit mention of acclamations is because these parts are included among those ad *populum spectant,* as it has been seen above.

However, some hesitation could perhaps arise for the formulas of dialogue, which fall in part directly to the priest or minister and in part to the people. But no one would wish to think of Latin for the first part and the vernacular for the other. In this situation it would seem to us that the people's part in the vernacular by reason of their active participation, is enough to draw also the part of the celebrant or minister.

2) The SCR says nothing concerning the other formulas actually listed under this third comma:

— for the formulas of Communion there should be no difficulty as they fall directly to the faithful;

— the same is to be said for the *Pater noster* changed from a presidential formula to a formula of the assembly with the *Instructio de Musica Sacra et Sacra Liturgia* of 1958;

— regarding the embolism (Libera nos), the vernacular seems justified by its nature of continuation and completion of the prayer of the *Pater,* even though this formula is recited by the celebrant alone.

4) In brief, it seems to us that number 55 of the Instruction is perfectly in keeping with article 54 of the Constitution, in the light of the authentic interpretation given to it in the Council Assembly; and that it is not even in contrast to article 36 §1. The SCR admits that article 54 requires interpretation: number 55 of the Instruction gives this interpretation, as the nature of the whole document demands.

5) Finally, it should be noted that the Instruction does not concede automatically and indistinctly the use of the vernacular in all the parts listed; but indicates only the different parts in which, in keeping with the Constitution, the competent territorial authority "pro condicione locorum" may decide on its use, "actis ab Apostolica Sede probatis seu confirmatis." And a clarification on the matter is necessary, as can be seen from the requests received by the Consilium on the part of numerous Bishops' Conferences.

n. 59   Also regarding this number of the Instruction, which deals with the use of the vernacular in the Sacraments and Sacramentals, the SCR, as already for the number relative to the introduction of the vernacular in the Mass, affirms that the Instruction "goes much further than article 63 of the Constitution."

Concretely, the objections and difficulties, on the basis of which the SCR asks that this article not be approved, are:
a) that the sacramental formula may also be in the vernacular;
b) that all Sacramentals, even major ones, including those contained in the Pontifical, such as consecrations, may be in the vernacular.
c) that finally, article 40 be referred to as a basis for obtaining a more ample use of the vernacular.

1. The answer to these three objections can be deduced from the conciliar Acts.

After the Conciliar Commission had discussed the observations made by the Council Fathers in assembly, a vote was taken on three proposed formulations of article 63 a). Of these three, one envisaged a distinction between rites contained in the Ritual and rites contained in the Pontifical, but it was not accepted. And so, after much debating it was agreed to put this text to the vote in Assembly: "In administratione Sacramentorum et Sacramentalium lingua vernacula adhiberi potest, sed quoad formam Sacramentorum, exceptis Matrimonio et aliis casibus expresse probatis, lingua latina 'generatim servetur.'" And the text was approved during the 48th General Congregation (October 15, 1963) with 2103 placet against 49 non placet.

During the comprehensive vote on chapter III (October 18, 1963) there were 1054 placet iuxta modum, of which 601 asked for the suppression of the final words regarding the preservation of Latin in the sacramental form.

On the basis of this high number of conditional votes, on November 21, 1963, the Fathers were asked if they thought opportune a modification of the text already approved by them, excluding the mention of Latin, for the sacramental form. And the reply was 1848 placet against 335 non placet, in favor of the present text of 63 a): "In administratione Sacramentorum et Sacramentalium lingua vernacula adhiberi potest ad normam art. 36." A text which is not of the clearest, it is true, but whose history is clear and whose significance cannot lend itself to ambiguous interpretations.

In conclusion:
a) from all the conciliar acts it is evident that the Fathers decided not to impose that the sacramental form be said in Latin, as it had hitherto been for bilingual Rituals approved by the Holy See. To return to a similar formulation of the problem would evidently be against the mind of the Council.
b) A distinction between the rites contained in the Ritual and rites contained in the Pontifical was refused by the Conciliar Commission itself and was not even presented to the Assembly.
c) There remains the question of the reference to article 40 of the Constitution in order to obtain in some cases a more ample use of the vernacular. The objection underlines that "article 40 regards not directly the vernacular, but the profound structural adaptations of a rite."

The answer is simple: the Instruction under this section simply returns to the text, including the reference to article 40, which the

Constitution places under article 54 for a more ample request of the vernacular in the Mass.

2. Lastly, as reasons which should reinforce the conviction that number 59 of the Instruction must not be accepted, the SCR puts forward two motives:

a) "Almost every country has for some time been in possession of the so-called bilingual Ritual, ritually approved, which foresees ample use of the vernacular, in the Sacraments, and even more so in Sacramentals and Funerals."

Answer: It was the Bishops of precisely these countries, who approved an "amplior locus" for the vernacular in the Sacraments and Sacramentals. And these Bishops, one may rightly suppose, had clearly in their minds the Ritual in use in their dioceses, therefore with all the vernacular conceded, not the Roman Ritual exclusively in Latin. Furthermore, from the observations made in the Council Assembly and the discussions by the Liturgy Commission it may also rightly be supposed that by means of this "amplior locus" for the vernacular the desire was to have a more logical use of the vernacular than before which would not exclude certain formulas, for which hitherto Latin was obligatory.

b) "Any nation lacking a bi-lingual Ritual may request one and it will be granted."

Answer: The observation is rather curious. The Constitution in article 63 b gives the competent territorial authorities the right not to ask, but to prepare the particular Rituals "singularum regionum necessitatibus, etiam quoad linguam, accommodata . . . actis ab Apostolica Sede recognitis." This is slightly different from "requesting" and "granting."

3. To conclude, not only do we see nothing in number 59 which goes against the spirit and the letter of the Constitution, but we consider it to be indispensable precisely because it interprets the text of the Constitution, which, due to the well-known vicissitudes mentioned above, is not clear.

It should also be noted that this article, like the one relative to the vernacular in the Mass, does not concede automatically and to all these parts the vernacular, but only indicates to the competent authority what it may decide within the limits of the spirit and the letter of the Constitution.

3. *Formula of approval and promulgation*

We propose that the formula of approval and promulgation be more similar to the generic formula communicated by His Eminence the Cardinal Secretary of State to the Consilium (letter of June 16, 1964, Prot. 3324/64) and to the S. Congregation for Rites.

We therefore propose the following formulation:

"The present Instruction, prepared by the Consilium ad exsequendam Constitutionem de sacra Liturgia by order of the Holy Father Pope Paul VI, was submitted to the Supreme Pontiff by His Eminence Cardinal Giacomo Lercaro, President of the said Consilium.

"The Holy Father, after having examined the Instruction with due care, assisted in this task by the said Consilium as well as this Sacred Congregation for Rites, has given his particular approval to the document as a whole and in its single parts, confirming it with his authority, during the audience conceded to Cardinal Arcadio Maria Larraona on the day _____and has ordered that the Instruction be made public and be diligently observed by all to whom it applies, as from January 1st 1965.

Notwithstanding any contrary dispositions.

Rome, . . ."

> There follow the signatures of the Cardinal Prefect and of the Secretary of the SCR and the "Visum" of the Cardinal President of the Consilium.

Rome, August 31, 1964

✠ Subject Index

✝ Names Index